AGRICULTURE AND THE STATE

Agriculture and the State

British Policy in a World Context

Edited by
BRIAN DAVEY, T. E. JOSLING and
ALISTER McFARQUHAR

for the
Trade Policy Research Centre
London

First published 1976 by
THE MACMILLAN PRESS LTD
London and Basingstoke
Associated companies in New York
Dublin Melbourne Johannesburg and Madras

SBN 333 21194 4

Printed in Great Britain by
WESTERN PRINTING SERVICES LTD
Bristol

Trade Policy Research Centre

The Trade Policy Research Centre in London was established in 1968 to promote independent analysis and public discussion of commercial and other international economic policy issues. It is a privately sponsored non-profit organisation and is essentially an entrepreneurial centre under the auspices of which a variety of activities are conducted. As such, the Centre provides a focal point for those in business, the universities and public affairs who are interested in international economic questions.

The Centre is managed by a Council which is headed by Sir Frank McFadzean. The members of the Council, set out below, represent a wide range of experience and expertise.

Having general terms of reference, the Centre does not represent any consensus of opinion. Intense international competition, technological advances in industry and agriculture and new and expanding markets, together with large-scale capital flows, are having profound and continuing effects on international production and trading patterns. With the increasing integration and interdependence of the world economy there is thus a growing necessity to increase public understanding of the problems now being posed and of the kind of solutions that will be required to overcome them.

The principal function of the Centre is the sponsorship of research programmes on policy problems of national and international importance. Specialists in universities and private firms are commissioned to carry out the research and the results are published and circulated in academic, business and government circles throughout the European Community and in other countries. Meetings and seminars are also organised from time to time.

Publications are presented as professionally competent studies worthy of public consideration. The interpretations and conclusions in them are those of their authors and do not purport to represent the views of the Council and others associated with the Centre.

The Centre is registered in the United Kingdom as an educational trust under the Charities Act 1960. It and its research programmes are financed by foundation grants, corporate donations and membership subscriptions.

Contents

List of Tables

List of Figures

Biographical Notes

JOHN ASHTON is Dean of the Agricultural Faculty at the University of Newcastle upon Tyne where he is Professor of Agricultural Economics and Director of the Agricultural Adjustment Unit. Professor Ashton has co-edited a number of the Unit's publications, including *Economic Change and Agriculture* (1967) and *The Remoter Rural Areas* (1971), and contributed to a number of other publications and journals. Until 1964 he was a senior principal economist in the British Ministry of Agriculture. Professor Ashton is a member of the Council of the Trade Policy Research Centre.

HUGH CORBET has been Director of the Trade Policy Research Centre in London since its inception in 1968. He was previously a specialist writer on *The Times* in London. Mr Corbet is author of *Raw Materials: Beyond the Rhetoric of Commodity Power* (1974), co-author of *Trade Strategy and the Asian-Pacific Region* (1970) and editor, with others, of *In Search of a New World Economic Order* (1974), *Commonwealth Policy in a Global Context* (1972) and *Europe's Free Trade Area Experiment: EFTA and Economic Integration* (1970).

BRIAN DAVEY, now a senior economist with the Canadian Department of Agriculture, was a Lecturer in Agricultural Economics at the University of Newcastle upon Tyne. He was earlier, from 1961 to 1966, an economist with the British Ministry of Agriculture. Mr Davey is the author of *Trends in Agriculture* (1970) and co-author of *Farmers and the Common Market* (1970) and *Farming Systems and the Common Market* (1971).

DONNA HAMWAY was a Trade Policy Research Centre Fellow at the London School of Economics and Political Science while working on the research programme reported in these pages. Miss Hamway was earlier an economist with a New York firm of management consultants.

A. C. HANNAH, now an economist with the GATT Secretariat in Geneva, was a Trade Policy Research Centre Fellow in the Department of Land Economy at the University of Cambridge while engaged on the research programme reported in this volume.

P. B. R. HAZELL was a Trade Policy Research Centre Fellow in the Department of Agricultural Economics, University of Newcastle upon Tyne, while on the research programme reported in this volume. Dr Hazell is now on the economic research staff of the International Bank for Reconstruction and Development in Washington.

JANE NIALL, a Research Officer at the Trade Policy Research Centre, London, was formerly on the research staff at the Institute of Applied Economic and Social Research, University of Melbourne. Mrs Niall is author of *General Aviation in Australia* (1974).

DONALD SILVEY is a Research Officer at the Department of Land Economy, University of Cambridge. His publications include *Milk Production: a Comparison of England and Denmark* (1972) and various articles in professional journals and other periodicals.

T. E. JOSLING has been Professor of Agricultural Economics at the University of Reading since 1974, having previously been a Reader in Economics at the London School of Economics and Political Science, which he joined in 1968. Professor Josling has been a consultant to the United Nations Food and Agriculture Organisation, the Commission of the European Community and, in the United Kingdom, to the Home Grown Cereals Authority and the Department of Prices and Consumer Protection. He is the author of *Interdependence among Agricultural and Other Sectors in the Canadian Economy* (1966), *The United Kingdom Grains Agreement* (1968), *Agriculture and Britain's Trade Policy Dilemma* (1970) and *An International Grain Reserve Policy* (1973).

ALISTER McFARQUHAR is a University Lecturer in Natural Resources in the Department of Land Economy at the University of Cambridge. He has been a consultant to the World Bank, the Organisation for Economic Cooperation and Development and the United Nations Food and Agriculture Organisation. In 1965, Dr McFarquhar was a Visiting Professor at the Food Research Institute, Stanford University. From 1955 to 1959, he was Agricultural Economist for the Ministry of Economic Planning, Government of Western Nigeria. Dr McFarquhar is the editor of *Europe's Future Food and Agriculture* (1971) and author of *Employment Creation in Primary Production* (1972) and of many papers in professional journals.

Preface

Agricultural policy is not only a domestic issue. In a very real sense it is also an international issue. This has not been universally recognised in the past. But the problems of international trade in temperate-zone agricultural products have now become vital.

With the development in the middle 1970s of world-wide shortages of major farm commodities, particularly of cereals (a key determinant of prices for livestock products), rural interests in the European Community, as elsewhere, have been lobbying more militantly than ever for increased government support for agricultural production. Many of these shortages have their origin in under-investment in the fields concerned – reflecting a serious distortion in the allocation of world resources.

Greater self-sufficiency at high cost is therefore not the appropriate answer to shortages of supply. International agreements should instead be sought on security of access to supplies and on security of access to markets. Such is the philosophy developed in this volume which reports on a three-year research programme which, in the context of the European Community and the international situation, examines agricultural policy in the United Kingdom, one of the largest importers of food in the world.

The programme was sponsored by the Trade Policy Research Centre with the help of a grant from the Leverhulme Trust Fund, in London, while funds made available by the Ford Foundation, in New York, were also used. The research was carried out in three universities: in the Department of Land Economy at the University of Cambridge, under the direction of Dr Alister McFarquhar; at the London School of Economics, under Dr T. E. Josling (who has since moved to the University of Reading); and in the Agricultural Adjustment Unit at the University of Newcastle upon Tyne, under Professor John Ashton. During the most intensive part of the programme, three TPRC Fellows were engaged full time: Mr A. C. Hannah, at Cambridge; Miss Donna Hamway, at LSE; and Dr Peter Hazell, at Newcastle. Mr Donald Silvey, at Cambridge, and Mr Brian Davey, at Newcastle, were also heavily involved, while Mrs Jane Niall, at the TPRC, became involved in the concluding stages.

With the uncertainties associated with the question of British membership of the European Community, which were no sooner resolved than fresh difficulties were created by the upheaval in world agricultural markets in 1972–73, the programme could hardly have been conducted in worse circumstances. The programme was able, however, to contribute to the Common Market debate in Britain with an interim report entitled *Burdens and Benefits of Farm-support Policies*, published by the Centre as Agricultural Trade Paper No. 1.

Reverting to the theme of the study, the opening of commercial markets for agricultural products is required, it is argued, in order to stimulate production in low-cost areas of the world. Increased production will not be undertaken without some assurance of a market for the resulting goods. But under the multilateral negotiating procedures of the General Agreement on Tariffs and Trade (GATT), the instrument by which the commerce of the free-enterprise world has been governed for more than a quarter of a century, agricultural products are placed in 'a special position' far less amenable to bargaining than industrial products. Indeed, no impact has been made, either in the Kennedy Round or in previous negotiations, on the long-run upward trend in the protection accorded to temperate-zone agricultural production, especially in the industrialised countries.

In the Tokyo Round of GATT negotiations, formally launched in Tokyo in September 1973, attention has been focusing more than ever before on the problems of international agricultural trade. That trade has been increasingly disrupted and distorted over the past decade by severe import controls and export subsidies and, more recently, by various export controls.

Weather conditions, declining foods stocks and changing diets, not to mention exchange-rate changes, have been major factors in the imbalances which have developed between world supply and demand. But in a sector of the economy as subject to government intervention as agriculture, politicians cannot absolve themselves from responsibility, at least in part, for the disarray into which world agriculture has fallen. For agriculture is supported by government interventions ranging from a variety of direct subsidies to fixed import quotas and variable import levies.

By the late 1960s the European Community's common agricultural policy began to make a substantial impact on international trade in temperate-zone farm commodities. Perhaps most affected was the world cereals market. Grain surpluses in the Common Market, generated by high support prices (protected by variable import levies), were being increasingly dumped with the help of export subsidies on the 'world' markets of the traditional exporting countries.

These last, such low-cost cereal producers as the United States, Canada and Australia, were thus confronted with depressed prices, which caused them to cut production. It was soon forgotten though that cuts in production contributed to the problem of tight supplies. An opportunity was also overlooked. For while commodity prices are buoyant, relieving governments of the pressures normally associated with depressed prices, the general climate for trade liberalisation improves. But higher prices for produce are followed by higher costs of production and many of the income benefits from higher prices get capitalised into higher values on farm assets – which farmers rapidly take for granted.

Agriculture is a vital source of earnings for many developed and developing countries. These countries have acknowledged over the years that in many industrialised countries the farming community poses difficult politico-social problems. While governments, clearly, have emphasised their national problems in international negotiations, they have not yet demonstrated any perceptible interest in reforming their national policies. Without such an interest in taking national action to correct at least some of the international disarray, discussions under the GATT stand little chance of achieving significant progress. What might then be jeopardised, apart from the interests of developing countries and others which enjoy a comparative advantage in agricultural production, is the further liberalisation of world trade in industrial products, especially if the United States makes progress on the industrial side conditional upon progress on the agricultural side.

It is therefore important that governments should be induced to examine the extent to which their farm-support policies are achieving their stated objectives. (a) How much have agricultural policies increased net farm incomes? (b) What effect have agricultural policies had on farm output and on domestic consumption of farm products? (c) How much do agricultural policies cost taxpayers and consumers? (d) How are the economic benefits of agricultural policies distributed between high- and low-income families in agriculture? (e) What part of the total costs borne by consumers and taxpayers actually accrues to farm people as additional income? These are the questions that need to be answered if ever the fundamental problems of agricultural trade are to be overcome. They are the questions which this study begins to address.

The volume is presented in three parts. In the first part, an introductory chapter sets the problems of European agriculture, and more particularly the British position, in an international context. The chapter briefly reviews the events leading to the Tokyo Round of GATT negotiations and the record of the GATT in earlier endeavours to liberalise trade in agricultural products. It then goes on to analyse the reasons – social, economic and political – for farm-support policies. The second chapter focuses on the United Kingdom, a major export market for most of the traditional agricultural-exporting countries, reviewing the various phases through which British agricultural policy has passed during the post-World War II period.

The second part of the volume is devoted to the results of the research carried out under the programme. Generally the work has focused on the effects on demand, domestic supply and trade patterns of British agriculture shifting from a deficiency-payments system of support to an import-levy system, and examines also the income-distribution effects and inter-country transfers involved. How the pattern of British consumption might be affected by the adoption of the European Community's common agricultural policy is projected to 1978 in the third chapter. Applying a different econometric technique, the fourth chapter examines the likely effect of the Community's system on the structure of British farming. In the fifth chapter, domestic supply is projected to 1978 so that, in conjunction with the demand projections, the consequences for imported supplies can be discussed. In a pioneering piece of research, the income-distribution effects, as well as the inter-country transfers, entailed in shifting to the Community's import-levy arrangements are analysed quantitatively in the sixth chapter.

The third part considers action at national and international level. In the seventh chapter is set out a formal and comprehensive framework in which the effectiveness of farm-support policies might be examined. The eighth chapter advances a set of proposals that might give greater assurance of access to supplies, on the one hand, and access to markets, on the other. In the ninth chapter the ramifications are explored of establishing an international system of nationally-held grain reserves. The concluding chapter draws on the empirical studies in Part II to discuss the effectiveness in particular of British farm-support policies and goes on to suggest further fields for enquiry.

Finally, while thanking all those engaged on the programme for their diligence and patience in trying times, it has to be emphasised as usual that the views expressed in this volume do not necessarily reflect the views of the Council or of others associated with the Trade Policy Research Centre. For the Centre, having general terms of reference, does not represent a consensus of opinion. Its purpose is to promote independent research and public discussion on international economic policy issues.

HUGH CORBET
Director
Trade Policy Research Centre

London
Spring 1976

List of Abbreviations

CAP	common agricultural policy of the European Community
c.i.f.	price includes cost, insurance, freight
EEC	European (Economic) Community
FAO	Food and Agriculture Organisation of the United Nations
FEOGA	Fonds Européen d'Orientation et de Garantie Agricole
f.o.b.	free-on-board prices
GATT	General Agreement on Tariffs and Trade
GNP	gross national product
IBRD	International Bank for Reconstruction and Development (World Bank)
IMF	International Monetary Fund
MAFF	Ministry of Agriculture, Fisheries and Food
OECD	Organisation for Economic Cooperation and Development
OEEC	Organisation for European Economic Cooperation, succeeded by OECD
OPEC	Organisation of Petroleum Exporting Countries
UNCTAD	United Nations Conference on Trade and Development
USDA	United States Department of Agriculture

PART I

Agriculture as an International Issue

CHAPTER 1

Multilateral Negotiations on Agricultural Trade

HUGH CORBET

Since 1947 the commercial system of the free-enterprise world has been governed by the General Agreement on Tariffs and Trade (GATT).[1] Its principles and rules guided the restoration, in the 1950s and 1960s, of some semblance of order in the world economy, following the disorders of the 1930s and 1940s.[2] These last were characterised by protectionist excesses which led, prior to World War II, to autarchic and discriminatory policies among the major trading nations.

By the late 1960s, however, mercantilist trends were reappearing and gathering force, almost encouraged by a loss of impetus in the movement towards an open world economy.[3] In commercial diplomacy the world does not mark time. Either it is moving forward or it is moving backward. With the completion in 1967 of the Kennedy Round of tariff-cutting negotiations, the sixth in the GATT series, governments failed thereafter to sustain the momentum of trade liberalisation through which international economic order had been restored.

The United States, preoccupied by the awful problems of a 'limited war' in Vietnam and by urban and communal problems at home, was growing weary of bearing on its own the primary responsibility for the maintenance of the international security, commercial and monetary systems. The European Community, caught between economic power and political impotence,[4] was preoccupied with the awkward problems of *achèvement, approfondissement et élargissement*. And Japan continued to be preoccupied by the awesome problems of adjusting, socially and industrially, to her increasing involvement in foreign economic activity.[5]

Eventually the international economic crisis of 1971 obliged governments to face up to the underlying tensions that had developed in the international system of trade and payments. The immediate crisis was settled at the end of the year in the Smithsonian Accord, which realigned exchange rates and in effect devalued the American dollar, with the United States agreeing to lift the 'temporary' import surcharge imposed as part of President Nixon's New Economic Policy measures of 15 August.

But the Nixon Administration had a further objective. For the 1971 crisis not only reflected, on the monetary side, the over-valuation of the American dollar. It also reflected, on the commercial side, the frustration of American efforts – over the previous two years – to initiate a new GATT round of multilateral trade negotiations.

In February 1972, after five months of economic confrontation, Washington finally induced the European Community and Japan to join in parallel declarations with the United States. The three agreed to embark on a 'comprehensive review of international economic relations' covering *inter alia* 'all elements of trade, including measures which impede or distort agricultural, raw material and industrial trade', with special attention being given to the problems of developing countries.[6]

Inter-governmental discussions focused for the rest of 1972 on the reform of the international monetary system and trade questions returned to their customary second place in the schedule of priorities. But preparations for a seventh round of GATT negotiations proceeded on their tortuous path amidst continuing monetary turmoil. No sooner though was the Tokyo Round of negotiations formally launched, in September 1973,[7] than the War of *Yom Kippur* broke out and the Organisation of Petroleum Exporting Countries (OPEC) shook the world economy to its very foundations by announcing in quick succession two large increases in oil prices.

Thus with the quadrupling of oil prices, the economic implications of which were clearly far-reaching, there was a quantum increase in the degree of uncertainty affecting the management of affairs at company, industry and national level. Consequently, the reform of the international system of trade and payments, far from having been overtaken by events, became overnight a matter of still greater urgency.

What therefore has to be understood about the Tokyo Round negotiations is that, unlike previous GATT rounds, they are not merely concerned with the further liberalisation of international trade within an accepted framework of rules. They are concerned with the rules as well.[8]

Need to Reform the GATT System

After the Kennedy Round of GATT negotiations were concluded in 1967, the Johnson Administration initiated in the United States a major review of international trade and investment policy, one in which the interests of the rest of the world figured very large.[9] Confidence in the GATT system was perceived to be weakening, perhaps chiefly in the United States, but also among the smaller countries which have to look to multilateral institutions for the protection of their interests. This was partly because some rules were being more honoured in the breach than in the observance, while others were aimed at problems which, over the years, had become considerably more complex.[10] No longer did the GATT system appear equal to the task of regulating change in a rapidly integrating world economy marked by growing interdependence between national economies.[11]

In the European Community there was resistance to the notion that the GATT system was in need of reform.[12] As the present writer observed at the time, 'growing prosperity had restored self-confidence and a sense of security to the countries of Western Europe, sufficient to encourage in them a tendency to pursue their interests with little regard for the interests of others. They have been inclined in recent years to take for granted the order in the world economy that – along with their prosperity, self-confidence and security – was also restored in the 1950s and 1960s.'[13]

By then, it had become evident, two other groups of countries were beginning to expect more, not less, from the international trading system. With economic relations among industrialised countries being conducted on a more orderly basis, the two groups entertained hopes, however crudely or subtly expressed, that a coordinated approach to their problems might at last be possible. The two groups overlap. First, there are the exporters of temperate-zone agricultural products, some of whom have been parties to the GATT from the outset, but have not benefited greatly to date from its rules and principles.[14] Then there are, secondly, the developing countries, most of which are not in a position to negotiate on a reciprocal basis with industrially advanced countries, but look to them for markets for their products.[15]

Persistent neglect of the first group's problems might be said to have contributed, in large measure, to the 'world food crisis' of 1972–74, although – as discussed below – it was the product of a coincidence of circumstances. Supplies of grain fell short of world demand, sending prices soaring to record levels, adding to the costs of livestock producers, whose products accordingly rose in price. At the end of 1974, the World Food Conference was held in Rome, under the auspices of the United Nations, and many fine speeches were made. The United States, on whose initiative the conference was held, advanced proposals for an international system of nationally-held grain reserves, for the twin purposes of famine relief and market stabilisation. It was agreed that the proposals, which are discussed in Chapters 8 and 9 below, should be pursued in the context of a new international grains arrangement.[16]

Turning to the second group's problems, with the dramatic increases in the price of oil at the end of 1973 the prices and supplies of other raw materials became a major issue in the conduct of international relations, forcing the governments of the developed countries to consider demands from the developing ones for a whole New International Economic Order.[17] As already indicated, however, the need to reform the world economic order was in the forefront of serious policy discussion, if not in all capitals, a good while before it was adopted as a slogan of the Third World. What the developing countries succeeded in doing, however, through the United Nations and its agencies, was to concentrate political attention in the developed countries on the questions involved.[18] More specifically they highlighted their stake in the international trading system. The danger was that the developing countries would get carried away by their own rhetoric and allow themselves to be diverted from the 'nitty gritty' of the GATT negotiations.[19]

Unfortunately the GATT negotiations had to mark time until the Congress of the United States could afford the Administration an authority to negotiate and until, too, the Council of Ministers of the European Community could approve negotiating directives for the Commission.[20] The ministers who met in the Japanese capital in September 1973 to finalise the Tokyo Declaration, which formally launched the negotiations, envisaged the negotiations being completed in 1975! But it was not until February 1975 that the negotiations began to get down to business in Geneva. And it was plain even then that they would take four or five years to conclude[21] – although, in a sense, if they succeed they should never end, since what should result is a continuing process of consultation and negotiation.

The slow progress of events, and the somewhat ambiguous commitment of governments to the success of the Tokyo Round negotiations, has been a reflection of the evident inability of political thought to keep pace with the rapid integration and growing interdependence of the world economy.[22] Six previous GATT rounds helped to produce a doubling of world trade during the 1960s and after; in fact, world trade was then expanding twice as fast as world production. Intense competition, large-scale capital flows, technological advances in both industry and agriculture, still greater economies of scale and the development of rapid transport and communications have been further factors exerting a profound and continuing influence on the pattern of international trade and production.[23]

FUNDAMENTAL ISSUE ON THE GATT AGENDA

In the final analysis, the Tokyo Round negotiations are between the European Community, Japan and the United States. Other industrialised countries and some developing ones are involved to varying degrees. Indeed, the roles of the smaller trading partners could be significant, if only they realise as much (as, in a way, they have come to do since the demands of the Third World for a New International Economic Order began to make a political impact on the major industrialised countries). Unless the big three are able to agree, however, there can be no overall agreement worth mentioning.

At the outset it was clear that two fundamental issues would need to be addressed constructively if the negotiations were not to come to grief or produce, what might be worse, an even deeper sense of frustration in economic relations among the major trading powers.

One issue relates to the division of the free-enterprise world into economic spheres of influence. That prospect has developed because of the multiplying number of discriminatory trading arrangements that have been appearing on the world scene since the mid-1960s. It is at the heart of the question of what is to be done about remaining tariffs on industrial products traded among developed countries.[24]

The other issue relates to the isolation of commercial markets for temperate-zone farm commodities. For little or no impact has been made, in either the Kennedy Round or previous negotiations, on the rising trend of protection accorded to relatively high-cost farmers in industrialised countries against the competition of relatively low-cost farmers in agricultural-exporting countries.[25]

Neither issue is discussed at inter-governmental level in such bald terms. That is the way both were posed though by those, not only in the United States but also elsewhere, who began calling for the reform of the GATT system of international trade in the mid-1960s.[26]

It is the second issue which is the concern of this volume. By what means are commercial markets for agricultural products being protected from international competition? Tariffs have been extensively used in the past. But now they are only of marginal significance, given that they do not exclude imports, which is what interests high-cost producers worried about their levels of income. Quantitative import restrictions, not to mention outright embargoes, and variable import levies have thus become the principal instruments of farm-support policies. Even so, the significance of other non-tariff measures, mostly relating to health standards, should not be overlooked. While the protection of public health is a legitimate objective, some food regulations go further than appears necessary. Some provincial regulations in federal countries exclude foreign products from the market for reasons that products from other provinces are not required to satisfy.

Agriculture is a vital source of earnings for many developed and developing countries. These countries have recognised that in many industrialised economies the farming community poses difficult politico-social problems. Those problems relate specifically to the position of low-income farmers. But it is not altogether clear how measures to restrict imports help low-income farmers relative to high-income farmers. Over the years, therefore, the agricultural-exporting countries have been pressing, and quite understandably, for a remedy to be brought to a situation that is both inefficient and inequitable.

Gatt Record on Agricultural Trade
The treatment of agricultural problems in the GATT framework, however, has been far from impressive.[27] Efforts by agricultural-exporting
countries to promote a coordinated approach to their problems have
always been resisted by more strongly-placed industrialised countries.
Almost from the outset the major signatories to the General Agreement, while acknowledging trade to be mutually advantageous,
deferred to immediate realities where agricultural products were concerned by allowing quantitative restrictions to be imposed on imports
that threatened those domestic farm-support policies which were of
the supply-control type.
    The exemption of agriculture from the general movement of trade
liberalisation was made in the early 1950s to avoid conflict with the
agricultural policy of the United States which, since the Agricultural
Act of 1933 (and legislation in 1938), had been based on the control
of agricultural acreage in production. The 1933 act contained a clause
which empowered the Administration to impose quotas where farm-
support programmes were endangered by imports and this clause,
Section 22, was later strengthened. In 1944 a formally-granted waiver
of GATT rules gave a general exemption to the United States. This
was taken as a sign that domestic farm-support policies took pre-
cedence over the principles laid down in the General Agreement. In
view of the damage done to the credibility of GATT principles it is
therefore ironic that since the later 1960s the United States has
resorted only sparingly to 'Section 22' measures.
    In the 1950s the countries of Western Europe, having inconvertible
currencies, were able to invoke the provision in the GATT for import
controls to be maintained on balance-of-payments grounds. (Japan
also exploited Article 12 when she acceded to the GATT in 1955.) With
all of them, however, the justifications were spurious, to say the least. As
the currencies of Western Europe became convertible the pervasive
protection accorded to agriculture became more and more apparent.
Other dimensions of the problem of international trade in temperate-
zone agricultural products became better known through a major GATT
enquiry and through the discussions that were held in consequence.
    For the difficulties associated with agricultural trade led in 1957
to the appointment by the signatory countries to the GATT of a panel
of experts – comprising four economists of international reputation[28]
– to enquire into trends and prospects in international trade with
particular reference to three points: 'the failure of the trade of less
developed countries to develop as rapidly as that of industrialized
countries, excessive short-term fluctuations in the prices of primary
products, and the widespread resort to agricultural protection.' It is
worth recalling the state of affairs that existed in the late 1950s.

The panel's report, usually referred to as the Haberler Report, was published in 1958.[29] It could not say precisely to what extent the relatively slow increase in agricultural trade in the post-war period was due to the protection of agriculture in both importing and exporting countries. But it pointed to two incontrovertible facts: (i) Agricultural protectionism existed at a high level in most of the highly industrialised countries. (ii) And as a result the net import of agricultural products into these countries was becoming increasingly marginal in relation to the development of domestic production and consumption. The Haberler Report thus established that agricultural protectionism in the industrialised countries was a major restriction on world agricultural trade.[30]

No drastic remedies were urged. Political leaders were not asked to put their political lives on the line. For the Haberler Report did not advocate any sudden or sharp reduction in the degree of protection. Rather the experts suggested that a moderate restraint on production and a moderate stimulus to consumption might over a number of years have a substantial percentage effect on the volume of imports.[31] Some protection was needed to ensure a decent living to uneconomic peasant farmers in Western Europe. But with suitable changes in organisation, the Haberler Report argued, the agriculture of Western Europe could become as efficient as any in the world. The reduction of protection, it continued, should be only one element in a combined operation, involving improvements in agricultural structure, social measures to guard against human distress and an expansion of employment opportunities in other occupations.[32]

The report recommended a gradual shift from systems of price support, which raise consumer prices, to systems of direct income support (it referred to 'deficiency payments as used in the United Kingdom, as explained below). Such a shift would have two advantages: First, the cost of direct income payments would be incorporated in national budgets and thus come under public scrutiny, which in itself might exercise a moderating influence on the degree of protection. Secondly, it could result in lower prices to consumers, which might stimulate consumption of some products.[33]

Getting governments to set up an expert enquiry and getting them to act on its findings are, however, two very different matters. The publication of the Haberler Report was accordingly followed by the setting up of a number of committees in the GATT framework. One of them, Committee II, was given the task of (i) assembling 'data regarding the use by signatory countries of non-tariff measures for the protection of agriculture or [for governments that were squeamish about the use of ten-letter words] in support of income of agricultural producers, and the agricultural policies from which these measures derive'.[34] It was also requested (ii) to examine the effects of these

measures on international trade, (iii) to consider the extent to which
the rules of the GATT were inadequate to promote international
trade, and (iv) to consider, also, appropriate steps that might be taken
in the circumstances. Finally it was asked (v) to suggest procedures
for further consultations on agricultural policies as they affect international trade.

After lengthy consultation on the farm-support policies of thirty-
four countries Committee II published its conclusions in 1962. The
reports were very revealing. Through the mass of diplomatic verbiage
seeped a sense of surprise and even shock at just how pervasive was
the protection of temperate-zone agricultural commodities. For each
of the six commodities studied, it was found, 'there has been extensive resort to non-tariff devices involving protection to an extent and
having consequences which were probably not fully recognized
earlier'.[35]

The GATT committee agreed that protectionism had seriously
affected agricultural trade in a variety of ways and had contributed
to inefficiency in the allocation of resources. Protection in the traditional importing countries was deemed to have placed a heavy burden
of adjustment on traditional exporting countries. The benefits which
the latter had expected from the GATT had been impaired or nullified
by non-tariff devices. 'These developments', the committee concluded, 'are of such a character that either they have weakened or
threaten to weaken the operation of the General Agreement as an
instrument for the promotion of mutually advantageous trade.'[36]

Impact of the European Community

That was before the negotiations of the European Community's
common agricultural policy (CAP). Because of the way it has been
managed, rather than because of the instruments it has employed, the
policy has made a substantial impact on international trade. It has
also diverted the attention of inter-governmental discussions which,
in the middle 1970s, seem to be back where they were in the late
1950s.

At this juncture it would be as well then to outline the common
agricultural policy of the 'new Europe'. Protection of the Community
market for agricultural commodities is based on three sets of prices
that are fixed by the Council of Ministers: 'target prices', 'intervention prices' and 'threshold prices'.

Target prices are theoretical prices fixed with the purported aim of
ensuring reasonable prices to consumers and reasonable incomes to
producers, as well as fostering the harmonious development of international trade. For some commodities, such as beef, 'guide prices'
are fixed instead of target prices, but these are similar in intent.

Intervention prices are guaranteed prices at which government agencies will undertake support buying of some commodities if necessary. They range from 40 per cent of the target prices for some of the fruits and vegetables to 95 per cent for sugar and some grains. Producer organisations may undertake support buying of some other commodities. The intervention price represents a floor to the market, although producers pay for the cost of transportation of their produce to the intervention centres.

Threshold prices are minimum prices at which imports can enter the Community market. If trade prices on the world market are below threshold prices, a (variable) levy is imposed to the extent of the difference. Imports entering at the threshold price should sell at around the target price on internal markets because the two prices are linked by the notional cost of transportation.

Farmers in the European Community are thus encouraged to produce, to the limit of their technical capabilities, commodities for which intervention prices are in force or support buying is conducted by their organisations. Sugar is the only commodity subject to production controls – actually an escalating price inhibition.[37]

About half the agricultural imports of the European Community are subject to 'variable import levies', the main commodities affected being grains, poultry, eggs, milk and sugar. Each variable levy is equal to the difference between the threshold price and the most favourable c.i.f. import price (including cost, insurance and freight) for the particular commodity. Other commodities are subject to fixed tariffs except for a few which are in deficit supply. In the case of beef, fruit and vegetables, fixed tariffs may be supplemented by variable levies equal to the difference between duty-paid import prices and threshold prices. Frozen beef is also subject to import quotas. (Restrictions on beef imports were temporarily lifted in 1973 in the face of world-wide shortages.) Levies on grain-fed products, such as pork, poultry and eggs, take account of differences between grain prices in the Community and in world markets; levies on processed products, such as milled rice, contain an element for the protection of processors in the Common Market.[38]

The European Community's machinery is completed by its provision for export subsidies or 'restitutions'. In principle the subsidy per unit of export may not exceed the import levy currently applying to the particular commodity. The common agricultural policy also has a safeguard clause for some commodities, allowing appropriate measures to be taken if imports cause, or threaten to cause, grave disturbances in members' markets which might interfere with the basic objectives of the policy. Finally, provision has been made, more recently, for export levies to apply when world prices rise above Community prices.

Under the common agricultural policy the tendency in the European

Community has been to set price levels high enough to satisfy the higher-cost farmers (mostly in West Germany).[39] The lower-cost farmers have thus been induced to expand production and, increasing their vested interest in high prices, the added profitability of their farms has been written into higher land values. In all commodities covered by the policy, the Community became increasingly self-sufficient and, as the 1960s progressed, even-lower-cost suppliers 'outside' were increasingly excluded from the market. What was worse, by the late 1960s the high prices of the European Community were generating large surpluses, which had to be either stored or destroyed at heavy cost or dumped, also at heavy cost, on 'world' markets.

As a result, the European Community's common agricultural policy came to be regarded as a major source of tension in international economic relations,[40] eventually affecting political relations. By dumping surpluses on 'world' markets, the Community was depressing the prices available to traditional exporters, obliging them to cut production. In this way, the Community has been, in effect, transferring its agricultural adjustment problems to other countries – without really doing much about them itself.

Kennedy Round a turning point?

Although tariffs on a number of agricultural commodities were lowered and 'bound' in the 1960–61 Dillon Round of GATT negotiations, it was not until the 1963–67 Kennedy Round negotiations that the United States insisted on concerted attention being given to agricultural trade problems. Even then, the Kennedy Administration apparently did not seriously believe that much could be achieved, in spite of the promise to Congress to make progress on the industrial side of the negotiations conditional on progress on the agricultural side.[41]

The Kennedy Round discussions on agricultural trade went through two phases. First there was a period of confrontation and clash of philosophy which put the entire negotiations at risk. Then there was a hurried attempt at the end to rescue from the deadlock some advantage for agricultural trade:

1. In the confrontation phase the United States argued for the modification of the European Community's variable import-levy system of agricultural support and for the lowering of protection thus accorded to European farmers. The European Community was then suggesting an organised world market where countries would agree to 'reference prices' for farm products entering international trade. It offered to freeze, along with other countries, the level of support given to these prices. To the United States the *montant de soutien* proposal was seen as simply a means of validating the variable import levy;

the proposition, it was thought, would contribute nothing substantial to the liberalisation of agricultural trade.[42]

2. The final phase of the Kennedy Round negotiations produced no more than an agreement on cereal prices, along the lines of successive international wheat agreements, with the addition of a food-aid scheme. But the International Grains Arrangement lapsed within months of the GATT negotiations being concluded.[43]

Agriculture has benefited, indirectly, from the success achieved on the industrial side of the Kennedy Round negotiations, as it has from previous GATT rounds, through the contribution to growth and prosperity of further trade liberalisation. But the outcome of the negotiations on the agricultural side was extremely disappointing. Even so, the Kennedy Round negotiations may be deemed to be, in the end, a turning point historically in the approach to agricultural trade problems. In all GATT negotiations to date the governments of industrialised countries have stressed their national difficulties. Yet they have shown little perceptible interest in reforming their farm-support policies. Towards the end of the Kennedy Round negotiations it began to be generally acknowledged that without such an interest in taking national action to correct at least part of the international disarray there would be little chance of achieving significant progress.[44]

In the preparations for the Tokyo Round negotiations Sir Christopher Soames, as the European Community's Commissioner for External Affairs, warned the European Parliament that unless significant progress is made in opening agricultural trade the further liberalisation of international trade in industrial products could be jeopardised.[45] Both the politico-economic and politico-strategic implications of a breakdown in the Tokyo Round negtiations are difficult to predict. But they would be serious. And they could be disastrous.

CHANGES IN THE CLIMATE OF NEGOTIATIONS

With the restoration of prosperity, self-confidence and security to Western Europe there has been an inclination among industrial countries to take for granted the continuance of order in the world economy. 'Without the bitter memory of the 1930s to spur them on,' wrote a commentator in the *Guardian* early in 1974, 'the industrial countries are likely to set less store by trade liberalisation than they did in the first two decades after World War II.'[46]

If it is the threat of dire consequences that in the end persuades governments to pursue sensible policies, having exhausted all other possibilities, it might not be necessary for them to remember back to the Great Depression. More recent events should be stimulus enough. For the precipitation of the oil crisis at the end of 1973 underscored, rather forcefully, the extent to which the international system of trade and payments has been in need of reform.[47]

Indeed, on top of the problems of world-wide inflation and food supply, the oil crisis has reinforced a spreading realisation that, with the growing integration of the world economy, many of the fundamental issues facing governments are international in character and require international solutions. In an age of rapid transport and communications around the whole world it is a paradox of contemporary politics that, as a guide to future action, emphasis is still put on geographical propinquity and on the political movements it has engendered. In the 1970s, as never before, it is necessary to think globally and acknowledge that the economic and political interests of countries are defined, not so much by their locations in relation to a continent or an ocean, but more by the network of their relations with other countries throughout the international commmunity.[48]

Since the early 1960s there have been several other developments in international economic relations that can be expected to influence the climate of the Tokyo Round negotiations and later GATT discussions. While the arguments have not changed much, the international situation has changed considerably. It is therefore worth dwelling on these politico-economic developments before turning to an examination of farm-support policies. Six might be cited.

First, mention has been made of the two groups of countries that were beginning in the 1960s to expect more from the international system of trade and payments: the exporters of agricultural products and the developing countries. When the industrialised countries failed to act on, *inter alia*, the Haberler Report and the recommendations of the GATT committees which followed, the developing countries commenced to organise themselves, first in the United Nations Conference on Trade and Development (UNCTAD) and then elsewhere.

Second, the United States embarked, in the mid-1960s, on a radical reappraisal of its farm-support policies. The purpose has been to return to a market orientation of agricultural policies that would dispense with the major elements of acreage control and income-support payments. This course has been presented in terms of removing government constraints on the decisions of farmers. But it stems from a need to control inflation and reduce the cost of government measures. For there is a widespread disenchantment in the United States with the present and past performance of farm-support policies.

Besides the reorientation of agricultural policies, several other factors, representing a third development, have been influencing the American position. As the United States becomes more and more a service economy, agricultural production is likely to assume greater importance *vis-à-vis* industrial production, particularly where foreign trade is concerned.[49] Manufacturing capacity can be, and is being, shifted abroad in response to competition in the home market from lower-cost foreign suppliers. But it is not possible to respond in that way with land. Because the labour unions are no longer strong upholders of liberal trade policies, now that they regard foreign investment as the 'export of jobs' (although that argument lost much of its force with the advent of more flexible exchange rates), the Administration has to rely more in its relations with the Congress on the support of the farm lobby in order to sustain an outward-looking commercial policy. Since the industrial exports of the United States, mostly high-technology products, are not greatly troubled by the remaining tariffs of other industrialised countries, the primary interest of the United States in international economic negotiations is in the agricultural field. After the Kennedy Round negotiations, and as the European Community's common agricultural policy began to make an impact on the rest of the world, intense official and public attention was brought to bear on the problems of agricultural trade. For the first time in the GATT's history, the United States was on the same side as Argentina, Australia, Canada and New Zealand in wanting steps taken to enlarge the opportunities for trade in temperate-zone foodstuffs.

In the European Community, as well, there has been widespread disenchantment – especially in West Germany – with the past and present performance of farm-support policies. Fourthly, then, the common agricultural policy has been under strain internally for reasons partly to do with the lack of progress towards monetary union and with the embarrassment, too, of surplus production in some commodities. The Commission has advanced proposals for agricultural policy. But they have concentrated on internal problems: (i) achieving a better balance between the relative prices of feed-grains; (ii) reducing wasteful production on the dairy side, especially butter; (iii) rationalising the structure of the agricultural sector; (iv) shifting the emphasis away from the production of cereals to the production of livestock products; and (v) reducing the overall costs of the whole farm-support system. But rapid advances are not expected.

The question of the effects of the common agricultural policy on world trade has mainly been seen as an annoyance which diverts attention from internal problems. Following its enlargement – with the admission of the United Kingdom, Denmark and the Irish Republic – the European Community looms too large though in international trade for it to eschew responsibility for the impact on the economies of other countries of its internal policies. This fifth development is something which individual member countries, not accustomed to considering 'international responsibilities', may have difficulty in accepting. Even so, some changes in the common agricultural policy would have positive effects on the trade problem, and hence might be orchestrated to coincide with the Tokyo Round negotiations.

Over the 1960s and early 1970s the composition of the councils
responsible for the international scheme of things has greatly changed
– the sixth development to be cited. In the immediate post-war period
the countries whose wealth and power gave them special responsibility
for world order and prosperity were concentrated in North America
and Western Europe. But during the 1960s the geo-political boun-
daries of the 1950s began to blur as new powers began to become
involved in international relations. No longer was it appropriate for
the institutions of the developed world to be confined to Atlantic
countries. Japan joined the Group of Ten and also the Organisation for
Economic Cooperation and Development (OECD), which Australia
and New Zealand have since joined, strengthening the agricultural-
exporting interest in the organisation. In addition, greater account now
has to be taken of Brazil, Mexico and South Africa.[50] Commodity
shortages and the oil crisis have strengthened the position of the
developing countries, especially the Arab oil producers, but they
remain basically divided in spite of appearances to the contrary.[51]

In inter-governmental discussions on agricultural trade questions
the balance of forces has therefore shifted. Moreover, the climate for
discussions has improved, following the high prices that prevailed for
a time in world markets for temperate-zone farm commodities after
1972/73. Shortages in many commodity markets relieved much of the
political pressure in the United States to push for greater access to the
European Community for American agricultural exports. And commodity prices in the Common Market itself have been closer to, and
in some cases even below, world prices. There has thus been less
reason than before for the United States and the European Community
to conduct negotiations in an atmosphere of mutual recrimination.
Governments have been obliged to think afresh on the whole nature
of the problems involved.

Outlook for Agricultural Trade
How long the sellers' market for farm produce would continue became
highly debatable in the aftermath of the 1972/73 season. Without
some sense of the direction of agricultural trade it was difficult to
prepare for international negotiations on the conduct of domestic
farm-support policies. Counsels have been divided and as a result the
making of policy – involving choices between options each having
wide implications – has been seriously hampered.

In the European Community some argued that high commodity
prices in world markets, in the mid-1970s, proved that the common
agricultural policy had been right in principle all along. Why, then,
did the Community's farmers still need so much protection? Why
weren't the instruments of the policy withdrawn? To those in Britain
who, at that time, bemoaned the excesses of the common agricultural

policy, and hankered after imports from low-cost Commonwealth sources, it was blandly said that 'the days of cheap food are gone forever'.[52] Did that mean – although nobody in the information media took the trouble to ask at the time – that the cost of food production in North America and Australasia had moved, fundamentally and on a permanent basis, to a higher level on a par with the cost of food production in the European Community? Had the United States, Canada, Australia and New Zealand – never mind Argentina, South Africa and others – lost their comparative advantage over the European Community in the production of temperate-zone agricultural commodities? Plainly not.

But the issues involved are too complicated for such superficial treatment and public discussion of them is not greatly helped by focusing on propaganda points. In this connection, a recent report, on the economic future of the European Community, recalled the old political adage that the lie is half-way round the world before the truth has got its boots on. 'It seems to be the motto of many apologists for the Community's shortcomings,' it observed, 'but it does not serve the cause of European unity any good, no good at all.'[53]

To go back to the start of the difficulties of the mid-1970s, let us consider the situation affecting grain prices, which are a key determinant of prices for livestock products. In 1972 world output of all grains, including rice, dropped 3 per cent to 1164m metric tons. Excluding rice, the figure was 879m metric tons, but consumption in that year was 919m metric tons. Stocks were running out and so, with demand apparently outstripping supply, there was world-wide concern that grain shortages were imminent. Would the shortages be temporary or continuing? Was it just an extraordinary coincidence of events in 1972 that shook confidence in the world's capacity to produce enough food to go round? Or was 1972 symptomatic of a new combination of forces making for a new world situation in which grain supplies would be chronically short, or would fluctuate widely, thereby requiring a new set of policies relating to the production and distribution of temperate-zone foodstuffs? For some guidance on these questions it is necessary to review the various factors which have been affecting supply and demand.

Supply factors

World production of grain in the period 1966–71 grew faster than world population. This was due in part to the Green Revolution in the developing countries. But it was due, too, to other technological advances in agricultural production in the developed countries. It was therefore thought that grain supplies could meet demand both for increased human consumption and for increased livestock production.

In the 1950s and early 1960s, the United States built up large stockpiles of grains, almost as a by-product of its farm-support policies. These stocks accounted for the bulk of world reserves and helped to moderate the price effect of fluctuations in production. But a number of developments contributed to the depletion of these reserves: famine relief, a succession of bad harvests in various major exporting countries, purchases in the world market by China and the Soviet Union and increased livestock production. By the late 1960s the world's reserves of grain were getting very low.

Also by the late 1960s, the European Community's common agricultural policy began, as already mentioned, to make a substantial impact on international trade in temperate-zone commodities. Surpluses generated by high support prices (protected by variable import levies) were being increasingly dumped, with the help of export subsidies, on the 'world' markets of the traditional exporting countries. These last, such low-cost producers as the United States, Canada and Australia, were thus confronted with depressed prices, which induced them to cut production. These cuts contributed to the problem of tight supplies.

By the same token, however, the resumption of former production levels should contribute to an improved balance between supply and demand. After the years of shortage, in 1973 and 1974, large increases in grain production, and in other commodities, were expected in the United States, Canada and elsewhere, as arable acres previously held out of production altogether began being brought back under the plough. And 'new' land began to be brought into production in many parts of the world. It should be noted, though, that land not regularly sown tends to be more marginal than land kept in production, for farmers 'put aside' their worst land first. Thus the yield on marginal land is usually lower and less viable.

Increased production may entail higher risks due to lack of crop insurance, storage capacity and transport facilities. Moreover, with the oil crisis, there has been uncertainty about the availability and cost of fuel for planting, harvesting and drying. And the availability and cost of fertilisers and other inputs has also been affected. These factors, combined with the tendency in all countries towards inflation, have added up to higher costs for food production.

Bad weather was the main cause of the fall in grain production in 1972. This factor is not susceptible to government intervention, but the probability of weather conditions reducing crops below 90 per cent of 'normal' is said by many climatologists to be of the order of one year in ten.

Demand factors

Turning to demand factors, the *de facto* devaluation of the American dollar, following the 1971 monetary crisis, made American grain a more attractive purchase and there have since been increased purchases from abroad. This has certainly been one of the lesser causes of tight supplies.

As real incomes improve consumers tend to turn to high-protein diets and eat more meat. In 1970–73 real incomes improved rapidly and pig and cattle numbers increased at twice the rate of the previous five years. There has hence been an expansion of demand for feed-grains; and this expansion is expected to continue with the rising level of real incomes, particularly in the developed countries.

Almost a factor on its own, but not to be exaggerated, has been the deliberate decision of the Soviet Union to develop livestock production and to purchase more heavily in the world market for feed-grains. The prospect of growing Soviet demand over the long term has been a source of considerable optimism that could transform the outlook for agricultural trade. This, however, remains to be seen.

One major query has hung over the long-term prospect of rising world-wide demand for grains. For the reduced rates of growth in national economies and the recession that resulted from, *inter alia*, the sharp increase in crude oil prices has affected the outlook.

On the basis of Arabian light crude, the revenue accruing to the governments of oil-producing countries rose from $0.91 in 1970 to $1.27 under the Tehran Agreement of 1971, to about $3.30 in October 1973 and to around $8.00 in January 1974. With further increases in revenue since then, the net liquid assets in the hands of the oil-producing countries could increase by up to $70,000m per annum, which compared with a total amount in the Euro-dollar market in the region of $100,000m early 1970s. At current prices, an 'oil-debt over-hang' of $200,000m to $400,000m could accumulate by 1980, assuming that the oil-importing countries are prepared to carry such debt.[54]

Oil-producing countries, however, will not be in a position for some time to absorb real transfers of goods as a counterpart to this debt, which means that unprecedented financial flows are going to be generated. These flows could have a distorting and disrupting effect on the exchange rates of major currencies. The fear has been that some countries may be tempted, and may even feel obliged, to achieve a balance on their current accounts by resorting – in spite of international commitments – to import restrictions, domestic deflation and competitive devaluations. Accordingly, the cause of concern has not only been the size of the transfer problem, which is small in relation to the total income of oil-importing countries, but how the transfer is managed by the industrialised countries.[55]

Need for flexible policies

In view of the uncertain outlook for international trade in temperate-zone foodstuffs, governments need to prepare for all eventualities, ranging from shortages to surpluses. And it only requires a change in supply or demand of a few percentage points to make the difference. Governments have in any case been developing a greater degree of flexibility in the use of instruments of farm-support policies – even if the arguments relating to such measures have hardly changed since the Haberler Report. That flexibility has to be developed further.

When considering the agenda of international discussions on the conduct of farm-support policies, it should be remembered that the *economic* purpose of trade liberalisation is not so much the expansion of trade *per se*, however much that may be politically necessary; rather it is to bring about a better allocation of resources, both domestically and internationally. There are now powerful reasons for encouraging resources to shift into the expansion of agricultural production in areas of the world where it enjoys comparative cost advantages. Shortages of key commodities need to be overcome. Rising food prices need to be checked in order to counter inflation. And in industrialised countries resources need to be made available for the development of alternative sources of energy. In an economic activity that is subject to so much government intervention it is impossible for governments to absolve themselves from responsibility for the disarray into which world agriculture has fallen.

REASONS FOR FARM-SUPPORT POLICIES

Why have governments intervened as much as they have? What are the social, economic and political reasons for farm-support policies? Social, economic and political factors interact. For the purposes of discussion, however, they will be treated under separate headings.

Social Reasons
Of the social factors, there are basically two, both based on value judgements, and therefore assessing their importance is extremely difficult. To varying degrees they are at work in the body politic of most Western countries.

1. Living on the land, under freehold conditions, is regarded for a start as 'a good way of life'. According to the tenets of 'agricultural fundamentalism' the small farmer should be helped to survive.[56] Are small farmers though the major beneficiaries of farm-support policies? The conclusion of Chapter 6 below is that in the United Kingdom they are not the major beneficiaries; instead, the major beneficiaries are the big farmers.[57]

2. There is an environmental interest in maintaining an open countryside – and not just for the benefit of the urban population. If farmers are prospering, they and their land will represent a social good in a modern industrial society, providing relief from pollution

and close living. But there can be a conflict between public and private interests. For as an observer of the French scene once mused: 'If prices are low, farmers cut the hedges to sow more seed; and then the wind blows and the land is spoiled. And if prices are high, farmers cut the hedges to sow more seed; and then the wind blows and the land is spoiled.'

Economic Reasons
In considering the economic arguments for farm-support policies, there is one overriding reason to do with farm prices, supported by three others relating to output, input and technology.

1. Because of the extreme inelasticity of demand for most farm products there tend to be wide fluctuations in prices for them. With producers on the one hand not liking low prices and consumers on the other not liking high ones, measures are devised to support commodity prices and/or farm incomes, reflecting a bias towards producer interests. These measures frequently have to be accompanied by programmes for distributing surpluses by fair means or foul.

2. Variations in weather conditions, in both space and time, lead to variations in the volume of farm production. The resultant fluctuations in prices can be quite dramatic – as in 1972/73.

3. In addition, the fixity of inputs – labour, machinery, fertiliser and so on – in family farming seriously obstructs adjustments in the allocation of overall resources that might otherwise result from general movements in the level of farm prices. This further contributes to the instability of price levels.

4. Finally, rapid advances in agricultural technology, supported by public finance, can force farm prices down and hold them down by a kind of 'treadmill' effect.

Political Reasons
In a sense there are no independent political reasons for agricultural-support policies. For political pressures to support farm prices and incomes are an expression of socio-economic problems in rural areas. And the larger and better organised the producer interest[58] the stronger is its political effect. Indeed, a point is reached when some socio-economic arguments, although by no means all, appear to be convenient rationalisations for measures largely decided on political grounds. But the decisions might be different if the consumer interest – giving vent to socio-economic problems in urban areas – was better organised.

Whether, in parliamentary democracies, the agricultural vote *per se* is an important factor influencing farm-support policies is rather a moot point. In Japan nearly half the members of the Diet represent rural constituencies although they only account for one-third of the electorate. This might account for the extreme caution of successive Japanese governments in contemplating changes in agricultural measures. In the United Kingdom opinion surveys of rural constitu- encies suggest that the farming community is so conservative it would vote for the Conservative Party however much the level of farm support was reduced.[59] But the Labour Party, having little strength in rural constituencies, has never made any serious proposals for shifting the bias of farm-support policies away from producer interests in the direction of consumer interests in urban constituencies.

The conservative nature of rural voters, even at times when their sense of grievance over prices is running high, was once remarked on by François Mitterand – just after the French general elections in 1973. 'On Monday', the Socialist leader said, 'the farmers of Brittany dumped their artichokes in the courtyard of the Prefecture. On Tues- day it was the turn of surplus potatoes. On Wednesday they barricaded the roads and protested still more. On Thursday they began breaking windows. On Friday they blocked the traffic around the Paris Opera and demonstrated outside the Ministry of Finance. On Saturday I don't know what they did. But on Sunday they voted for the Government!'[60]

Whatever view is taken of specific political reasons for affording support to the agricultural sector of the economy, there are – in another sense – general political reasons for doing so, ones rooted in general economic policy. For over the post-war period governments have been assuming a wider range of responsibilities or obligations which have significant implications for agriculture.[61]

1. First, there is the responsibility they have assumed for the distri- bution of population within a country, in particular for the balance between different regions and between urban and rural employment. One of the dominant considerations in the discussion of rural develop- ment in the United States has been the link between 'the urban crisis' and the exodus of people from the land.

2. What is more, governments have accepted an obligation, where they are rich enough, to maintain a balance in income between dif- ferent sectors in their economies. But keeping agricultural incomes in some politically acceptable relationship to industrial incomes has far- reaching implications – as the Haberler Report made clear. What needs to be examined more is the income-distribution effects among the farming population of the measures taken to lift agricultural incomes nearer to industrial levels.[62]

3. The commitment on the part of governments to maintain full employment has been carried much further since the immediate post- war period. Now there appears to be a commitment not only for every man to be employed, but for him to be employed in the occupation of his choice, in the location of his choice and, it would sometimes seem, at the income of his choice.

4. Governments are also undertaking responsibility for the distribution of income as a whole. The work of economists in recent years has shown that the distribution of income is related fundamentally to the distribution of income-producing assets and skills. Until governments provide greater educational opportunities for farming communities the problems of rural poverty will persist irrespective of interventions in the market place.

5. There is governmental interest, too, in the redistribution of the gains from technical change. This provides a powerful explanation for many farm-support policies. For it is felt that in an unregulated economy farmers would not benefit from technological advances in production.

6. Governments are interested in the general stability of incomes and, in particular, in the presumption that agricultural incomes are more unstable than incomes in other sectors. Concern over the instability of agricultural incomes declined for a time, but it has been coming back into prominence, especially in the European Community. Indeed, there is no way of understanding agricultural policy in Western Europe, either nationally or at Community level, except in terms of the premium placed on stability of incomes and of the need to insulate the agricultural sector from 'outside' economic forces.

7. From time to time, governments have used particular sectors to defend the exchange rate of their currency, although not always successfully. In several West European countries, and in Japan, agriculture has been induced to engage in import substitution and export expansion.[63]

8. The general movement of governments towards comprehensive incomes policies also has important implications for agriculture. It might be said, in fact, that agriculture has already been subject to an incomes policy and that other sectors are being brought into line.

9. Then governments are interested in the stability and adequacy of food supplies. The issue has been most potent in times of international tension and threat to security. But it has been revived with the development of world commodity shortages – as discussed above.[64]

CONSTRAINTS ON POLICY OBJECTIVES

In pursuit of these policies, governments operate under constraints, some more pressing than others. These might be briefly stated.

Limitations on Expenditure
Most governments are obliged to limit expenditure. And such limitations influence the type of policies that are pursued. Governments are accordingly biased in the direction of import controls. These greatly inhibit them in negotiations on the liberalisation of international trade.

Import restrictions play a role in farm-support policies in three important ways.[65]

First, import restrictions enable governments to pursue income-support schemes in a convenient way by limiting – even eliminating – competition from overseas producers. This has the additional benefit of producing government revenue through an indirect tax on consumers, whereas many other forms of income support, such as deficiency payments, necessitate an outlay of funds from the treasury. Governments will only give up the convenience of import controls when consumers and their political champions (i) object strongly to indirect income-support based on high prices protected from low-price competition and (ii) show a willingness to bear the tax burden of direct income support.

Secondly, import restrictions enable governments to stabilise prices in domestic markets against the influence of fluctuations in world price levels. This, at any rate, is the rationale for variable import levies as opposed to fixed customs duties. The attractiveness of such devices will diminish only with the introduction of direct measures designed to stabilise world market prices.

Thirdly, import restrictions act to stop re-importation which would otherwise defeat the measures aimed at removing surplus production from the domestic market. The import levies of the European Community on butter, sugar and soft wheat at present act in this way, as do the 'Section 22' quotas of the United States. There seems little chance of abolishing import levies and customs duties of this type so long as domestic farm-support policies persist.

While governments are biased towards import controls, they are biased away from export subsidies, however much they may resort to them from time to time. Export subsidies, and other aids, are used as devices to boost farm incomes, but they have none of the advantages of import restrictions. They are expensive in terms of government expenditure and, moreover, they are politically vulnerable to the charge that foreign consumers benefit at the expense of domestic taxpayers.

It should therefore be possible for governments to reach an international agreement on the elimination of export subsidies. For it is more satisfactory to remove export subsidies on a multilateral basis than by a unilateral decision where the fall in export sales is likely to be greater.

Interdependence of Policies

Another major constraint on governments is the interdependence of their policies and those of other countries. For the farm-support policies of one country amount to a limitation of domestic demand for farm products from abroad. They have the effect, in other words, of limiting employment and incomes in the agricultural sectors of other countries.

Olivier Long, the Director-General of the GATT, in stressing the importance of the agricultural problem, has urged the recognition of two principles:[66]

(a) The cost of governments of maintaining a reasonable relationship between farmers' incomes and those of other sections of the population should not be shifted on to foreign producers.

(b) International cooperation in the broadest sense – extending from consultation to negotiation – is the only way of avoiding such shifts in the burden of farm-support costs.

In an increasingly interdependent world the international implications of farm-support policies are being felt more and more. As a result, agricultural issues are affecting international economic relations, which themselves have been moving nearer the centre of the world stage.

Necessity for Consistency
Turning to a third constraint, agricultural-support policies have to be consistent with other policies, if only to avoid conflicts and contradictions.

In the United Kingdom, for example, policies with respect to agriculture are having to be adjusted, not to comply with purely British objectives, but in order to be consistent with the wider purposes of membership of the European Community.

Mythologies
Finally, governments have to operate under less tangible constraints, which might be called mythologies. It is not that these constraints are necessarily untrue, but they are inclined to acquire a momentum unrelated to their truth value. One such mythology is the state of the world supply situation.

Indeed, the uncertainties about the world supply situation – whether there will be continuing shortages or a return to glut conditions – have made it extremely difficult to assess how the above factors might influence farm-support policies in the remainder of the 1970s.

POLICY IMPACT OF CURRENT TRENDS

Difficult as it is to determine the outcome on balance, there are a number of trends – both economic and political – that are likely over the 1970s to affect the various factors influencing policy.

1. To begin with, the decline in farm populations throughout the developed world, and the decline in the relative political importance

of the agricultural sector, is likely to continue. This trend can be expected slowly to erode the political power of producer interests which cannot therefore continue to rely on the kind of support they have enjoyed in the past.

2. With the increasing commercialisation of agriculture, especially in North America, the fixed-input argument – of significance in family farming – will become less important. Since agricultural corporations hire their labour they can lay it off as circumstances dictate.

3. There is a possibility, no more than that, of a sustained shift in the terms of trade in favour of agricultural production if world supplies lag behind a rapidly expanding demand for food. If the demand for beef in Japan, the Soviet Union and Western Europe continues to grow, as it has been doing in line with rising levels of real income, increased resources will have to be employed in the production of carcases.

These three trends would tend to moderate the pressure for agricultural support. But there is a fourth trend which is serving to accentuate fluctuations in farm prices.

4. This fourth trend is the relative price-inelasticity of demand for food under conditions of rising real incomes in developed countries at large. The marginal utility of money declines as incomes rise. As consumers become better off they are prepared to pay more for what they want.

5. As for trends in the making of farm-support policies, the discussion of objectives and constraints has already underlined their complexity, calling for numerous instruments. Any attempt to meet those objectives by a limited number of instruments is liable to encounter problems. In fact, this partly explains the difficulties being experienced with the European Community's common agricultural policy – currency problems apart. Too much has been expected of price-support measures.

In this connection, a group of leading European agricultural economists, meeting in 1973 under the auspices of the Trade Policy Research Centre and the Agricultural University of Wageningen, concluded that 'another source of stress [under the CAP] is the growing recognition that even a policy of high prices is insufficient to provide an acceptable minimal standard of living for many elderly families on small farms – especially those who live in the industrially less developed regions of the Community.[67] The distribution of human skills and physical assets is unequal in all European countries. Just as a free market system rewards roughly in proportion to the amount of labour and productive assets held by households, so an administered price system benefits most those who have more to sell.

'The need to improve the incomes of small farmers', the group continued, 'has to be reconciled with the necessity to avoid over-commitment of resources and excessive capitalization on the largest farms. While present price policy has enabled a significant number of medium-sized commercial family farms to adapt to changing conditions and to finance their growth, it has also brought disproportionate benefits to those large and highly specialized farms which would be able to adjust to a changing environment, even under a lower price level. . . .

'Political decisions tend to be based on short-run considerations, but their effects are long lasting. The European Community needs explicitly to accept responsibility for long-run development policy. Immediate decisions should moreover be consistent with long-run aims. Agricultural adjustment is a continuous process. The need for a consistent policy to share the benefits and to distribute the burdens of growth is perhaps more important in agriculture than elsewhere in the economy.

'Price policies alone are unsuited for such functions, particularly where price decisions are unduly influenced by short-run considerations. The variety of demands made on the common agricultural policy requires a more flexible use of present instruments and the possible use of additional policy measures,' the group concluded.

6. There appears to be a growing awareness, and as is argued in Chapter 7, that agricultural policies should be part of an overall social and economic policy for the development of an economy. In the European Community it is necessary to achieve equality of education in, and extend social services to, rural areas and then the adjustment problems besetting agriculture would be less severe.

7. In addition, it is being increasingly accepted that the traditional mechanisms of farm support are inefficient, even if it is difficult to make comparisons between the systems deemed appropriate in different countries. They all suffer from high external costs. Over the years, though, there have been improvements in methods of policy analysis in ministries of agriculture and these should lead, in due course, to the evolution of more efficient measures.

8. Governments have also recognised the need to think more in terms of food-supply policies to supplement farm-income policies. When in 1973 the United States imposed export controls on soya beans, even though in the end all orders were satisfied, a doubt was implanted in Western Europe about the assurance of future supplies. The episode has been used to argue the case for greater self-sufficiency. More emphasis has to be put on stockpiling and on the coordination of stock policies for the purposes of both development and price stabilisation.[68]

Such are the issues, and the factors influencing them, that need to be addressed in multilateral negotiations on trade in temperate-zone agricultural products.

SIGNIFICANCE OF TOKYO ROUND NEGOTIATIONS

Emphasis was placed at the beginning of this chapter on the deterioration in international economic relations that has been evident since the conclusion of the Kennedy Round negotiations. One of the main purposes of the Tokyo Round negotiations is to mend relations between the major trading powers – most notably the United States, Japan and the European Community – by getting to grips with the industrial and agricultural policy issues that have been dividing them. By negotiating, the risk of further deterioration is minimised; but it will not be enough to avoid a breakdown in the negotiations.

Whatever might be superficially agreed for the time being, if the negotiations result in disappointment and an even deeper sense of frustration in some countries, the long-term direction of their policies is likely to change. If none of the major trading powers is prepared thereafter to champion the GATT system – the only one we have – it would be difficult to contain the further loss of confidence in the international economic order that would ensue.

NOTES AND REFERENCES

1. This chapter is based on Hugh Corbet, *Agriculture's Place in Commercial Diplomacy*, Ditchley Paper No. 48 (Enstone: Ditchley Foundation, 1974).
2. For an account of the events leading to the General Agreement, and of subsequent negotiations, see William Adams Brown, *The United States and the Restoration of World Trade* (Washington: Brookings Institution, 1950); Richard N. Gardner, *Sterling–Dollar Diplomacy: Anglo-American Collaboration in the Reconstruction of Multilateral Trade* (Oxford: Clarendon Press, 1956); Gerard Curzon, *Multilateral Commercial Diplomacy* (London: Michael Joseph, 1965); Karen Kock, *International Trade Policy and the GATT 1947–67* (Stockholm: Almqvist & Wicksell, 1969); and Kenneth W. Dam, *The GATT Law and International Economic Organization* (Chicago and London: University of Chicago Press, 1970).
3. An analysis of the situation prior to the international economic crisis of 1971 is provided in Corbet, 'Global Challenge to Commercial Diplomacy', *Pacific Community*, Tokyo, October 1971, reproduced in the *Congressional Record*, Washington, 16 December 1971, pp. E 13590–3.
4. Curt Gasteyger, *Europe and America at the Crossroads* (Paris: Atlantic Institute for International Affairs, 1971) p. 37.
5. G. C. Allen, 'Japan's Place in Trade Strategy', in Corbet *et al.*, *Trade Strategy and the Asian–Pacific Region* (London: Allen & Unwin, for the Trade Policy Research Centre, 1971; and Toronto: University of Toronto Press, 1971) pp. 92–110.
6. *GATT Press Release*, Geneva, 10 February 1972.
7. The negotiations were formally launched with the Tokyo Declaration, which set out the 'terms of reference', so to speak. The text of the Declara-

tion can be found in *GATT Activities in 1973* (Geneva: GATT Secretariat, 1974) pp. 5–10.

8. The major issues to be addressed in the negotiations are analysed in Corbet and Robert Jackson (eds), *In Search of a New World Economic Order* (London: Croom Helm, for the Trade Policy Research Centre, 1974; and New York: Wiley, 1974).

9. The review began with the enquiry by William Roth, as President Johnson's Special Representative for Trade Negotiations, who produced *Future United States Foreign Trade Policy*, Roth Report (Washington: US Government Printing Office, 1969). But the Congress and a host of business organisations and research establishments also participated in the public debate, the culmination of which was the massive report of the Presidential Commission on International Trade and Investment Policy, *United States International Economic Policy in an Interdependent World*, Williams Report (Washington: US Government Printing Office, 1971).

10. What is mainly meant here is the erosion of the principle of non-discrimination, through abuse of the GATT's Article 24 which provides for departures from the principle to form customs unions and free trade associations, while the whole question of emergency protection against 'market disruption' has become too complex to be coped with adequately under the provisions of the GATT's Article 19.

11. By way of exemplifying the interest that was developing in the United States in the late 1960s in the implications for international economic organisation of the rapid integration of national economies, see Richard N. Cooper, *The Economics of Interdependence* (New York: McGraw-Hill, for the Council on Foreign Relations, 1968).

12. Commenting on the relatively small number of continental European contributions to the literature on contemporary international economic issues, Gunther Harkort, the former State Secretary for Foreign Affairs in the Bonn Government, remarked in 1973 that Europeans have taken more interest in the establishment and enlargement of the European Community. 'Besides,' he added, 'they are not quite as dissatisfied with the world trading system as are – at present – the Americans.' See Harkort, 'A Concept for an Open World Economy', *Intereconomics*, Hamburg, April 1974, p. 110.

13. Corbet, *loc. cit.*, pp. 224–5.

14. *Ibid.*

15. This point was emphasised by the Director-General of the GATT, Olivier Long, in 'Reflections on Changes in International Trade', a lecture to the Institut Universitaire de Hautes Etudes Internationales, Geneva, 6 October 1970.

16. The United States advanced more detailed proposals to a preparatory meeting of the International Wheat Council in London on 29 September 1975.

17. See the *Declaration on the Establishment of a New International Economic Order*, and the programme of action, drawn up at the sixth special session of the General Assembly of the United Nations, New York, April–May 1974.

19. For an analysis of the Third World's demands for the organisation of commodity markets, see Corbet, *Raw Materials: Beyond the Rhetoric of*

Commodity Power, International Issues No. 1 (London: Trade Policy Research Centre, 1975).

20. In the United States, the Trade Act of 1974 was signed by President Ford on 3 January 1975, while in the European Community the Commission secured its negotiating directives a few weeks later.

21. Under the Trade Act of 1974 the negotiating authority of the United States is limited to five years, as it was under the Trade Expansion Act of 1962, but the Kennedy Round negotiations were only just completed before the American negotiating authority expired.

22. This was plain in the late 1960s, if not earlier, as remarked in Corbet, 'Role of the Free Trade Area', in Corbet and David Robertson (eds), *Europe's Free Trade Area Experiment: EFTA and Economic Integration* (Oxford and New York: Pergamon Press, for the Trade Policy Research Centre and the Reading Graduate School of Contemporary European Studies, 1969) p. 47.

23. In this connection, see Cooper, *op. cit.*; Lester Brown, *World Without Borders* (New York: Random House, 1972); and Harry G. Johnson, *Technology and Economic Interdependence* (London: Macmillan, for the Trade Policy Research Centre, 1975; and New York: St. Martin's Press, 1976).

24. The issue is discussed in Theodore Geiger, 'Towards a World of Trading Blocs', *The Atlantic Community Quarterly*, Washington, winter 1971–72, and in Corbet, 'The Division of the World into Economic Spheres of Interest', *Pacific Community*, January 1974. Also see Ernest H. Preeg, *World Economic Blocs and US Foreign Policy* (Washington: National Planning Association, 1974), and Geiger, John Volpe and Preeg, *North American Integration and Economic Blocs*, Thames Essay No. 7 (London: Trade Policy Research Centre, 1975).

25. For a selection of the literature on the subject, see the titles listed in the Bibliography at the end of this volume.

26. It was clear during the Kennedy Round of GATT negotiations, from 1964 to 1967, that the system was in need of revision, which was why when the negotiations were completed President Johnson had his Special Representative for Trade Negotiations, William Roth, begin a major review of international trade policy in which the needs of the world economy figured large.

    But a glance through the literature of the time on international trade reveals a widespread awareness among professional observers of the GATT's weaknesses. See, for example, Gerard and Victoria Curzon, *After the Kennedy Round*, Atlantic Trade Study No. 2 (London: Trade Policy Research Centre, 1968).

27. The GATT record on agricultural problems is briefly reviewed in Dam *op. cit.*, pp. 257–73. Also see Brian Fernon, *Issues in World Farm Trade*, Atlantic Trade Study No. 11 (London: Trade Policy Research Centre, 1970) pp. 54–61.

28. They were: Professor Gottfried Haberler (Chairman), then of Harvard University; Professor James Meade, of the University of Cambridge; Professor Jan Tinbergen, of the Netherlands Institute of Advanced Economic Studies; and Professor Roberto de Oliveira Campos, then of the University of Brazil.

29. Panel of Experts, *Trends in International Trade*, Haberler Report (Geneva: GATT Secretariat, 1958).
30. *Ibid.*, para. 246.
31. *Ibid.*, para. 251.
32. *Ibid.*, para. 253.
33. *Ibid.*, paras. 267–9.
34. *Trade in Agricultural Products*, Second and Third Reports of Committee II (Geneva: GATT Secretariat, 1958), p. 7.
35. *Ibid.*, pp. 135 and 140–1.
36. *Ibid.*, pp. 21–46.
37. Simon Harris and Ian Smith, *World Sugar Markets in a State of Flux*, Agricultural Trade Paper No. 4 (London: Trade Policy Research Centre, 1973) p. 49.
38. Michael Butterwick and Edmund Neville Rolfe, *Food, Farming and the Common Market* (London: Oxford University Press, 1969).
39. Hermann Priebe *et al.*, *Fields of Conflict in European Farm Policy*, Agricultural Trade Paper No. 3 (London: Trade Policy Research Centre, 1972), p. 6 *et seq.* Included in this study are three critiques of the European Community's common agricultural policy from German, French and Dutch points of view.

    Also see Priebe, *Landwirtschaft in der Welt von Morgen* (Düsseldorf: Econ Verlag, 1970).
40. The American position was reflected in Hubert Humphrey, 'Agriculture's Place in International Trade', an address to the Trade Policy Research Centre, London, 30 July 1971. Senator Humphrey said the common agricultural policy had become a major disruptive force in world agricultural markets. The former Vice-President of the United States went on to say that unless the policy was reformed the enlargement of the European Community could have 'a further disillusioning effect on the United States attitude towards the new Europe'.
41. See the testimony of John Schnittker, formerly Under Secretary of Agriculture in the Johnson Administration, in Hearings before the Joint Economic Committee of the United States Congress, *A Foreign Economic Policy for the 1970s*, Part 2 (Washington: US Government Printing Office, 1970).
42. *Report of the Agricultural Negotiations of the Kennedy Round* (Washington: US Department of Agriculture, 1967).
43. An account of the agricultural side of the Kennedy Round negotiations can be found in Preeg, *Traders and Diplomats* (Washington: Brookings Institution, 1971). For a European view, see Gian Paolo Casadio, *Commercio attraverso l'Atlantico: dal Kennedy Round al neoprotezionismo* (Rome: Italian Institute of International Affairs, 1972).
44. John O. Coppock, *Atlantic Agricultural Unity: Is it Possible?* (New York: McGraw-Hill, for the Council on Foreign Relations, 1966) pp. 17 and 47.
45. Statement to the European Parliament, Luxembourg, 4 April 1973, when introducing proposals for the European Community's mandate for the Tokyo Round of GATT negotiations.
46. *Guardian*, London, 14 February 1974.
47. The implications of the rise in oil prices is examined systematically in

T. M. Rybczynski (ed.), *The Economics of the Oil Crisis* (London: Macmillan, for the Trade Policy Research Centre, 1975).

48. H. G. Johnson and Corbet, 'Pacific Trade in an Open World', *Pacific Community*, April 1970.

49. This point is developed in Lawrence B. Krause, 'Trade Policy for the Seventies', *Columbia Journal of World Business*, New York, January–February 1971.

50. Corbet *et al.*, *Trade Strategy and the Asian-Pacific Region, op. cit.*, p. 28.

51. For a brief discussion of the divided interests of commodity-producing countries, see Corbet, *Raw Materials: Beyond the Rhetoric of Commodity Power, op. cit.*, pp. 7–14.

52. This kind of assertion fell from the lips of Conservative, Labour and Liberal leaders alike at the time of Britain's accession to the European Community.

53. Sir Alec Cairncross, Herbert Giersch, Alexandre Lamfalussy, Giuseppe Petrilli and Pierre Uri, *Economic Policy for the European Community: the Way Forward* (London: Macmillan, for the Institut für Weltwirtschaft an der Universität Kiel, 1974) p. 101.

54. For a brief outline of the reasons why the 'oil-debt overhang' by 1980 is likely to be lower than originally feared, see Chauncey E. Schmidt, 'The Middle East: a $200 Billion Challenge', an address to the Trade Policy Research Centre, London, 16 October 1975. Mr Schmidt gave the address as President of the First National Bank of Chicago.

55. The economic implications of the rise in oil prices is examined closely in T. M. Rybczynski (ed.), *The Economics of the Oil Crisis* (London: Macmillan, for the Trade Policy Research Centre, 1975).

56. An interesting discussion of the influence of 'agricultural fundamentalism' on the agricultural policies of the United States can be found in Don Paarlberg, *American Farm Policy* (New York: Wiley, 1964).

57. Since Chapter 6 only summarises the study, under the research programme, on the income-distribution effects of British farm-support policies, the reader should also turn to the full results reported in T. E. Josling and Donna Hamway, 'Distribution of Costs and Benefits of Farm Policy', in Josling *et al.*, *Burdens and Benefits of Farm-Support Policies*, Agricultural Trade Paper No. 1 (London: Trade Policy Research Centre, 1972).

58. Besides those engaged on the land, the producer interest includes suppliers of agricultural inputs (machinery, fertiliser and so on) and, too, the distributors of agricultural produce.

59. See, for example, Peter J. O. Self and Herbert J. Storing, *The State and the Farmer*, revised edition (London: Allen & Unwin, 1971).

60. *Evening Standard*, London, 16 March 1973.

61. The implications for manufacturing industry are discussed in Geoffrey Denton, Seamus O'Cleireacain and Sally Ash, *Trade Effects of Public Subsidies to Private Enterprise* (London: Macmillan, for the Trade Policy Research Centre, 1974).

62. See Josling and Hamway, *loc. cit.*; and, also James T. Bonnen, 'The Distribution of Benefits from Selected US Farm Programs', and Vernon G. McKee and Lee M. Day, 'Measuring the Effects of US Department of Agriculture Programs on Income Distribution', in Presidential Commission

on Rural Poverty, *Rural Poverty in the United States* (Washington: US Government Printing Office, 1968) pp. 461–505 and 506–21 respectively.

63. In the United Kingdom, for instance, there was heavy emphasis on import substitution after the balance-of-payments crisis of 1964. The arguments, pro and con, are dealt with in Asher Winegarten and Josling, *Agriculture and Import Saving*, Occasional Paper No. 5 (London: Hill Samuel, 1970). The arguments were revived after Britain joined the European Community, but for slightly different reasons, in order to minimise intra-Community imports. Also see Michael Tracy, *Japanese Agriculture at the Crossroads*, Agricultural Paper No. 2 (London: Trade Policy Research Centre, 1972), for a discussion of import substitution in Japan.

64. See Chapters 8 and 9 below.

65. This section draws on *European and American Interests in the Multilateral Negotiations on Agricultural Trade*, Staff Paper No. 2 (London: Trade Policy Research Centre, 1972).

66. Olivier Long, 'International Trade in the 1970s: Some Immediate Problems', address to the Bundesverband der Deutschen Industrie, Bonn, 26 January 1970.

67. Group of European Agricultural Economists, *Reform of the European Community's Common Agricultural Policy*, Wageningen Memorandum (London and Wageningen: Trade Policy Research Centre and the Agricultural University of Wageningen, 1973), pp. 6 and 8. The memorandum was reproduced in *European Review of Agricultural Economics*, The Hague, Vol. 1, No. 1, 1973.

68. This is urged in Cairncross *et al.*, *op. cit.*, pp. 92–107.

CHAPTER 2

Post-war Development of British Agricultural Policy

BRIAN DAVEY

Agriculture is a vital source of earnings for many developed and developing countries with policies affecting trade in agricultural products becoming more and more under scrutiny. Because Britain is one of the world's largest importers of food, she has had a major influence over world agriculture, with several countries developing industries largely to supply the British market. Before analysing British agricultural policy in Part II, of this volume, it would help to review briefly its development in the period since World War II.

Four Phases of British Policy
The development of British agricultural policy over this period can be divided into four phases. In the immediate post-war period, the emphasis was on the expansion of output, without much regard for costs. By the mid-1950s, however, it had become apparent that the world supply situation had eased, and was likely to remain that way. At this time the direction of domestic farm-support policy changed towards the containment of Exchequer expenditure and greater economic efficiency. Early in the 1960s, policy shifted in new directions, as the British Government made a greater effort to control external access to the United Kingdom's market. Subsequently, import-saving arguments were invoked, with the burden of the higher level of protection placed more directly on the consumer. Then, in the late 1960s and early 1970s, issues related more specifically to the question of Britain joining the European Community.

During the whole of this period the basic philosophy underlying agricultural policy has been for the government to assume continuing responsibility to intervene in the free working of economic and social forces. The aims of policy were: (i) to ensure food supplies at reasonable prices while the parties involved in agriculture received equitable treatment; and (ii) to ensure that agriculture made an appropriate contribution to the development of the British economy as a whole. The preamble to the Agriculture Act 1947 laid down as the objective

34

of policy the promotion and maintenance, by the provision of guaranteed prices and assured markets for the main commodities produced on farms, of 'a stable and efficient agricultural industry capable of producing such parts of the nation's food and other agricultural produce as in the national interest it is desirable to produce in the United Kingdom and of producing it at minimum prices consistent with proper remuneration and living conditions for farmers and workers in agriculture and an adequate return on capital invested in the industry'.

The main, but by no means the sole, instrument of policy has been the system of guaranteed prices implemented through the Annual Review procedure. During the early post-war period world prices were often relatively high and the guarantees were largely open-ended. During the second phase, from the mid-1950s to early 1960s, the extent of the guarantee was restricted for a number of commodities by means of 'standard quantities'. At the same time, the Annual Review economic arithmetic was formalised by the Agriculture Act of 1957 and, with continuing increases in domestic output, it became increasingly difficult for the Government to find room to manoeuvre between the existing commitments to domestic agriculture and international arrangements.

Later in the 1960s, under the umbrella of continuing balance-of-payments difficulties, the Government moved towards an expansion programme aimed at saving imports. This led to the relaxation of quantitative limitations on domestic output; import volumes were regulated by means of market-sharing agreements of various types and, in consequence, it became possible to transfer more of the cost of support from the Treasury (and taxpayer) to the consumer. In addition, it was during these years that entry to the European Community became a serious possibility and some of the changes in policy which took place then can be rationalised retrospectively as preparation for this major change in agricultural policy. During the period after the Heath Government accepted the terms of entry to the Community, agricultural policy was aimed at adapting to the Community's system of farm-support so that, in effect, the 'transition period' began at the time of the agreement.

TECHNOLOGICAL ADVANCES IN THE 1960s

During the 1960s agricultural technology continued to develop at a rapid rate. Yields of most enterprises increased. For example, between 1960–63 and 1969–72 average yields of wheat rose by 10 per cent, of barley by 7 per cent, of potatoes by more than 20 per cent, and of sugar beet by 10 per cent. On the livestock side, the annual milk production per cow rose by 10 per cent and the number of eggs laid per bird by 15 per cent. In addition, there were further improvements in farm machinery and the trend towards mechanisation continued. For instance, there were about 20 per cent more farmyard manure spreaders, balers and combine harvesters in 1970 than in 1961 and three times as many drying machines. Most of this new machinery incorporated improvements in design.

It is not easy to determine how much of the increased mechanisation of agriculture could be attributed to independent technological progress and how far it had been fostered by government policies. At one extreme it can be recognised that some technological improvement would have taken place whatever policy had been pursued, while at the other it can be argued that government policy contributed to the creation of an economic environment which allowed the adoption of new techniques to continue.

Over the decade, the balance of resources used in agriculture changed, with more capital and purchased inputs applied with less labour to about the same area of land. Thus the annual rate of gross capital formation in agriculture nearly trebled in money terms between 1961–63 and 1972. At the same time, the active population in agriculture declined from 896,000 to 709,000 (falling still further to 678,000 in 1974), while the total area of land devoted to agriculture fell by 4 per cent. Meanwhile the net product of agriculture rose by over a quarter.

Not only did the total pattern of resource-use change, so did the structure of farm businesses. The total number of agricultural holdings in the United Kingdom declined from around 450,000 in 1960 to less than 290,000 in 1972 (in 1974 there were 273,000 holdings). Within holdings enterprise specialisation continued, so that between 1967 and 1972 the average dairy herd increased from 24 to 34 cows, the average cereal enterprise from 55 to 71 acres, the average pig breeding herd from 10 to 17 sows and the average broiler enterprise from 9800 to 20,700 birds.

Agricultural prices also changed during the 1960s and early 1970s, with wheat and meat products rising more rapidly than barley, dairy products and others. Increases in production did not necessarily follow these relative price changes. Wheat production stayed at much the same level for several years, but increased substantially in 1970/71 and 1971/72, while barley production rose over the period except for the short year in 1970/71. Between 1964/65 and 1971/72 the value of fat cattle and calf production rose from £269m to £297m; revenue from fat sheep and lambs fell from £86m to £72m and from fat pigs it rose from £206m to £236m; and returns from milk and milk products rose from £406m to £431m – all at constant prices. But there was no simple relationship between price changes and domestic production. This was a reflection, on the one hand, of differential rates of technological change and, on the other, of complementarities in production. The overall effect of this complex pattern of input and output changes on aggregate farming net income (which is the income from the national farm on a tenant basis) was an increase from £469m to £668m between 1964/65 and 1971/72.

TABLE 2.1

Index Numbers of Agricultural Prices in the United Kingdom
(1964/65 to 1966/67 = 100)

Commodities	1964/5	1970/71	1972/73
All products	98.8	116.1	141.4
Wheat	101.6	123.5	137.6
Barley	103.5	114.0	123.8
Cattle (clean)	98.8	133.0	189.6
Lambs	100.3	124.9	160.6
Pigs (bacon factory)	97.7	124.5	146.1
Milk	98.6	113.1	126.8
Eggs	96.4	102.8	103.7

Source: *Annual Abstract of Statistics*, No. 111 (London: HM Stationery Office, 1974) Table 425.

Retail prices of food rose by 44 per cent over the period, whilst total personal income rose by 70 per cent. There was also a shift in income distribution in favour of the lower income groups. These changes, along with the changes in relative prices shown in Table 2.1 gave rise to the new patterns of food consumption (see Table 2.2).

During the 1960s, changes were made to British international trade arrangements covering such commodities as cereals, butter, cheese, bacon and beef. The general effect was to control imports into Britain and to keep wholesale prices at a somewhat higher and more stable level than would otherwise have been the case. These arrangements, together with changes in domestic agricultural production and in consumer habits, affected the volume of the United Kingdom's international trade in food and agricultural products (see Table 2.3).

The combination of changes in policies and producer and consumer responses had an effect on the distribution of income. The parties affected can be conveniently grouped into consumers, producers, government, exporting nations and distributors. Some of these distributional questions were examined in the interim report of this study.[1] One conclusion was that under the deficiency payments policy, farmers with the most to sell gained most, as is inevitable with a policy based on market prices, although low-income farmers benefited significantly from production grants and subsidies on milk, sheep and

TABLE 2.2

Consumption of Food per capita in the United Kingdom: 1964 and 1971
(lb. per head)

Commodity	1964	1970	1973
Flour	156.1	146.0	141.6
Sugar	108.0	106.0	103.7
Fresh and frozen meat	93.9	92.8	86.4
Bacon and ham	25.3	25.2	22.3
Poultry	15.8	23.6	25.8
Liquid milk (pints)	251.0	241.5	240.7
Cheese	10.6	11.8	12.7
Eggs (number)	249.0	251.0	244.0
Butter	19.8	19.4	16.7
Margarine	13.4	11.9	12.8
Fresh fruit	74.0	76.4	71.0
Potatoes	226.9	228.2	216.5
Fresh vegetables	115.3	115.5	119.3
Canned vegetables	13.1	16.9	20.1

Source: *Annual Abstract of Statistics*, No. 111 (London: HM Stationery Office, 1974) Table 240.

Note: The figures given in the above table are for estimated food supplies (i.e. production plus imports minus exports).

TABLE 2.3

British Net Imports of Major Commodities: 1961/62 to 1963/64 and 1971/72
('000 tons)

Commodity	Average of 1961/62 to 1963/64	1971/72	1973/74
Cereals	8,752	8,009	7,004
Sugar	1,961	1,758	1,601
Beef and veal	311	215	189
Mutton and lamb	329	325	181
Pork	10	18	−8
Bacon and ham	390	372	304
Poultry meat	3	10	4
Butter	413	368	297
Cheese	134	162	98
Eggs (million dozen)	69	16	44

Source: *Annual Review of Agriculture*, Cmnd. 5254 (London: HM Stationery Office, 1973), and Cmnd. 5977 (London: HM Stationery Office, 1975).

cattle. The burden of support was shared, under this policy, approximately in accordance with income.

The agricultural sector reacts with the rest of the economy in a number of ways. As a production sector agriculture buys from, and sells to, other industries. As a significant part of consumer spending, expenditure on food not only affects consumption of other foods and services but, as prices increase, it creates inflationary pressure in so far as higher food prices are one of the factors leading to demands for higher wages and salaries. During the period under review, however, all prices were rising, so that it is not possible to isolate, except notionally, the agricultural element of inflation.

Some Undesirable Features of Policy

In seeking to evaluate the appropriateness of agricultural policy from 1964 to 1970, it can be argued that it was consistent with the intention to enter the European Community.[2] Aside from this, however, a change in agricultural policy took place which had several undesirable features.

First, at a time when international trade negotiations under the General Agreement on Tariffs and Trade (GATT) were liberalising trade for industrial products, agricultural policies were becoming more protectionist.

Secondly, there was a move to switch the burden of agricultural protection from the Exchequer to the consumer, by moving towards minimum import prices and agreements on the volume of trade. In this respect, it is interesting to observe the relative stabilisation in money terms of Exchequer expenditure on agriculture which in 1955/56 was £206m, in 1964/65 £265m and in 1970/71 £273m. Consumer prices were allowed to increase to limit this direct cost to the Treasury. In welfare terms it is not difficult to demonstrate that this was to the detriment of the economy as a whole.

Thirdly, the import-saving role ascribed to agriculture overstated the response which it was within the capacity of the industry to make, so that it was never likely that agricultural import-saving would replace more conventional policy instruments – like devaluation – for tackling balance-of-payments problems.

EUROPEANISATION IN THE 1970s

On 1 January 1973, Britain became a member of the European Community. This meant adoption of the common agricultural policy (CAP) and all its regulations. A transition period was envisaged during which British farm prices would be harmonised with European prices through the mechanism of transitory prices and monetary compensation. Member governments of the Community retain considerable national freedom in determining agricultural structure and some other aspects of policy (such as research and extension programmes), but price and international trade policies are determined centrally, as explained in Chapter 1 (pp. 10–12). Prices are administered by means of threshold prices and variable levies, which broadly determine the upper limit, while intervention buying determines the lower limit. Imports from third countries are governed by the threshold/variable levy system, while exports usually attract restitution payments. There are also a number of agreements covering specific commodities or countries.

Dissatisfaction has been voiced about the CAP from a number of quarters. To the United States, the CAP is seen as posing a severe problem of market access, whilst in Western Europe there has been growing concern about the cost of the policy. Among the problems confronting the CAP are: (i) its failure to tackle low incomes in agriculture; (ii) the lack of balance between the rapid progress which has been made in the liberalisation of internal agricultural trade in the European Community and the small steps that have been taken towards monetary and economic union; (iii) the inability of the agricultural price system to contain surplus production; (iv) the problems posed by the enlargement of the Community, particularly the economic and political difficulties facing the United Kingdom in view of the need to raise prices; and (v) the change in market balances brought about by enlargement.[3] The CAP also has its effect on the Community's external relations with both developed and developing nations, particularly the members of the Organisation for Economic Cooperation and Development (OECD), and this will be examined as part of a wider consideration of agricultural trade problems in the Tokyo Round of the GATT negotiations.

The Community has undertaken its own examination of the CAP in the light of criticisms raised in the Council of Ministers during the 1973 round of negotiations on farm prices. It is generally accepted, however, that because of political difficulties the policy's principles and instruments of the early 1970s are likely to prevail throughout the rest of the decade. But some modifications may be made in the direction, for example, of direct income support for low-income farmers (in which connection, see Chapter 6, below) and changes in the relative prices of crops and animal products in favour of the latter.

Entry into the European Community was associated with higher food prices in the minds of British consumers. The contribution of agriculture and high food prices to general inflation had been a matter of concern in Britain, as well as in other countries, and this led to the suggestion that food subsidies should be introduced.

There were a number of political difficulties attached to the suggestion. One was whether it would be possible to operate a policy of wage restraint without control of food prices. Another was whether the control of food prices was consistent with the principles of the CAP. There was, also, the question of the link between food prices and the depreciation of sterling in international foreign exchange markets, a factor clearly of importance to a major food-importing nation like the United Kingdom. The relationship between sterling and the currencies of other member states was a further item in the food-price equation. Finally, there was the question of whether the problem of higher food prices in Britain was sufficient reason for making changes to the CAP, bearing in mind that food prices on the Continent had traditionally been much higher than in the United Kingdom. A point which had to be remembered, however, was that one effect of the import-levy system had been to cushion Community consumers against higher world prices for agricultural products, while the United Kingdom had been fully exposed to such increases.

In spite of the anticipated rise in prices resulting from acceptance of the CAP there are several factors which will limit the potential increase in British agricultural production. When considering the response of producers to a regime of higher prices, it is necessary to bear in mind that some farm costs will increase at the rate of inflation, while the costs of labour may increase somewhat faster if real incomes increase. This rise in costs will reduce the benefits from the increased prices.

In addition, there are two important characteristics of British agriculture which must be taken into account when future production is being considered. The first is that most of the land which is capable of supporting agriculture is already doing so, and there are no major tracts of unexploited land to bring into production. The second is that most British farming systems are subject to some technical limitations and are fairly insensitive to price changes. For example, the dairy farmer in Cheshire will remain in dairy farming, even if beef prices rise; similarly the upland beef and sheep farm will continue on much the same pattern as before the price rise.

Given these two conditions there is a limited amount of change expected in the pattern of farming, and most of this will be the result of intensification. Some of this intensification will come from capital injection, facilitated by higher farm incomes; some will be related to management ability. Intensification by purchasing animal feedstuffs, which has been a traditional British technique for expanding farm businesses, will be less attractive during times when cereal prices are high, although livestock producers may find suitable substitutes. (See Chapter 5.)

The effects of changes in prices and production will vary between farms of different types and different sizes. Structural change in agriculture is likely to continue and, as a result, by 1978 the number of full-time farm businesses in England and Wales will have fallen significantly. One of the factors influencing this structural change is the value of land. The dramatic increases in the early 1970s were due partly to the anticipated increase in farm incomes after Britain's entry into the European Community and partly to an increased demand from institutional buyers associated with a lack of confidence in the ordinary equity market. Before then it had been possible to explain most of the changes in the value of agricultural land by reference to farm profitability and tax concessions and, in consequence, structural change could be expected to be in harmony with these factors. With land values in excess of £1000 per acre, however, and even poor-quality land commanding £300 per acre or more, it became clear that a new set of forces, such as those generated by industrial and domestic requirements, had entered the market and that these would affect the future rate and direction of structural change. (See Chapter 4.)

Higher retail prices and changes in relative prices will lead to changes in the pattern of food consumption. (See Chapter 3.) The changing nature and size of the domestic market, combined with the expansion in domestic agricultural output, will have an impact on Britain's trade in agricultural products. Moreover, of the produce which is required from overseas, the price relativities will change between Common Market and non-Common Market sources as a result of the imposition of import levies and so on, so that a switch to produce of Community origin can be expected; this will affect different commodities differently. This modification of trading patterns will also affect Britain's contribution to Fonds Européen d'Orientation et de Garantie Agricole (FEOGA) and the cost to FEOGA of supporting exports from the European Community.

The general picture which emerges for the late 1970s is that the British consumer will be paying higher prices for a different basket of food goods. Some of the additional revenue will accrue to the British farmer. Importers of non-Community goods into Britain are likely to lose revenue, except where there are special agreements covering this eventuality. In addition, the CAP will have some impact on the non-agricultural sectors of the economy. In most cases the effects will be small in the aggregate. Thus it seems unlikely that the ancillary industries will benefit or lose materially in total, although particular firms may find that the new environment creates more extreme conditions.

It appears unlikely that the expected increases in food prices will be an irresistible inflationary force, although the pressure will exist, as experience has shown during the early 1970s. Perhaps the most important effect will be upon the balance of payments, where the contribution to FEOGA, the switching to more expensive (pre-levy) Common

Market sources and the possible loss of reciprocal exports to traditional suppliers will all contribute to a worsening of the balance-of-payments position.

Earlier it was argued that the CAP was likely to remain broadly in its present form throughout the 1970s. No doubt negotiations will be started on alternative arrangements, some possibilities for which are discussed in the next section, at which the United Kingdom will carry some weight, but that is for the future. In the meantime there is the question of whether joining the European Community and adopting the CAP has changed British objectives.

The direct and simple answer is that British interests would be best served by responding to the CAP in particular ways. For example, although costly to the Community as a whole, it may be in the United Kingdom's national interest to increase wheat production at home. Similar arguments might apply in the dairy sector. It is tempting to make this a moral issue. But it is quite unnecessary. Just as the basis of a free-enterprise system is some search for rational, long-term and legal profit maximisation, so in a governmental sense it is the function of any body with regional responsibilities to seek advantages for its electorate. It must be assumed that if the sum of the interests of the parts is less than the interests of the whole, then policy will be amended appropriately. There is the question therefore of what is in Britain's best interests within the room for manoeuvre permitted under the CAP. This is rather a different policy objective from that of adjusting the underlying policy as was done previously.

Over the course of the 1970s pressures are likely to build up for the reform of the CAP. Externally the European Community will be hoping for the liberalisation of trade in industrial goods and will be asked to concede something on agricultural products by the United States and other traditional agricultural exporters. In addition, the developing countries will be asking the European Community for improved market access so that they can take full advantage of Community aid and other development assistance.

Internally, other calls on the Community's budget will put the cost of the CAP under even closer scrutiny, while the consumer and tax-payer may become more conscious of the direct and indirect costs of supporting domestic agriculture. Farmers, farm workers and rural communities will no doubt have a voice in any decisions that are taken, but since the farm/non-farm income disparity will remain, farming interests are unlikely to be unanimously behind the CAP. There will be a set of strong, if not compelling, forces for reforming the CAP, yet at the same time, the difficulty of renegotiating such a complex policy has to be recognised.

A number of alternative policies and policy instruments can be suggested. But they need examining in some detail and should be subject to a wide-ranging debate, so that some consensus can be reached, or at least a range of options provided. The final part of this chapter introduces some thoughts on this debate; that is, some speculation about new directions and policies for the 1980s.

TOWARDS THE 1980s

The root of the agricultural policy problem is that to attempt to meet an objective about incomes of farmers and farm workers it is deemed necessary to redistribute income to the agricultural sector from consumers and taxpayers. Third countries are also affected by such a policy. The procedure under the CAP is to maintain high product prices, allowing output to remain at high levels and encouraging expansion.

It has been generally conceded that this procedure is at best ameliorative while causing distortions in the pattern of resource use. In the long run there must be a withdrawal of resources from agriculture and a restructuring of the resources that remain in the industry. The argument then becomes, on the one hand, a matter of how best to achieve the structural reform and, on the other hand, what constitutes equitable treatment during the period of adjustment, assuming without any historical evidence, that ultimately agriculture should be afforded no more protection or redistributive assistance than any other sector of the economy.

But there are other factors to be considered as well as how best to tackle the farm-income problem. Most important among these is the integration of agricultural policy and general economic policy. Among the factors involved here are: (i) the contribution of agriculture to economic growth and employment; (ii) recognition of the consumer interest in the determination of farm policy; (iii) regional problems, including in particular the effects of rural depopulation on the rural economy; and (iv) the whole question of agricultural trade and the balance of payments. This integration of policy has been lacking hitherto in the United Kingdom. Because agriculture constitutes such a small sector of the British economy, it has been regarded virtually as a self-contained sector, with the links between the agricultural sector and the rest of the economy largely overlooked. (These last are discussed in Chapter 7.) Agricultural policy has been regarded mainly in terms of transferring income from the non-farm to the farm population.

In the European Community, on the other hand, agricultural policy has been used as the primary tool for the achievement of European integration. The movement towards union has limited the scope for rationalising agricultural policy as there are clearly greater problems in reforming a harmonised policy than in reforming the policies of an individual country. In this sense, the price and surplus problems that have arisen in the European Community can be regarded as one result of the commitment to economic union.

At the same time, the CAP is not – or should not be – the only means of reaching a true European community, even though so much emphasis has been placed on the development of a common policy for agriculture. Other areas – regional, social and transport policy for example – are equally worthy of attention. If the Community is to develop, the focus of economic union must shift to those other areas thereby making agricultural policy questions relatively less important.[4] Indeed, more attention to these other areas of policy, particularly regional policy, would be of considerable advantage to the agricultural sector.

Agriculture must therefore become a less dominant policy issue in the Community. This argument is reinforced by Britain's interest in seeking something – such as a Community policy for the regions – in return for the price she is paying for membership by accepting the CAP. But even if areas other than agriculture do become more important policy issues in the Community in the future, the need for reform of the CAP cannot be disregarded.

Before embarking on any discussion of alternative policies for agriculture it is necessary to recognise that the situation is inherently one of conflicting interests. Producers want high prices; consumers want low prices. Overseas suppliers want market access at favourable prices; domestic suppliers want limited imports and profitable export opportunities for surpluses. Livestock producers want low cereal prices; arable farmers want high cereal prices. Landlords and owner-occupiers prefer buoyant and perhaps rising land values, while tenant-farmers prefer low rents. Domestic ancillary industries sometimes have a community of interest with farmers, but sometimes not. In consequence, there can never be complete agreement on the principles or details of a new policy and the best that can be achieved is some consensus of opinion which reflects a compromise between the highest expectations and the worst fears of the several parties involved.

One aspect of consumer bargaining power which cannot be overlooked is that substitutes for temperate-zone commodities can be sought and this process will be assisted by non-agricultural entrepreneurs. Thus there is an upper limit within which the market will and should be allowed to operate. In such a situation one can rule out as unrealistic any policy proposals of an extreme nature, whether these take as their starting point *either* that the Community's agricultural policy should be aimed solely at domestic farmers' objectives, therefore demanding an extension of the CAP's high price policies, *or* that the Community should solely pursue consumers' objectives and therefore legislate for world prices and an open market.

One possibility, within the realm of practicality, but perhaps somewhat pessimistic, is that the Community acknowledge its inability to devise and administer any detailed common agricultural policy – given the administrative complexities, the diversity of farming and of consumer behaviour in the nine member countries and the problems attendant upon having, or not having, a common currency. In such an event, the only policy which would be appropriate would be one of delegating responsibility back to member governments, with some overriding legislation concerning trade within the Community and possibly with third countries as well, although the latter would not be necessary. While the possibility of fragmenting the policy exists, it has wider ramifications concerning the Community as an entity and, for this reason, it is not intended to develop this argument any further. Within the framework of a unified common agricultural policy, new possibilities can best be discussed under the separate headings of price policies, structural policies and trading policies, bearing in mind the interrelationships between them.

The main disadvantages of the existing pricing policy are two-fold. First, by their nature the arrangements are open-ended, so that there is no disadvantage to the farmer in expanding output, even where the extra output may give rise to an expensive disposal problem. Secondly, the margin between intervention and threshold prices is often narrow, so that the range of prices within which Community-produced goods are competitive is reduced, and trade within the Common Market may not be profitable. In addition the relativities do not move sufficiently to encourage shifts of production and changes in processing and marketing. This second point could be partially remedied by widening price bands and making bolder relative price changes.

On the first point, the open-ended nature of the policy, there are more difficulties. In the original proposals, it was suggested by the Commission that price support should be channelled through producer groups who would themselves have to tackle and finance any problems of surplus production. This suggestion, similar to the Dutch method of operating their auctions, was apparently not acceptable at the time and it may well be that it is too difficult to operate.

As an alternative there is much to commend the deficiency-payments scheme that was generally used in the United Kingdom. The lower consumer prices under such a system encourage consumption, particularly by the lower income families. The free market allows for innovation and development. The deficiency payments can be tied to a standard quantity of output in some way, so that producers bear the cost of surplus production; at the same time the taxpayer's liability is limited. There are a number of ways in which the standard quantity relationship can be established. In Britain it was calculated on a global basis with adjustments made to the deficiency payment rate. It would also be possible, however, to introduce production or marketing quotas, either allocated to a farm (which would be easy to administer but would generate production rigidities) or on a saleable basis.

Linked to a deficiency-payments and standard-quantity system, or as an alternative, a scheme of direct income support could also be considered. Since one of the objectives is to protect farmers' incomes, preferably without generating surpluses, direct income transfers have several advantages. They are simple to administer. They can be attached to the existing population of farmers, so that the cost is automatically reducing. They can be focused on the low-income farmers, whereas any price support policy inevitably benefits larger farmers more than smaller farmers, simply because the larger farmers have more to sell.

The above three suggestions offer several variations of price policy which might provide an appropriate level of income support without some of the concomitant disadvantages of the existing arrangements.

Notwithstanding any improvements in price policy, problems of surpluses and inefficiencies in production are likely to remain. It is necessary to look to structural policies for the remedy to these problems. The relationship between surpluses and agricultural structure is such that reducing the number of farms does not, as some optimists believe, provide the panacea for the problem of excess production. The amalgamation of farms, particularly at the size-levels prevailing in the European Community in general, will result in a similar output per acre, or an increase in output if the amalgamation is accompanied by an improvement in management. (There is the political point, too, that more big farmers would strengthen the farm lobby.) The root of the problem of surpluses lies in technological advancement, with new varieties, increases in the quantity and quality of purchased inputs, better strains of livestock and improved husbandry methods leading to higher yields per unit. Moreover, the improvements in yield do not have to be sacrificed under large-scale farming operations, because the new technology has also affected the economies of scale. Clearly, there is a level of labour input per acre below which a relative labour shortage will affect yields, but this limit is substantially beneath the ratio commonly found in the Community.

The most effective method of containing total production lies in reducing the total amount of land available to agriculture. There are a number of ways of implementing a land retirement programme. For example, in the United States individual farmers have been compensated for resting crop land, but this can prove both expensive and ineffective. Retiring whole farms, or groups of farms, may be economically preferable and offer a more permanent long-term solution, but at the same time it may give rise to fundamental political and social objections concerning property rights. It also has implications for the rural economy. It may well be that the pressure of the growing urban population for more land for housing, roads and recreational facilities will, if allowed to express itself in the market, contribute to land retirement from agriculture. At all events, this is not an issue which can be dismissed, for there is no sign that agricultural technology is at a standstill.

The other aspect of structural change concerns efficiency in relation to farm incomes and economies of scale in agriculture. In the early 1970s new structural policies were formulated by the Community, but it is too early to pass detailed judgement on their likely effectiveness. It can be asserted, though, that structural policies are generally slow to work and expensive to implement, particularly at the small-farm end of the spectrum.

One of the advantages of a deficiency-payments and production-quota system is that it can be discriminatory with respect to size of farm. Within such a system it would be possible not only to define non-viable farms (a step which the Community has under way in its existing structural policies), but to go a stage further by denying the non-viable sector price support, substituting instead direct income payments.

Perhaps of greater concern in the long run is the large farm. The capital requirement of an arable farm of 2000 acres, by no means too large to take advantage of economies of scale, at 1973 land values would have amounted to over £1m, but the return to capital, for a variety of reasons (many of them non-agricultural), would have been relatively modest. If it is envisaged that agriculture in the Community will move, albeit slowly, towards a structure consisting mainly of such large units, then it may be necessary to consider some organisational changes to facilitate their development and survival. The key to such organisational changes is likely to be the separation of land ownership from farming, but this opens up a wide range of issues and is not discussed further here. In brief, under the ambit of structural change, the best that can be expected as a result of policies is a modest reduction in the number of farmers and a modest increase in the average size of farm, still leaving a substantial number of farmers dependent upon a farm business of inadequate size for a living. It is at least open to question whether that is sufficient.

The future of international trade policies depends very much upon the related questions of price and structural policies discussed above and the resulting producer and consumer responses. Within the existing CAP, imports and exports are encouraged or discouraged by policy, largely in order to stabilise prices within the Community, without due regard to stability – whether of prices or of earnings – outside the Community. At best such behaviour does nothing to help stability in world markets, while at worst it can have a considerable destabilising influence. In looking to the future, potential suppliers will be seeking not only some overall improvement in market access, but also some concession towards the need for orderly trade and stability.

In seeking policies to improve stability, it should be borne in mind that most of the causes of disequilibrium are beyond government control. Volumes of production, and therefore exportable surpluses or import requirements, still depend upon climatic and disease variables beyond the control of not only governments but also producers. Even when volumes are stable, seasonality of production and marketing can vary, and consumption patterns are influenced by factors such as weather and fashion. Given these unavoidable fluctuations of demand and supply, it might be in the Community's best interest – as well as in the interests of other trading nations – to move from an objective of stable prices to one of stable incomes and, in consequence, to regard international trade and policies for storage and disposal of surpluses in a somewhat broader context. Proposals to establish an international system of nationally-held grain reserves can be seen as recognition of this problem. (See Chapter 9.)

So far as improved market access for imported produce and better conditions for exports from the European Community are concerned, interest is often expressed, mainly by Community countries, in a series of market-sharing agreements for different groups of commodities. These agreements would need to take account of comparative advantage and of variations in supply. (The alternative of free trade, politically impracticable in the short run, is generally ruled out of consideration from the outset.) Under such a series of agreements the share allocated to domestic producers would be a reflection of price and structural policies, but it could be slanted towards providing larger markets both for developing countries or for some of the traditional suppliers if this were considered desirable. These last, however, have little confidence in such proposals, which seemed designed to maintain the *status quo*. (See Chapter 8.)

Implicit in the pronouncements on the structural policies of the CAP is that an additional financial burden is to be imposed on both Community and national budgets in order to reduce the number of farmers. This is largely a once-for-all burden, against which can be offset the eventual savings which will accrue as price support for agricultural commodities become less expensive. As has already been argued, there is no evidence to suggest that structural change will lead to a decrease in production, nor that the larger farmers would be willing to receive substantially lower prices for their produce. The entry of three new members to the Common Market has relieved pressure on FEOGA in the short run, but it seems likely that by the 1980s the combined requirements of structural and price policies will be imposing a substantial financial burden on the Community's budget at a time when competing claims – for example of regional policy – are growing. Thus any new directions of policy will have to be accommodated within a tight budgetary situation. Since much of the cost of structural policies is already borne by member governments, the room for manoeuvre by the Community is limited and any major budgetary saving is going to have to be found from the guarantee section of the Fund, which is concerned with commodity price support. The major costs arise from intervention buying, which is then followed either by storage or by subsidised exports; it is these two elements which will have to be tackled, hence the pressures for changing price policy are reinforced.

NOTES AND REFERENCES

1. T. E. Josling, Brian Davey, Alister McFarquhar, A. C. Hannah and Donna Hamway, *Burdens and Benefits of Farm-Support Policies*, Agricultural Trade Paper No. 1 (London: Trade Policy Research Centre, 1972).
2. For a discussion of the issues posed for agricultural policy by British membership of the European Community, see Josling, *Agriculture and Britain's Trade Policy Dilemma*, Thames Essay No. 2 (London: Trade Policy Research Centre, 1969).
3. The general consensus on what is wrong with the CAP is reflected in Group of European Agricultural Economists, *Reform of the European Community's Common Agricultural Policy*, Wageningen Memorandum (London: Trade Policy Research Centre, 1972).
4. See Sir Alec Cairncross *et al.*, *Economic Policy for the European Community: the Way Forward* (London: Macmillan, for the Institut für Weltwirtschaft an der Universität Kiel, 1974).

PART II

British Agriculture in the European Community

CHAPTER 3

Projected Pattern of British Food Consumption

ALISTER McFARQUHAR and A. C. HANNAH

Rising food prices in the United Kingdom have proved to be one of the greatest economic problems of the 1970s.[1] Britain has pursued a low-cost food policy since the end of World War II and a dramatic increase in the price of food was always reckoned to be one of the major costs of British membership of the European Community. Opponents of British entry to the Common Market argued that the increase in the price of food, by its effect on wages, would be highly inflationary. Supporters of British entry argued that the increased price of food would be offset by a decrease in the cost of other commodities which account for a higher proportion of the family budget.

Not foreseen was the increase in the price of food that would take place before the United Kingdom entered the Common Market and that after entry the rate of increase would be accelerated by high world commodity prices and by high rates of inflation over the economy as a whole. The position in 1974, about two years after Britain's entry to the Community, was that the price of foodstuffs had been rising at the rate of 25 per cent per annum, based on monthly estimates, and that the price of some foods was as high as, or higher than, projected figures for 1978 at the end of the period of Britain's adjustment to Community market conditions. These rapid price increases have had a strong effect on the level and pattern of food consumption in the United Kingdom although the added cost of food can be offset by quite moderate rates of economic growth. Whether a sufficient rate of growth, however, can be maintained on average over the period 1972–78, in view of the recession which began in 1974, is another matter. At the same time the rapid rise in the cost of food up to the middle of 1974 effected a considerable redistribution of income in favour of the rich and away from the poor and also, at the same time, accelerated wage demands and pressure upon the inflation spiral.

Meanwhile, the Tokyo Round of multilateral trade negotiations under the auspices of the General Agreement on Tariffs and Trade (GATT) emphasises the major importance of agricultural trade in the future relationships of the European Community, particularly with the United States and with the developing world. Historically the United States has put considerable political and economic emphasis on finding a market for its exports of agricultural products.

In the early 1970s, a series of poor crop yields, notably of grain in Russia, India and South-east Asia, led to an abnormally high world trade requirement. Stocks had been run down, particularly in the case of wheat and maize in North America, the world's reserve granary. These factors led to exceptionally high prices. An annual increase in the demand for grain of around 25m tons, mainly due to the increase in population, exacerbated the shortage, but higher prices for agricultural products should induce increases in production. Measures to assist such increases have been taken in the United States, for example by releasing land for the cultivation of more cereals. The situation has been similar for many primary commodities, with shortages and high prices. It seems likely that the chronic cycle with periodic surpluses will continue with a possible surplus before 1978 even if only because poor countries are less likely to be able to pay the higher prices for grain which some could certainly consume.

Periodic instability must be the pattern of the second half of the 1970s, particularly if the United States maintains its policy of refusing to hold large stocks like those of the 1950s and 1960s. Considerable buffer stocks would be necessary to even out supply over a period of years given the fluctuations in annual cereal yields associated with the changes in weather patterns from year to year. If buffer stocks in the West should be held only by the trade, as opposed to government authorities, large fluctuations in prices can be expected with periodic shortages.

The United Kingdom has traditionally been a major net importer of food and will continue to be so. The European Community's common agricultural policy (CAP) is such that when world food prices exceed the threshold prices no levies are paid on imports and, of course, suppliers abroad benefit from the high prices. When world prices fall, however, the benefits do not accrue to the United Kingdom since the difference between the lower import price and the threshold price for each commodity has to be paid directly into the Fonds Européen d'Orientation et Garantie Agricole (FEOGA) in order to support the Community budget. When world prices actually fall, as they are expected to do, although not perhaps to the pre-1972 levels, these import levies could reach such proportions that they will outweigh the benefits of economic growth. They could put such an additional burden on the balance of payments that a huge decline in the value of the pound would result. Historically, short periods of growth in Britain's economy have put a strain on the balance of payments and the added effect of penalties for important agricultural products may well be critical.

Against this background the essential need to have the best possible estimates of the future demand for food and the pattern of imports must be obvious. This chapter concentrates on reviewing the expected position of Britain's food and agricultural sector in 1978, using econometric models which have been developed at the University of Cambridge.

The initial discussion in this chapter concentrates on estimating the response of the demand for food to expected changes in food prices by 1978, the end of the transitional period of adjustment covering Britain's entry to the Common Market. The pattern of food consumption is studied in detail in terms of over thirty food commodities and one non-food commodity. Although similar estimates have been produced regularly at Cambridge,[2] the estimates published here take account of the statistics available in 1974 for food prices and consumption and of estimates of 1978 food prices. The work described here also involved a major reconstruction of the model to take advantage of developments in econometric methodology for estimating demand for food and other consumption goods.

In Chapter 5 of this study the 1974 projections of trends in the supply of agricultural products in the United Kingdom are compared. During the late 1960s and early 1970s considerable research effort has been devoted at Cambridge and elsewhere to the development of econometric models for projecting the supply of agricultural products in the United Kingdom. These models involve the identification of secular trends and the estimation of the response of supply to the critical variables which affect it. The entry of Britain to the European Community, however, poses such major problems of adjustment that projection of historical trends is a particularly dangerous process. Consequently the authors of Chapter 5 have been diverted from the normal principle of insisting that projections of future supply should follow logically and rigorously from the assumptions made about the situation in which production takes place. The supply forecasts are 'best guesses' of what is likely to happen considering all relevant projections, but also take account of the views of various institutions concerned with the supply of agricultural products in the United Kingdom.

In the second part of Chapter 5 an input-output model is used to relate final demand, through intermediate demand, to supply. This in turn produces estimates of the positive or negative balances which determine the pattern of trade in agricultural products in 1978. The demand models show how the pattern of demand is likely to vary with alternative expected rates of growth. When discussing likely trade patterns, however, it seemed unwieldy to consider many alternative projections and the estimated trade pattern is based on a single assumption about the average rate of growth in Britain over the period 1974–78.

It may be argued that the discussion does not explore in enough detail the policy implications which emerge from the projections. It is, however, difficult enough to make projections of supply, demand and trade in agricultural products for 1978 at a time when the situation is changing so rapidly that price expectations may appear out of date a few months after they are made. Most studies of this kind have a gestation period of years rather than months. In this study our demand projections take account of price behaviour up to 1974 and expectations at mid-1974. The supply forecasts are based on projections made during the early 1970s as well as expectations current at mid-1974. Major efforts to produce up-to-date projections for 1978 in a very fluid situation have been perhaps at the expense of deeper analysis of the results. Other studies in this volume, however, concentrate specifically on issues of income distribution and agricultural policy.

FOOD CONSUMPTION AND PRICES

The rapid increase in the cost of food in 1973–74 was associated with a major change in British economic policy. By 1958 the pattern of demand for food had settled after the termination of rationing and throughout the 1960s expenditure on food in the United Kingdom remained more or less constant. Indeed, by 1972 expenditure on food,[3] measured at 1958 prices, was only 4 per cent above the 1958 level. During the same period expenditure on non-food commodities,[4] measured at constant prices, rose by over 50 per cent (Figure 3.1).

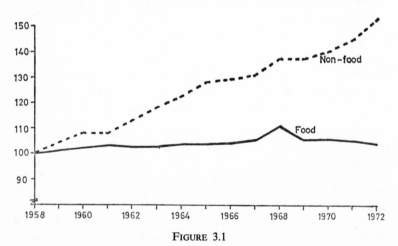

FIGURE 3.1

Index of Expenditure on Food and Non-Food in the
United Kingdom at 1958 Prices

During this period the real price of food fell steadily up to 1968, but by 1969/70 an upward trend in prices developed, as Britain began to adjust to her probable entry to the Common Market. During the period 1958–72 the prices of non-food commodities rose by only 2 per cent in real terms (Figure 3.2). As shown below, the position of food and non-food prices will be reversed, and the real price of food is expected to rise more rapidly than real non-food prices.

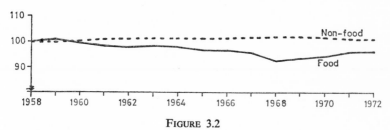

FIGURE 3.2

Index of Real Prices of Food and Non-Food Commodities

Trends in Food Prices

It is shown in Figure 3.2 that the real price of food fell steadily between 1958 and 1968 when the real price of non-food commodities remained more or less constant. In 1968 a steady upward movement in the trend of food prices relative to non-food prices began to emerge. In Table 3.13 on p. 82 in the Appendix to this chapter, an index of deflated retail prices of food commodities in the United Kingdom shows how the prices of individual commodities have changed in relation to the general level of prices.[5] The relatively steady relationship between the price of food and other commodities does, however, conceal quite marked differences in the prices of foods in various sectors.

Milk and Milk Products. Price trends for milk and milk products in Figure 3.3 show that the price of fresh milk remained relatively constant up to 1970, but rose by 11 per cent in the two years to 1972. The price of cheese, after a rapid initial rise in 1959, had returned to its 1958 level by 1970. The price of cream appears to show a cyclical trend but by 1972 had fallen to two-thirds of the 1958 level. In 1970/71 there was a rapid change in the trends for all of these commodities except cream. By the end of 1972 the United Kingdom had anticipated the money price rise expected to develop over the full period of adjustment to Community conditions.

Meat and Poultry. Over the period 1958–72 prices of pork, mutton and lamb, bacon and ham and other meats fluctuated within upper and lower limits of about 10 per cent with no indication of an upward or downward trend. The price of beef, however, had been rising on a

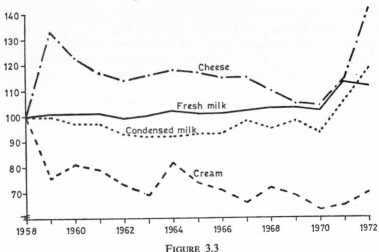

FIGURE 3.3

Trends in Real Prices of Milk and Milk Products in the United Kingdom

cyclical trend and had increased by 22 per cent in real terms between 1958 and 1970. By 1972 the price was one-third or 33.5 per cent higher than in 1948. (The considerable decreases after 1972 in the price of beef and veal are not shown in Figure 3.4.) By contrast to the price of beef and veal, the price of poultry fell markedly over the period from 1958 to 1972, to about two-thirds of the 1958 level. Indeed, the

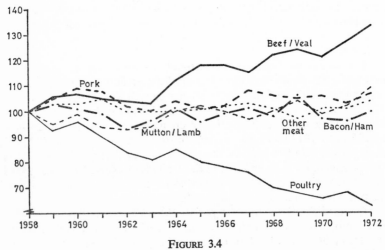

FIGURE 3.4

Trends in Real Prices of Meat and Meat Products in the United Kingdom price of poultry-meat has fallen further, and more rapidly, than any other price during the period. As will be shown below, a fall in price has been associated with a rapid increase in consumption in the case of poultry, and also in the case of cream and fruit, two other products wich have experienced falling real prices over the period studied.

Fish and Eggs. The behaviour of the prices of these commodities shows an interesting contrast. Both may be regarded as substitutes for meat, but while the price of fish has risen to 23 per cent above its 1958 level, the price of eggs, fluctuating around a downward trend, by 1972 had declined to two-thirds of the 1958 level (Figure 3.5).

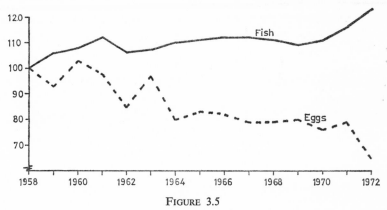

FIGURE 3.5

Trends in Real Prices of Fish and Eggs in the United Kingdom

Butter and Fat. The price of butter fluctuated markedly during the 1960s, but the downward trend after 1964 was reversed in 1970, as prices rose to the peak levels of the early 1960s. Over the same period, the prices of margarine and other fats fell steadily, and consistently, until 1969. There was an upward trend after that date; however, by the end of 1972 prices for these items had reached only 90 per cent of their 1958 levels (Figure 3.6).

Sugar Products. Prices of sugar products behaved more inconsistently than prices for other products as shown in Figure 3.7. By the 1970s sugar prices had dropped to 80 per cent of the levels maintained in the late 1950s and early 1960s. The most spectacular change took place in the price of sugar confectionery, which followed a steadily rising trend up to 1969 with the price at the end of the period being 30 per cent above the level of the late 1950s. A sudden increase in 1970 and 1971 brought these prices up another 60 per cent, but by 1972 the price had returned to the level of the late 1960s.

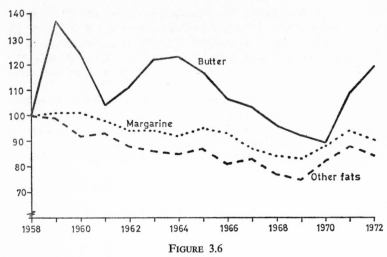

FIGURE 3.6

Trends in Real Prices of Butter and Fats in the United Kingdom

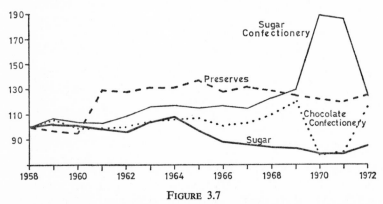

FIGURE 3.7

Trends in Real Prices of Sugar and Sugar Products in the United Kingdom

Trends in Food Consumption

Food consumption patterns are not necessarily related to prices in a simple way. The main factors involved, in addition to prices, are changes in real income per head and changes in taste. Over the period 1958–72 real income per head increased by about one-third whereas real expenditure on food, as shown in Figure 3.1, remained more or less constant. Certain foods which account for a large proportion of total food consumption can be regarded as basic in the sense that they provide a cheap source of essential nutrients or bulk in the form of carbohydrates. As incomes grow it is usual for the consumption of these foods to remain steady or even to decline because consumers prefer foods of better quality. For example, the consumption of products such as milk, margarine, bread and potatoes would be expected to decline as incomes increase.

In fact, an index of per capita household consumption shows that food commodities fall into three groups. The first group, including bread, potatoes, sugar, jam, lamb, beef, fish, butter and margarine, has shown a decline in consumption over the period examined. The case of beef is curious since it is always regarded, even by experts and albeit without much statistical support, as having a relatively elastic response to increasing income.

The second group of commodities comprises milk, bacon, eggs and vegetables. Consumption of foods in this group has remained static. Cream, pork, poultry and fruit are included in the third group, where consumption has increased remarkably since 1958. An index of consumption of individual commodities is given in Table 3.14 on page 83 in the Appendix to this chapter. Over the period 1958–72 it can be seen that the consumption of poultry has increased fivefold and the consumption of cream has doubled. Consumption of these two commodities shows a response to rising income and falling relative prices. The only anomalous behaviour occurs in the case of beef consumption which was affected by the world shortage of beef from the early 1960s to the early 1970s, associated with the considerable increase in the price of beef over the period studied.

TABLE 3.1

All Food and Beverages: Share of Total Expenditure[a] (per cent)

1958	1963	1968	1970	1971	1972
36	36	31	31	30	30

[a] Including alcoholic beverages.

Considering aggregate food consumption patterns it is clear that food has become cheaper in real terms over the period since 1958 to the extent that by 1972 it was 5 per cent cheaper than non-food goods (Figure 3.2 above). As shown in Figure 3.1, there was very little increase in food consumption over this period, in contrast to the rapid increase in consumption of non-food goods. In fact, all food and beverages taken together accounted for 36 per cent of total expenditure over the period 1958–1963, declining to 30 per cent in 1971 and 1972 (see Table 3.1). This picture, reflecting a steady decline in the percentage of expenditure on food and drink, does, however, hide quite marked trends in the expenditure on individual commodities discussed below.

Milk and Milk Products. The pattern of expenditure on milk and milk products has remained fairly stable over the period 1958–70 as shown in the first column for each year shown in Table 3.2. By 1972 expenditure on fresh milk had stabilised at around 6 per cent of total food and drink expenditure, while expenditure on cheese and cream, expressed as a percentage of expenditure on all food and drink, had increased by 50 per cent. Between 1958 and 1972 total expenditure on milk and milk products (excluding butter) rose from 8.5 per cent to 9.0 per cent of total expenditure on food and drink.

TABLE 3.2

Milk and Milk Products: Share of Total Expenditure (per cent)

	1958		1970		1972	
	Com-modity group	All food and drink	Com-modity group	All food and drink	Com-modity group	All food and drink
Fresh milk	77	6.5	72	5.9	69	6.2
Condensed and dried milk	5	0.4	7	0.6	7	0.7
Cream	3	0.2	4	0.3	4	0.3
Cheese	15	1.2	17	1.4	20	1.8
Total for all milk products (excluding butter)	100	8.5	100	8.2	100	9.0

Meat, Fish and their Products. Taken as a group, expenditure on these products exhibited a very consistent pattern during the 1960s (Table 3.3). The most outstanding changes were a decline in lamb and a rise in expenditure on pork from 5 to 8 per cent of total expenditure on meat and fish products. At the same time the share of expenditure on poultry meat almost trebled over the 14 years from 1948 to 1972. It is interesting to note though that the total expenditure on meat and fish products was maintained as a constant proportion of the total expenditure on food and drink up to 1970. It then declined from 22 to 21.5 per cent of total expenditure on food and beverages in 1972. Over the period, however, the share of expenditure on all meat and fish accounted for by beef, veal and lamb fell from 39 to 33 per cent.

Butter and Fat. The pattern of expenditure within this group has remained fairly constant during the period considered. By 1970, there had been a slight movement away from margarine towards butter, but in 1972 the original pattern of expenditure within the group re-emerged. The share of total expenditure on fats, however, between 1958 and 1972 declined from 4.1 per cent to 3.3 per cent of total expenditure on food and drink (see Table 3.4).

TABLE 3.3

Meat, Fish and Meat Products: Share of Total Expenditure (per cent)

	1958		*1970*		*1972*	
	Com-modity group	*All food and drink*	*Com-modity group*	*All food and drink*	*Com-modity group*	*All food and drink*
Beef/veal	25	5.5	22	5.0	22	4.7
Lamb	14	3.1	11	2.4	11	2.4
Pork	5	1.2	7	1.5	8	1.7
Poultry	3	0.6	8	1.8	8	1.8
Bacon/ham	18	4.0	16	3.7	15	3.3
Meat products	22	4.8	23	5.2	23	4.9
Fish	13	2.8	12	2.7	13	2.7
Total for meat and fish	100	22.0	100	22.0	100	21.5

TABLE 3.4

Butter and Fats: Share of Total Expenditure (per cent)

	1958		*1970*		*1972*	
	Com-modity group	*All food and drink*	*Com-modity group*	*All food and drink*	*Com-modity drink*	*All food and group*
Butter	60	2.5	62	2.0	60	2.0
Margarine	23	1.0	20	0.6	24	0.8
Other fats	17	0.7	19	0.6	16	0.5
Total for all fats	100	4.1	100	3.2	100	3.3

Other Food Products. The pattern of consumption expenditure on other food products shows some interesting trends. Expenditure on eggs, sugar, jam, potatoes, fresh vegetables, bread and flour and other cereal products all experienced a declining share of total expenditure on food and drink over the period considered. Expenditure on bread and flour fell from over 5 per cent to 4.2 per cent of total expenditure on food and drink, whereas the share of expenditure on potatoes halved, over the 1958–72 period. Fresh fruit, which might be expected to have a higher income elasticity, has experienced almost no increase in expenditure. On the other hand, the proportion of expenditure on sugar has declined to scarcely more than half of the 1958 level (Table 3.5).

Following from the relationship between the pattern of consumption, prices and expenditure, it is clear that the pattern of demand is the result of a complex interplay between several factors. In some cases demand has been rising as prices fall and in other cases the reverse has happened. Consumption of certain commodities increases with income; however, in other cases it may fall or remain constant. At first sight most products appear to respond to both price and income changes but to varying degrees. In order to measure the degree and direction of response, a simple review of past trends, although interesting, cannot be expected to give a coherent picture of what may happen in the future. A comprehensive econometric and statistical analysis is required and two alternative methods of procedure may be considered.

TABLE 3.5

Other Food Products: Share of Total Expenditure (per cent)

	1958	1970	1972
Eggs	3.4	2.5	2.0
Sugar	1.9	1.2	1.1
Jam and preserves	0.8	0.5	0.5
Potatoes	3.0	2.0	1.6
Fresh vegetables	3.4	3.5	3.1
Fresh fruit	2.5	2.4	2.5
Bread and flour	5.1	4.6	4.2
Other cereal products	5.8	5.2	5.1
Total	25.7	21.9	20.2

The first would involve the statistical study of the relationship between prices and incomes for individual commodities studied in isolation. The second method involves an attempt to examine the relationships simultaneously. The behaviour of food consumption patterns in response to price and income changes can be examined using models of expenditure systems to measure past behaviour and project future trends. This latter approach has been pursued at Cambridge University during the late 1960s and the results of the econometric models developed in the early 1970s are described below.

PROJECTING THE DEMAND FOR FOOD

A series of models have been used in Cambridge for estimating consumer behaviour and these models are fully described in a series of references.[6] In the model used for this study there is included a major

adaptation which has led to considerable improvement in the estimation of consumer behaviour. In this model thirty-two items were taken
to represent total consumer expenditure rather than a part of it.
Twenty-nine were food commodities, two referred to drink and one
category contained all non-food elements of expenditure. The use of a
simultaneous system meant that when projections were made of the
sum of expenditure on each of the commodities, the total projected
expenditure did not exceed the total amount of income available. In
each of the thirty-two commodities a change in the quantity demanded
of any commodity was taken to be a function of the change in price
of that commodity, changes in the prices of the other thirty-one commodities and any change in income. Criticism of previous models for
estimating consumer expenditure has centred on the point that any
expenditure system being used may be satisfactory to mirror changes
in broad categories of consumption but is not sufficiently flexible to
estimate changes in a highly disaggregated set of commodities.

Two major improvements were included in the model discussed
here. First, instead of using annual data of household food consumption derived from the British Ministry of Agriculture's *National Food
Survey*, quarterly observations have been used to give a time-series
four times as long as in previous models and, at the same time, to
allow the estimation of elasticities taking account of seasonal behaviour in consumption patterns. Second, and more important, the
linear expenditure system has been remodelled to take account of the
work by A. P. Barten, set out in *Econometrica*,[7] in which constraints
are imposed on the behaviour of individual commodities. This constitutes a major advance on the application of linear expenditure
systems to demand estimation as a whole, and the work reported here
represents a first attempt to incorporate this development in the
estimation of consumer behaviour in the British food sector. The
details of the model are described in Appendix 2 to this chapter
(pp. 84–5).

Estimates of per capita consumption have to be related to future
prices and incomes. In the case of incomes, projections assume alternative rates of growth ranging between a minimum of −1.5 and a
maximum of 0.0 per cent. The upper limit can now be regarded a
realistic target for the United Kingdom over the later 1970s in view of
the energy crisis and the economic recession in the mid-1970s. Assumption of a lower growth rate may seem unduly conservative, but considering performance in Britain – the 1974 rate of inflation of 20 per
cent or over, a balance-of-payments deficit and the resulting value of
sterling, the likelihood of zero or negative growth in 1974 and 1975 –
it seems unlikely that growth rates *averaging* more than 0.0 per cent
will be achieved over the period 1975–78. The assumption of an *average* growth rate of 0.0 per cent does not preclude higher rates in the

later years of projection. Nevertheless, on average, taking the period 1975–78 as a whole, the United Kingdom would be fortunate to reach an average growth rate of this order.

ESTIMATION OF 1978 PRICES

Estimates of the consumption of food over the period 1975–78 have to be related to estimates of the trend in retail prices up to 1974. This raises major difficulties. Estimates in 1970–72 of expected prices in 1978 have already been overtaken by events up to the end of 1974. Changes in the prices of food have far exceeded expectations in calculations made at a time when Britain was assessing the increase in food prices and costs which would be associated with full membership of the Common Market. A fresh attempt, however, has been made here to estimate probable real prices for foods in 1978 on the basis of information including 1974. As far as possible estimates of retail prices have been based on independent estimates of the farm prices which are likely to obtain in the United Kingdom at the end of the full period of adjustment to conditions of the Common Market.[8] Estimates were made of expected trends in the margins which have to be added to farm prices to produce future retail prices and from this a set of expected margins in 1978 was obtained.[9] These were to be added to the expected farm prices in 1978. In cases where information on farm prices or margins was not available for some commodities, estimates of 1978 prices were made, after considering likely supply and demand trends and the price in 1974 for the appropriate commodity in the European Community.

Relative prices between all food and non-food commodities are more important than the absolute price level in determining the price influence on demand. In this study all prices are given in 1972 terms rather than current prices. If money prices in 1978 were to be calculated, an additional assumption would have to be made about the rate of inflation over the period concerned. The difficulties of estimating future prices under the unstable circumstances prevailing in the United Kingdom during the mid-1970s have been increased with the rapid rises in food prices in 1973/74. The rise over the 12 months ending mid-1974 was around 20 per cent. It must be remembered, however, that most of the changes in prices were due to inflation and price relatives did not change as much.

Emphasising that only *relative*, not absolute, price changes are relevant, a set of 1978 prices has been calculated and is shown in Table 3.6. These prices have been checked with institutions concerned with planning and projection and, in some cases, have been adjusted appropriately in the light of their views. It must be emphasised that the prices shown in Table 3.6 are deflated to show the real change in the price of a commodity after the effect of inflation has been removed. Nevertheless, taking 1972 as a base period, some quite large changes in prices are predicted. For example, much of the 15 per cent increase expected in the price of beef had already occurred before 1974. Beef prices have since steadied and it is likely that little further adjustment will occur before the end of the transition period.

TABLE 3.6

Index of 1978 Deflated Retail Prices used in the Projection of Demand
(1972 = 100)

Fresh milk	85	Preserves	115
Condensed and dried milk	96	Sugar confectionery	103
Cream	105	Chocolate confectionery	111
Cheese	104	Potatoes	115
Beef and veal	115	Fresh vegetables	95
Mutton and lamb	116	Vegetable products	91
Pork	102	Fresh fruit	89
Poultry	118	Fruit products	98
Bacon and ham	105	Bread and flour	99
Meat products	106	Other cereal products	97
Fish	111	Beverages	98
Eggs	106	Other miscellaneous food	94
Butter	134	Food outside the home	108
Margarine	105	Beer	84
Other fats	115	Wine and spirits	82
Sugar	143		

The prices of lamb, pork, poultry and meat products are also expected to rise considerably by 1978, in particular lamb and poultry by 16–18 per cent. In the case of dairy products, butter is expected to rise by 34 per cent above the 1972 price with more moderate increases expected in the case of cheese (4 per cent above 1972) and cream (5 per cent above 1972). Only a major change in the policy of price support for milk products will alter this expectation. Milk prices, however, are expected to fall by 15 per cent in real terms by the end of the adjustment period. A 43 per cent increase in sugar prices is expected.

Increases are also expected in the real prices of fish (11 per cent), margarine (5 per cent) and cheese (4 per cent), but the prices of fruit products are expected to remain about the same in real terms, while prices of vegetable products and fresh fruit are expected to decline by just 10 per cent. The price of eggs is expected by 1978 to be 6 per

cent above the 1972 level. With the effect of inflation removed, however, these changes in food prices appear less spectacular than they
would if quoted in money terms. For example, if the annual rate of
inflation were to average 15 per cent – a moderate rate for the mid-
1970s – this would lead to a 90 per cent increase in the money price
which, in addition to the 20 per cent increase in the real price over
the period, would make a total price increase of over 100 per cent.

Considering the overall relationship between the price of food and
non-food products, Table 3.7 shows that the real price for all food
products taken together is expected to rise by 5 per cent over the
period 1972–78. This table also shows that food prices are expected to
rise by 6 per cent *in relation to* non-food prices. The rich, who spend
a higher proportion of their budget on non-food goods, will be less
affected than the poor, who spend a relatively high proportion of their
income on food. The increase in food prices relative to non-food prices
may therefore have a serious effect on the welfare of the poorer classes
of society. Inflation is of less concern to the rich and to the well-
organised groups in society who are able to increase incomes *pari
passu* with the cost of living. But for the pensioners, large families and
the less-organised trade and professional unions and those working in
positions where strike action has small strategic or political effect, the
outlook may be very bleak indeed.

TABLE 3.7

1978 Food and Non-Food Prices[a] (1972 = 100)

Food	105
Non-food	99
Ratio food, non-food	106

[a] The value of the index actually depends on the income growth because
the prices are calculated using current quantity as weights. The growth rate
used, however, makes little difference. The index resulting from a 0.0 per cent
growth rate is given here.

BRITISH FOOD CONSUMPTION 1978

Using the assumptions, data and models discussed in detail above, a
projection has been made of the per capita consumption of food commodities in 1978. This was done assuming two alternative levels of
growth, namely −1.5 and 0.0 per cent per annum. Only the projections
in which a 0.0 per cent rate of growth in income was assumed are discussed in detail in the sections below since this was thought to be the
most likely of the two alternatives over the period 1975–78. The effect
of different growth rates can be seen in Table 3.8 and the response of

individual commodities to income changes will be referred to in detail
below.

TABLE 3.8

Food and Beverages: Projected Index of per capita Consumption for 1978
compared for Different Rates of Growth in Consumer Expenditure
(1972 = 100)

	Growth in Consumer Expenditure[a]			Growth in Consumer Expenditure[a]	
	−1.5	0.0		−1.5	0.0
Fresh milk	100	100	Sugar confectionery	104	102
Condensed and dried milk	99	99	Chocolate confectionery	100	101
Cream	95	95	Potatoes	92	92
Cheese	104	104	Fresh vegetables	117	117
Beef and veal	105	105	Vegetable products	103	103
Mutton and lamb	97	102	Fresh fruit	105	108
Pork	114	114	Fruit products	97	97
Poultry	85	85	Bread and flour	105	103
Bacon and ham	104	104	Other cereal products	100	100
Meat products	89	89	Beverages	97	97
Fish	92	92	Other miscellaneous food consumed in the home	106	106
Eggs	117	114			
Butter	82	82			
Margarine	103	101	Food consumed outside the home	109	109
Other fats	103	103			
Sugar	65	65	Beer	104	110
Preserves	129	125	Wine and spirits	144	167

[a] Growth in consumer expenditure refers to the years 1975–78. Projections
take into account actual growth for the years 1973 and 1974.

Fresh Milk and Milk Products
Income seems to have very little influence on the consumption of milk
and milk products. Consumption of fresh milk is expected to vary
very little from the 1972 level since it seems to be insensitive to price
changes and negligibly sensitive to changes in income. Consumption
of condensed and dried milk, however, is expected to fall by about
1 per cent. These products are quite sensitive to price changes with
an elasticity of −0.57, but prices are expected to fall 4 per cent in
real terms by 1978. In response to an expected 5 per cent increase
in price, and with an estimated elasticity of −0.88, the consumption of
cream is expected to fall by 5 per cent by 1978.

In the case of cheese there was no evident response to changes in
income and, with a quite negligible price elasticity and the assumption

of a 4 per cent increase in price by 1978, consumption is up by 4 per cent. Movements in cheese prices in 1972–73 raise doubts about the reliability of the price projections for 1978. At the same time, with an increase in the price of meats, cheese began to recover its position as a relatively cheap source of protein.

The price elasticity for cheese is negligible, but it has a cross-elasticity with pork of 0.38, which suggests that if there is a 1 per cent increase in the price of cheese there will be an increase of 0.38 per cent in consumption of pork, other things remaining equal. Additionally, a 1 per cent rise in the price of cheese leads to a 0.30 per cent increase in consumption of fish; and a 1 per cent rise in the price of cheese leads to a 0.11 per cent decrease in consumption of bread – a complementary product.

Consequently the model is showing that cheese consumption is affected considerably by the price of pork which has traditionally been considered by consumers to be one of the cheaper sources of meat protein. If cheese prices go up, however, pork consumption will rise unless the price of pork also rises. In fact, the estimates for 1978 show that the prices of both cheese and pork are expected to rise, by 4 and 2 per cent respectively, and as a result the expected consumption of cheese rises by 4 per cent.

Meat and Meat Products

Traditionally meat and meat products, in particular beef and veal, are supposed to have a high income elasticity; that is to say, consumption per capita will increase by a relatively large quantity with income, other things remaining constant. In fact, the data extending over the period 1958–1972 for the United Kingdom suggest that lamb is the only meat item which responds to changes in income. All the others, including beef and veal, have negligibly low income elasticities. In the case of mutton/lamb a 1 per cent increase in income is associated with a 0.87 per cent increase in consumption, but this results in a projected increase in per capita consumption by 1978 only if income rises with economic growth.

The price of poultry-meat is expected to rise appreciably by 1978, but poultry-meat has a relatively high price elasticity of −0.35 so that changes in price are likely to have considerable effects on consumption. The price of poultry-meat affects the consumption of other meat products, pork and lamb. Time-series data suggests that it is a common substitute for pork so that a 1 per cent rise in the price of poultry leads to a 0.25 per cent increase in the demand for pork.[10] Consequently, the projections suggest a large increase in the per capita consumption of pork meat in 1978 compared with 1972, with an equivalent increase if the economy experiences a higher growth rate than the average rate of 0.0 per cent assumed (Table 3.8).

It has not been possible to extract from time series data evidence to support the prejudice that beef has a high income elasticity. Table 3.9 below shows that the price elasticity of beef is, however, extremely high at −1.63. The table also shows a strong effect between beef and veal and pork to the extent that a 1 per cent increase in the price of beef as associated with an increase of 0.91 per cent in pork consumption. These estimates lead to the projection of an increase in the per capita consumption of pork of 14 per cent in association with a price rise of 2 per cent by 1978. The recent evidence of consumer indifference to rising beef prices lends plausibility to the beef figures. But once consumption increases as a result of lower prices, beef consumption will tend to stabilise at current levels. All that can be said is that the evidence since 1958 suggests that beef consumption in the home does not respond to income changes, but does respond considerably to rising prices.

TABLE 3.9

Response in British Consumption to 1 per cent
Price Change in Meat and Fish (per cent)

Per cent change in consumption in	*Price change of 1 per cent in*					
	Beef and veal	Mutton and lamb	Pork	Poultry	Fish	Other meat products
Beef and veal	−1.63	0.4				0.48
Mutton and lamb		−1.41		0.30		1.46
Pork	0.9	0.36	−1.21	0.25		1.32
Poultry				−0.35		
Fish			0.19		−0.40	
Other meat products						−0.47

The diagonal figures show response of a meat commodity to a 1 per cent change in its own price. All elasticities measured at 1978 prices.

In the case of lamb, it was assumed that prices will increase in real terms by 16 per cent over the period 1972–78. Because of its very high price elasticity (Table 3.9), lamb consumption is projected to rise by 2 per cent of its 1972 level by 1978. Pork consumption seems to be relatively closely correlated with the consumption of other meats, as shown in Table 3.9, since increases in consumption follow increases in prices of poultry, beef and lamb. Pork shows also a high cross-price elasticity with meat products, which suggests that if the price of meat products rises, as is estimated here, people consume more beef and mutton/lamb, while pork consumption falls against preferred meats.

It is already clear that meat may become relatively more expensive in the United Kingdom and this trend is likely to continue even with steady reductions in producer prices. It might be expected therefore that consumption would be switched to cheaper meat products such as sausages and pies since these products use less meat and more offal per unit of production. The price of meat products does not usually rise as quickly as the prices of meats themselves. Judging, however, by the data and its interpretation this is not likely to occur, because meat products are quite price-elastic and a 1 per cent increase in price leads to a 0.5 per cent fall in consumption. Since the price of meat products is expected to rise because of increases in the price of raw materials including the rising demand for offals, consumption is projected to fall by 11 per cent by 1978.

In the case of bacon and ham, real prices may be 5 per cent above the 1972 levels. Bacon and ham are highly price-elastic in respect of their own prices since a 1 per cent increase in price leads to a 1 per cent fall in consumption. But operating against this pressure is the fact that both are substitutes for other meat products, the prices of which have been rising faster than that of bacon and ham. Bacon and ham consumption tends not surprisingly to be associated with the consumption of eggs which is expected to rise as prices rise slightly, and the net effect of these factors gives a projection of a 4 per cent increase in bacon and ham consumption by 1978.

In 1972 household consumption of meat and meat products reached 123 lb per head per annum. The projected figure for 1978 is 119 lb per head per annum, a fall of 3 per cent. Since these products are not usually correlated with changes in income, increasing consumption may be taken as a reflection of consumer response to changing price relatives.

Fish and Eggs

It has been shown above that consumption of fish has been declining steadily over the 1960s, and a fall of 8 per cent is projected by 1978. Like meat, fish consumption surprisingly shows no correlation with income level but the price elasticity is of the order of -0.4 and prices are expected to rise by more than 11 per cent by 1978. The consumption of eggs is strongly (-0.6) related to income but eggs are weakly price-elastic (-0.2) and their consumption is complementary to the consumption of bacon and ham. Relative to prices of beef/lamb, the price of eggs is expected to fall as is the price of bacon and ham, and the joint effect is a projected increase for egg consumption of 14 per cent by 1978 compared with 1972 (Table 3.8).

Butter and Fats

Projection of the demand for butter and fats involves the assessment of a number of conflicting factors. Despite the large difference between butter and margarine prices until the subsidies on butter were brought in during 1973/4, the fact that margarine is a possible dietary substitute for butter, and given the recent publicity against the consumption of animal fats, there is still a distinct consumer preference for butter. Margarine enjoys a strong income elasticity of −0.6 per cent. It is often assumed that butter consumption is related to bread consumption. Over the period 1958–71, however, bread consumption fell by 25 per cent, but butter consumption by only 9 per cent. By 1972 the consumption of bread continued to decline, reaching a level of 28 per cent below the base period, while butter consumption – affected by high prices – slumped suddenly to 23 per cent of the base period level, almost catching up with the decline in bread consumption.

By 1971 margarine consumption had fallen by 9 per cent, but margarine accounts for less than one-third of the total consumption of butter and margarine, taken together. In 1972 margarine consumption had recovered, reaching a level 4 per cent above the base period.

Faced with an increase in the price of butter, consumers would substitute margarine. In 1971 butter prices increased by 17 per cent above prices in the previous year and butter consumption fell by 8 per cent. At the same time margarine consumption increased by 10 per cent. The price and quantity demand relationships for butter and fats are given in Table 3.10. The table indicates that butter has quite a high price elasticity of −0.6. Butter is clearly a substitute for margarine since a 1 per cent increase in the price of margarine leads to a 0.4 per cent increase in butter consumption, whereas a 1 per cent increase in the price of butter leads to a 0.9 per cent increase in margarine consumption. At the same time, margarine is a weak substitute for other fats, since a rise in the price of other fats is associated with a rise in consumption of margarine. Margarine is a complement to cheese since, if margarine prices rise by 1 per cent the consumption of cheese is expected to rise by 0.3 per cent. Since bread consumption reacts inversely to changes in its own price, it is expected that the consumption of both bread and margarine will move in the same direction. Furthermore, other fats are a weak substitute for butter and a weak complement to margarine. Margarine also exhibits a negative income elasticity of −0.6, showing that as income rises the demand for margarine falls. Other fats are of food made up largely of cheap sources of fat – such as lard, dripping and vegetable oils – which would be expected to be 'inferior' commodities, in the sense that as income increases consumption would decrease.

The main effect of prices and income on projected consumption is the expected increase of 34 per cent in the price of butter. Consequently the projections indicate some substitution of margarine for butter. In fact, butter consumption is projected to fall by 18 per cent by 1978, and margarine consumption to remain stable. A check on these projections shows that the consumer would be remarkably consistent in respect to the total intake of fat purchased in the form of butter and margarine. In 1972 the total consumption of butter and margarine was 27 lb per head per annum and projections show, by quite independent estimates, that the combined consumption in 1978 would be 24 lb per head. The consumption of other fats is projected to rise slightly (3 per cent above the 1972 level), assuming a 0.0 per cent growth in income. Low or negative rates of growth in income would result in a similar increase in consumption although these products are inferior commodities.

TABLE 3.10

1974 Elasticities of Demand for Fats

Per cent change in consumption	Price change of 1 per cent in			Income elasticity
	Butter	*Margarine*	*Other fats*	
Butter	−0.6	0.4		0.0
Margarine	0.9	−1.0	0.2	−0.48
Other fats	0.1	−0.25		0.0

Sugar and Sugar Products
Consumption of sugar and sugar preserves has declined by 19 and 44 per cent respectively between 1958 and 1972. For sugar this trend will continue with consumption down by one-third, but with confectionary consumption up by 2 per cent by 1978 in comparison with 1972 figures. Both products respond slightly to changes in prices with elasticities of −0.3 and 0.18 respectively. The consumption of sugar preserves, however, is projected to increase; and chocolate confectionery, with an income elasticity of 0.2, to increase by 1 per cent (Table 3.8).

Vegetables and Potatoes
Projected demand for potatoes shows an 8 per cent decrease in consumption by 1978, given a 0.0 per cent growth in income. Potatoes are clearly an 'inferior' commodity in the sense that, at higher rates of income growth, consumption is reduced. Vegetable products, largely tinned and dried vegetables, are expected to follow a different trend to that of potatoes with small increases in consumption independent

of rates of income growth. If there were a 0.0 per cent growth in income up to 1978, the consumption of vegetable products would stabilise around the level in 1972. On the other hand, fresh vegetables show a negative price elasticity of -0.9, although consumption is expected to increase by 17 per cent by 1978 on the assumption of a 0.0 per cent growth rate (Table 3.8).

Fruit
Fresh fruit and fruit products have income elasticities of 0.6 and zero respectively. Fruit products are highly price elastic at -0.7. Assuming a 0.0 per cent growth rate, consumption is therefore projected to rise by 8 per cent in the case of fruit, and fall by 3 per cent in the case of fruit products, by 1978. At a growth rate of -1.5 per cent the comparative changes in consumption would be 5 per cent and -3.0 respectively (Table 3.8).

Bread and Cereal Products
The decline in the consumption of bread and flour is projected to reverse between 1972 and 1978, when it is expected that these two items account for less than 4 per cent of expenditure on food and drink, but the consumption of other cereal products, including breakfast cereals, biscuits, cakes and buns, is expected to remain at just about the 1972 level (Table 3.8).

Beverages, Beer, Wine and Spirits
Beverage consumption, including tea, coffee and cocoa, is expected to fall slightly to 97 per cent of the 1972 figure by 1978. Beer consumption shows up at 10 per cent above the 1972 level, which reflects a balance given very moderate growth rates between the high income elasticity of 0.9 and the price elasticity of -0.6 (Table 3.8). In the case of wine and spirits, a very high (2.4) income elasticity effect was found, but there was a small (-0.3) response to price, expected to fall in real terms by 1978, leading to a projection of a 67 per cent increase in consumption by that date.

Other Categories of Food
The major items in this category are convenience foods, the consumption of which has increased rapidly during the 1960s at the rate of almost 2 per cent per annum. The projections suggest that this trend is likely to level off with the influence of falling prices, and consumption is expected to increase by 6 per cent in 1978 compared with 1972. The consumption of food outside the home, which includes consumption in canteens and institutions as well as in restaurants, was, not surprisingly, found to be slightly income-elastic, since a 1 per cent increase

in income leads to a less than 0.2 per cent increase in consumption. This figure is low since it does seem plausible that food consumption outside the home is very sensitive to changes in income, particularly at the margin. The result of this effect is that consumption outside the home will be 9 per cent above the 1972 level at a growth rate of zero. At lower growth rates consumption could still be considerably above 1972 levels.

Even if this estimate seems exaggerated, there is no doubt that the consumption of food outside the home is extremely sensitive to changes in 'taste'. It is also sensitive to changes in prices which are expected to rise very rapidly by 1978, partly because of the rise in the prices of materials and partly because of the effect of value-added tax and the increase in labour costs. The net result on the projections is that a 0.0 per cent growth in income could result in a 9 per cent rise in the consumption outside the home. This net effect would result by off-setting the decrease in consumption resulting from the large increase in prices against the increase associated with changing habits.

Other Goods excluding Food and Drink

The inclusion of this non-food category in the model makes the sum of the estimated expenditure on each commodity equal to total expenditure which is in turn related to the assumed rate of growth in total income. Any substitution which occurs between food and non-food goods is automatically taken into account. Non-food goods are estimated to have an income elasticity of 1.2 so that consumption in 1978 is expected to be 1 per cent less when relative prices are taken into account than in 1972, given a 0.0 per cent growth in income. This estimate is influenced by the relatively high prices of food compared with non-food goods predicted by 1978. Deflated overall food prices (excluding alcoholic beverages) are expected to rise by about 5 per cent above the levels of 1972 and the deflated prices of all other goods (including alcoholic beverages) to fall by 1 per cent with a consequent substitution between these two categories. It must be emphasised that only the relative prices of food and non-food goods affect the share of expenditure on each. In money prices, non-food goods may increase by 70–80 per cent between 1972 and 1978 due to inflation but this does not affect the projections of the model as these are dependent on relative price increases.

SUMMARY OF PROJECTIONS

The results discussed above assume that growth in real income will average 0.0 per cent per annum between 1974 and 1978 and this, combined with the effect of a different price structure will determine the pattern of food consumption during that period. A reduction in consumption varying from 10 to 35 per cent is projected for each of butter, sugar and poultry. It is anticipated that potatoes, cream and fish will fall by between 5 and 10 per cent. Consumption of fruit, cheese, beef and veal, bacon/ham, and beer is expected to rise between 4 and 10 per cent and the consumption of vegetables and pork by 10 per cent or more. The consumption of bread, lamb, margarine, fruit and cereal products, beverages and milk are all projected to remain within plus or minus 3 per cent of the 1972 level.

Total food expenditure (excluding alcoholic beverages) is expected to increase by 0.75 per cent per annum in association with a 0.0 per cent increase in real income per annum. It is anticipated that the consumption of non-food goods (excluding alcoholic beverages) will decrease less than 1 per cent over the same period, 1974–78. If real income were not to grow at all during the period, food consumption would be reduced by nearly 2 per cent compared with 1972. Since food prices were projected to increase by 5 per cent by 1978, this implies an overall expenditure elasticity of about −0.4 whereas income elasticity is something over 0.4.

It must be emphasised that these projections deal with household consumption of food per capita plus an aggregate commodity to represent consumption outside the home. Even if consumption per capita remained static, total consumption would, of course, rise in proportion to the increase in total population during the projection period. In estimating the total demand for food by 1978, to which reference is made later, the population projections published by the Central Statistical Office have been used. These indicate an increase of something under 2 per cent between 1972 and 1978.[11]

Total expenditure in the United Kingdom is expected to have risen by 3.4 per cent by 1978 taking into account the expected increases in per capita incomes and population. Table 3.11 shows that expenditure is expected to rise by 3 per cent on food and stabilise on non-food goods over the 1974–78 period. The share of food in total expenditure

TABLE 3.11

Expenditure on Food and Non-food in 1978[a]

	Expenditure index 1974 = 100	Share of total expenditure (%) 1972	1978
Food	103	22	22
Non-food	100	70	69
Alcohol	107	8	9

[a] Assuming a growth rate of 0.0 per cent per annum.

will be 22 per cent in 1972 and just under 22 per cent in 1978, whereas expenditure on non-food goods will fall by 1.0 per cent from 70 to 69 per cent.

CONSUMER BEHAVIOUR 1972 TO 1978

In Table 3.12 there is a comparison between the projected pattern of consumption in 1978 at expected real prices (see Table 3.6) and the pattern for the year 1972. Table 3.12 shows the percentage share of each particular commodity in (*a*) total expenditure within the commodity group and in (*b*) total expenditure on all food and drink. Considering commodity groups it is remarkable how little change is likely to take place in their contributions to total expenditure over the period considered. Expenditure on milk and milk products is likely to decrease from 9 to 6.5 per cent of total expenditure on all food and drink. For meat and fish a decrease from 21.5 to 20.5 per cent is likely and for butter and fats an increase from 3.3 to 3.4 per cent. For other commodities listed in Table 3.12 there is unlikely to be any significant change.

Expenditure on groups of commodities, however, can conceal quite marked changes in expenditure on particular commodities *within* the group. Expenditure on fresh milk, for example, is likely to decrease considerably from 6.2 to 3.8 per cent of all food and drink expenditure, whereas share of cheese is projected to rise from 20 to 28 per cent, an increase of about 40 per cent. In the meat and fish group, expenditure is expected to remain steady in the case of mutton and lamb, whereas for beef and veal, poultry, meat products and fish it is expected to fall very slightly. In the butter and fats group expenditure on butter is projected to decrease by about 20 per cent although it appears that the distribution of expenditure within that group itself will remain fairly constant between butter, margarine and other fats (see Table 3.12).

In the group listed under 'Other commodities' in Table 3.12, expenditure is expected to fall slightly in the case of eggs, fruit and fresh vegetables, to rise a little in the case of sugar and preserves and fall about 10 per cent in the case of bread and flour. In summary, therefore, although quite marked changes are expected in the pattern of physical consumption of food and food products by 1978, the pattern of expenditure on these products is not expected to show a very marked change when the effects of inflation have been removed. It should be emphasised of course that inflation will simply raise the value of money expenditure in 1978 without disturbing its pattern in percentage terms as shown in Table 3.12.

Finally it should be noted that where projections appear implausible it is usually due to the fact that results are expressed on a 1972=100

TABLE 3.12

Share of Commodity in Total Expenditure (per cent)

	1972		1978	
	Com- modity group	All food and drink[a]	Com- modity group	All food and drink
Milk and Milk Products				
Fresh milk	69	6.2	58	3.8
Condensed and dried milk	7	0.7	10	0.6
Cream	4	0.3	4	0.3
Cheese	20	1.8	28	1.8
Total for Milk and Milk Products				
(excluding butter)	100	9.0	100	6.5
Meat and Fish				
Beef and veal	22	4.7	22	4.5
Mutton and lamb	11	2.4	11	2.4
Pork	8	1.7	9	1.8
Poultry	8	1.8	8	1.6
Bacon and ham	15	3.3	17	3.4
Meat products	23	4.9	20	4.2
Fish	13	2.7	13	2.6
Total for Meat and Fish	100	21.5	100	20.5
Butter and Fats				
Butter	60	2.0	54	1.8
Margarine	24	0.8	26	0.9
Other fats	16	0.5	20	0.7
Total for All Fats	100	3.3	100	3.4
Other Commodities				
Eggs		2.0		1.7
Sugar		1.1		1.4
Jam preserves		0.5		0.7
Potatoes		1.6		1.6
Fresh vegetables		3.1		3.0
Fresh fruit		2.5		2.4
Bread/flour		4.2		3.8
Other cereal products		5.1		5.1
Total		20.2		19.7

[a] Including beer, wines and spirits.

Agriculture and the State

base. In the event the projections include the effect of actual events up to the end of 1974. Consequently where a zero growth is assumed this means zero growth in consumer expenditure 1974–78, but would include the effect of actual growth in 1973–74.

NOTES AND REFERENCES

1. The authors acknowledge the contribution made by Donald Silvey, of the Department of Land Economy at the University of Cambridge, after Mr Hannah left the project in 1972, in updating statistical material which formed the basis of the results published below and also in the preparation, in collaboration with Dr McFarquhar, of the final drafts of the paper. Acknowledgement is also due to G. B. Aneuryn Evans, of the Faculty of Economics at the University, for help in the development of computable models and for programming and computation. Debt is expressed to Joan Maskell and R. Butcher, of the Department of Land Economy, for assembling and checking statistical material.
2. T. E. Josling, Brian Davey, Alister McFarquhar, A. C. Hannah and Donna Hamway, *Burdens and Benefits of Farm-Support Policies*, Agricultural Trade Paper No. 1 (London: Trade Policy Research Centre, 1972); and McFarquhar and M. C. Evans, 'Projection Models for UK Food and Agriculture', *Journal of Agricultural Economics*, Manchester, September 1971.
3. Food = food + non-alcoholic beverages.
4. Non-food commodities = alcoholic beverages + all non-food goods.
5. All the prices in Table 3.13 have been deflated by an index of the following form:

$$\frac{\sum_{i} p_{it} q_{io}}{\sum_{i} p_{io} q_{io}} \qquad \begin{aligned} &i = 1, 2, \ldots n \text{ commodities.} \\ &t \text{ is the current year.} \\ &o \text{ is the base year.} \end{aligned}$$

This index measures the cost of purchasing the base year quantity at current year prices. By summing over all commodities (including goods other than food) movements in the general level of prices are recorded.
6. McFarquhar and Evans, *op. cit.*; McFarquhar (ed.), *Europe's Future Food and Agriculture* (Amsterdam: North-Holland, 1971); and Josling *et al.*, *op. cit.*
7. A. P. Barten, 'Estimating Demand Functions', *Econometrica*, London, No. 2, 1968; Barten, 'Consumer Demand Functions under Conditions of Almost Additive Preference', *Econometrica*, No. 1–2, 1964; and Barten, 'Maximum Likelihood Estimation of a Complete System of Demand Equations', *European Economic Review*, London, Vol. 1, 1969.
8. A number of calculations of farm prices have been made by Ian Sturgess at the University of Newcastle. These estimated prices have been subject to periodic revisions and the set included here reflects discussions with Sturgess and others.
9. An estimated set of margins was provided by T. E. Josling when at the

London School of Economics, based on the work done on margins published in John Ferris *et al.*, *The Impact on US Agricultural Trade of the Accession of the United Kingdom, Ireland, Denmark and Norway to the European Community* (East Lansing: Institute of International Agriculture, Michigan State University, 1971).

10. In the projections pork prices rise by 2 per cent and the price of poultry increases by 18 per cent.

11. Strictly, the projection for food consumed outside the home should be broken down into the various food types and added to the relevant category to obtain total consumption figures. Although the aggregate data for food consumed outside the home is published in the *National Income Bluebook* (London: HM Stationery Office, annually), no breakdown is available. It has proved extremely difficult to estimate a plausible breakdown and finally it was decided to assume (*a*) that the study's estimates of total supply moving into consumption were reasonably accurate and (*b*) that response to changing demand conditions would be the same both in and out of the home. Total supplies moving into consumption (that is, final demand) for each commodity in 1968 were therefore adjusted *pro rata* the change in household demand between 1968 and 1978 for use with the input-output model which is discussed in Chapter 5.

Appendix 1 to Chapter 3

INDICES IN THE CAMBRIDGE STUDY

Set out below are the indices for deflated retail prices and per capita household consumption used in the Cambridge part of the project.

TABLE 3.13

Index of Deflated Retail Prices in the United Kingdom (1958 = 100)

	1963	1968	1970	1971	1972
Fresh milk	100	103	102	114	111
Condensed and dried milk	92	95	93	107	118
Cream	68	72	63	66	70
Cheese	116	111	103	117	141
Beef and veal	103	122	122	127	133
Mutton and lamb	94	101	99	102	109
Pork	100	106	106	104	107
Poultry	81	71	66	68	63
Bacon and ham	96	98	96	96	100
Meat products	101	101	101	101	104
Fish	107	111	111	117	123
Eggs	97	78	76	78	64
Butter	121	96	89	113	119
Margarine	94	84	88	94	91
Sugar	100	84	79	79	85
Jam and preserves	131	129	121	120	124
Potatoes	94	68	81	66	73
Fresh vegetables	124	110	116	114	116
Fresh fruit	88	95	81	87	93
Bread and flour	111	124	124	125	127
Other cereal products	95	92	89	89	93

TABLE 3.14

Index of per capita Household Consumption (1958 = 100)

	1963	1968	1971	1972
Milk	104	100	99	96
Condensed and dried milk	109	128	136	142
Cream	185	214	230	218
Cheese	106	114	122	118
Beef and veal	99	81	83	71
Mutton and lamb	105	94	88	80
Pork	111	133	144	146
Poultry	244	447	453	525
Bacon and ham	105	103	102	96
Meat products	104	110	111	110
Fish	102	100	90	88
Eggs	104	105	103	101
Butter	98	101	91	77
Margarine	96	81	91	104
Sugar	100	88	85	81
Jams and preserves	69	61	59	56
Potatoes	103	94	88	83
Fresh vegetables	96	98	101	91
Fresh fruit	117	122	132	118
Bread and flour	90	79	75	72
Other cereal products	106	111	109	106

Appendix 2 to Chapter 3

CAMBRIDGE DEMAND MODEL

The demand model is based on the work of A. P. Barten (see n. 7 above for references). It is a system of single equations of the following form:

$$\frac{p_{i,t}(q_{i,t} - q_{i,t-1})}{\mu_t} = b_i z_t + \sum_j c_{ij} \log (p_{j,t}/_j p_{,t-1})$$

for $i, j = 1, 2, \ldots n$ commodities

where $p_{i,t}$ = price of commodity i in period t

$q_{i,t}$ = quantity consumed per head of commodity i in period t

$$\mu_t = \sum_i p_{i,t} q_{i,t}$$

$$z_t = (\mu_t - \sum_i p_{i,t} q_{i,t-1})/\mu_t$$

$$= 1 - \frac{\sum_i p_{i,t} q_{i,t-1}}{\mu_t}$$

μ_t is total expenditure (or income) in period t. z_t reflects the proportional change in income by measuring the effect of purchasing the quantity of the previous time period at current prices. Thus the term $b_i z_t$ represents the income effect of price change as well as the effect of changes in total expenditure (income) on changes in the quantity of commodity i consumed. b_i and c_{ij} are the parameters estimated. b_i, the income parameter equal to $(p_i \delta p_i)/\delta \mu$ and the income elasticity is therefore given by b_i/w_i where w_i is the share of good i in total expenditure. o_{ij}, the price parameters, are given by

$$o_{ij} = \frac{p_i p_j}{\mu} \left(\frac{\delta q_i}{\delta p_j} + \frac{\delta q_i}{\delta \mu} q_j \right)$$

They are therefore compensated for the income effect of a price change the compensated elasticity being given by o_{ij}/w_i.

The normal restrictions on demand systems are enforced, that is

$$\sum_i b_i = 1, \ \sum_i o_{ij} = 0 \text{ and } \sum_j c_{ij} = 0$$

The first are the additive restrictions imposed by the budget constraint and ensure that the sum of all the changes in expenditure equals the change in total expenditure. The third, or homogeneity restriction, precludes money illusion.

Some of the c_{ij} have been set to zero on the grounds that an implausible price relationship is not a good basis for projection. In order to enforce the budget constraint under this condition only $n - 1$ equations were estimated, the nth equation being determined by

$$c_{nj} = -\sum_{i=1}^{n-1} o_{ij} \text{ and } b_n = 1 - \sum_{i=1}^{n-1} b_i.$$

This was not considered unreasonable because the nth commodity is a conglomerate of all non-food goods, the implication being that food expenditure is allocated first according to price and income changes and then the remaining income is spent on non-food goods.

The system was estimated using quarterly food consumption data from the National Food Survey of household consumption (a system of dummy variables was used to absorb purely seasonal consumption effects) and total consumer expenditure information from the National Income Bluebook. There are twenty-nine food, two drink and one non-food categories in the system. All prices are deflated by an index of the form

$$\frac{\sum_i p_{i,t} q_{i,o}}{\sum_i p_{i,o} q_{i,o}}$$

where O is the base year and t is the current year.

CHAPTER 4

Adjustment in British Farm Production

BRIAN DAVEY and P. B. R. HAZELL

In order, *inter alia*, to predict organisational adjustments in British farming, following the United Kingdom's accession to the European Community, a model of agricultural supply was developed at the University of Newcastle upon Tyne.[1] Emphasis was placed on adjustments over the transition period to the end of 1978 at both micro (or individual farm) and macro (or aggregate) levels.

The study has been concerned with the major adjustments for the main types of British farm enterprises and with the prospects for farm incomes. The purpose of the model is to produce projections of aggregate agricultural production in the United Kingdom, providing information on levels of output of the main crop and livestock commodities produced on British farms and, too, on changes in the structure of British agricultural production in response to changes in relative prices.

NEWCASTLE MODEL OF SUPPLY

Delays between the production of the first results from the model, as published here, and the publication of this volume reporting on the programme of studies has had two major consequences which should be mentioned at the outset.

First, unforeseen changes in cereal and livestock prices since the autumn of 1972 meant that the price levels assumed, in the model, for the end of the projection period (1978/79) have been surpassed in less than two years. This inevitably reduces the utility of the results as a guide to the future. But that is not the aim of this chapter, which is to give an indication of the type of information that the model can generate, as an analytical tool for policy-making purposes.

Second, since the generation of the first results from the model, a considerable amount of work has been done on its revision. Unfortunately, at the time the present programme of studies was being finalised it was not possible to detail a more up-to-date set of assumptions, and produce an improved set of results. For a more detailed discussion of the further work, see the Appendix to this chapter, pp. 123–24.

Methodology[2]
The Newcastle study used the basic methodological approach of linear programming a set of farm models selected to represent groups of farms of different types and sizes in different parts of the country. The objective is the construction of a comprehensive microeconomic model of British agriculture that will assist in the evaluation of policy changes at the farm, regional and national levels.

The analysis contains a number of steps. First, all farms in the population are classified by homogeneous groups and a representative farm defined for each group. Second, supply estimates are derived for each farm model using linear programming. Ideally the models should be solved simultaneously to take account of connections between the various groups, such as the flows of intermediate goods of production (for example, store livestock), but, at the time of writing, this feature had not been incorporated into the model. Finally, aggregate group and national supply estimates are obtained through the application of an appropriate weighting procedure on the representative farm solutions.

This method was adopted for a number of reasons. First, a mathematical programming model necessarily embodies an explicit explanatory system of the functioning of the individual farm. Therefore it is not so susceptible to the problems which arise when the policies to be evaluated involve either extrapolation of explanatory variables beyond the range of past experience, or structural changes in the economic environment. This consideration is particularly relevant in examining the British transition to the European Community's common agricultural policy (CAP) which involves considerable changes in relative prices. Secondly, the method can take formal account of the fact that most farms produce many products using many resources; hence it is well suited to examining the *total* impact of changes in relative prices on the supply of individual products. Thirdly, suitable time-series data for an econometric approach are not available at the disaggregated level.

On the other hand, there are a number of difficulties inherent in using this approach to supply analysis. For example, considerable data are required about individual farms in order to permit proper farm classification and specification of the representative farm models. These requirements are not only taxing in relation to the availability of data, but also pose a very considerable computational burden in handling the necessary data for a complete model of British agriculture. Moreover, the optimising feature of the mathematical programming approach tends to lead to results which are more normative than predictive, that is the results are more indicative of what *should* happen given a specific government policy rather than predictive of what *would* happen.

A mathematical programming model, however, need not be normative. Normative choice implies both rational decisions in relation to specified goals and perfect knowledge about the consequences of alternative decisions. If it is accepted that farmers tend to act quite rationally in relation to given goals, and within the realms of limited rather than perfect knowledge, then predictive results can be obtained from a mathematical programming model according to the degree in which the true decision environment is successfully simulated.

Another serious problem in using a representative farm approach to obtain estimates of aggregate commodity supplies is that of aggregation bias – which is defined as the discrepancy obtained in estimating aggregate supply from weighting the solutions of representative farm models compared with the straight sum of solutions obtained by separately programming every individual farm – for aggregation bias characteristically leads to overestimates of supply for the more profitable enterprises. It should be noted that there may still be a discrepancy between actual supply and the programmed supply even when aggregation bias is zero; such a discrepancy could be caused by model specification errors and the normative nature of the approach.

Classification of Farms

An important and integral part of the study involved the derivation of homogeneous groups of farms for which representative farm models were developed. The major objective in defining the groups was to minimise problems of aggregation bias while keeping computational requirements to an acceptable level. The degree of choice was constrained by the availability of data and by the need to estimate the number of farms in each group for each year of the supply forecast period to 1979.

In order to minimise aggregation bias it is necessary to satisfy a number of theoretical requirements regarding the homogeneity of farms in a group. These requirements are that only farms which have identical technology, proportional gross margin expectations and proportional resource levels should be grouped together. Identical technology means that all the farms in the group have the same production alternatives to choose from, the same types of constraints and the same technology and managerial performance. The second condition holds if all the farms in the group have identical expectations about the relative profitability of their enterprises. Given that for the major agricultural products in both the United Kingdom and the European Community there are fixed 'policy' prices which apply over large areas, then as long as yields and costs are the same (or proportional) for all farms in the group, the condition will be satisfied. The third condition requires that if, for example, one farm has twice the land area of the average farm for the group, then it also must have twice all the other resources. Because the model is dynamic (see below), it is required that these conditions hold not only in the base year (1970), but also in every year of the forecast period.

It was recognised at an early stage that these requirements were not likely to be fully met without involving a number of farm groups which were too large for the computing capacity. Thus classification procedures were used which attempted to approximate the three conditions as far as possible, while maintaining a computationally feasible number of groups. The analysis was severely constrained by existing data sources and by the need to adhere quite closely to the Ministry of Agriculture's farm classification scheme so as to have the use of suitable data for forecasting the numbers of farms in each group in each year. The Ministry's scheme for England and Wales is composed of thirteen farm types, six size groups and eight regions; a total of 624 cells.

An initial classification was carried out for the base year of 1970. Using aggregate census data on twenty-three variables for each cell in the Ministry's farm classification scheme, the aggregate data were classified on the basis of resource proportionality using statistical cluster techniques. The twenty-three variables included information on numbers of workers, crop acreages and livestock numbers. No attempt was made, however, to handle the requirements of proportional gross margin expectations and technological homogeneity on a systematic basis because of the absence of relevant data. It is assumed that these conditions are accounted for in the farm type-size-regional breakdown. This may not be unreasonable in that technological performance and yields are closely associated with characteristics of farm type, size and regional location. Furthermore, the high degree of government involvement in farm price determination can be expected to lead to fairly homogeneous price expectations amongst farmers.

The groups resulting from the analysis for England and Wales are summarised in Table 4.1. Forty-two groups were identified, horticultural farms having been excluded from the analysis. Representative farm models were constructed for fourteen dairy groups, eleven livestock groups, four pig and poultry groups, nine cropping groups and four mixed groups. In a similar analysis for Scotland seven homogeneous farm groups were identified. In general, the results of the classification procedure showed that differences between different types of farms were always more important than either size or regional differences. Of the size and regional differences, it was usually the case that, within a type, size differences were more important than regional differences.

Agriculture and the State

TABLE 4.1

Farm Classification in England and Wales for
Micro-Economic Supply Analysis: 1970

Type of farming	Number of cells	Number of farms represented	Average number of farms per cell
Dairy	14	49,823	3,559
1. Predominantly dairy	6	29,860	4,977
2. Mainly dairy	8	19,963	2,495
Livestock	11	21,387	1,944
1. Mainly cattle	3	5,925	1,975
2. Mainly sheep	3	3,149	1,050
3. Cattle and sheep	5	12,313	2,462
Pigs and Poultry	4	9,271	2,318
1. Poultry	1	3,367	3,367
2. Pigs and poultry	3	5,904	1,968
Cropping[a]			
1. Cereals without intensive horticulture	2	8,905	4,452
2. Cereals, with intensive horticulture	2	703	351
3. Cropping, without intensive horticulture	3	10,519	3,506
4. Cropping, with intensive horticulture	2	3,546	1,773
Mixed	4	12,472	3,118
Total	42	116,626	2,777

[a] Cropping farms were sub-divided into those with and without more than 10 acres of field-scale vegetables and other horticultural activities.

Structural Change

It should be recalled that the objective of the model is to project the domestic supplies of agricultural commodities in the United Kingdom for a number of years assuming progressive adoption of the CAP. For any one commodity, total supply is given by the sum (taken over all the representative farms which produce the commodity) of the product of the farms' output of the good and the number of actual farms the model farm represents. It was necessary, therefore, to predict the numbers of holdings and the total acreage within each of the forty-two groups for each and every year of the supply forecast period in order to have an appropriate set of structural weights or raising factors for aggregating the individual farm solutions.

There are two ways in which these structural weights could change through time, namely by changing the type of farming (production patterns) or the size of farm (resource levels). It would be inappropriate to include changes in the type of farming in any measurement of the weights. Since the programming models are used for the explicit purpose of predicting type changes, to include such changes would involve double counting. So far as size changes are concerned, farms can switch from one size category to another in two ways: (*a*) by acquiring or selling land; and (*b*) by acquiring or disposing of inputs other than land. Like the type changes, this latter size change is predicted by the linear programming models which allow for investments to be made in machinery and buildings and for labour to be hired or not used. It follows, therefore, that in projecting the structural weights, the only changes that should be measured are those involving size changes and more specifically the acquisition or sale of land.

Structural weights were estimated for each year of the forecast period using Markov methods. These methods involve the estimation of a transition probability matrix *P*, which shows the probability that a farm or acre of land moves from state *i* in one period to state *j* in the next period. Having calculated such a matrix, the projection of numbers in succeeding periods is achieved by powering *P* and multiplying it by a base year vector of numbers in each state. The data on which the analysis was based consisted of time series on the number of holdings and the crops, grass and rough grazing acreage by region, size and type of farm for the three years 1968 to 1970 inclusive.

The analysis involved projecting the total crops, grass and rough grazing acreage in each group for each year to 1980. The numbers of holdings in each group were estimated from the total acreage projections by making assumptions about average size of farms. The results of this analysis for England and Wales are summarised in Table 4.2.

It was pointed out earlier that the only type of structural change which is relevant to the microeconomic supply model is that concerning acreage changes. Thus the weights attached to each group must be interpreted extremely carefully. For example, the projected change in the number of sheep farms implies nothing about the relative popularity or profitability of sheep farming in 1979; the size structure of sheep farms is such that if the trends of the early 1970s continue, there will be fewer of these farms in the future, but on average they will be larger. For this reason it is perhaps somewhat confusing to refer to the groups of farms by their early 1970s output pattern, such as 'sheep', since this might change over the forecast period (and if so, it will appear in the programming solutions).

Projected numbers of farms by size of business groups are summarised in Table 4.3.

The number of full-time farms in England and Wales is projected to fall by 19,000 between 1970 and 1979. By 1979 it is expected that there will be only 109,000 farms providing a full-time livelihood for their occupiers compared with 128,000 in 1970. Within this overall decline, changes in the distribution of farms between the various size categories will be occurring. The number of one-man and two-man farms is projected to fall by 22,000 over the period, but this will be partially offset by an increase in the number of large farms in the 1800 standard-man-day (smd) and over size group.

TABLE 4.2

Structural Weights of England and Wales Supply Model: 1970 with Projections for 1979

Type of farming group	1970		1979	
	Acres of crops, grass and rough grazing	*Number of farms*	*Acres of crops, grass and rough grazing*	*Number of farms*
	million	*thousand*	*million*	*thousand*
Predominantly dairy	3.28	29.7	2.82	23.2
Mainly dairy	3.46	19.9	3.31	16.5
Cattle	1.18	5.8	1.00	4.5
Sheep	1.39	3.2	1.38	2.6
Cattle and sheep	3.24	12.4	3.01	9.9
Pigs and poultry	0.52	8.7	0.54	7.6
Cereals, without horticulture	3.00	8.6	2.8	7.2
Cereals with horticulture	0.38	0.7	0.44	0.7
Cropping, without horticulture	2.37	10.8	2.39	9.3
Cropping, with horticulture	1.41	3.5	1.52	3.4
Mixed	3.09	12.5	3.27	11.0

TABLE 4.3

Standard Man-Day (smd) Size of Farms in England and Wales: 1970 with Projections for 1979 (thousand)

Size group (*smd*)	1970	1979
275–599	56	42
600–1,199	44	36
1,200–1,799	14	14
1,800–2,399	6	6
2,400–4,199	5	7
4,200 and over	3	4
Total, all sizes	128	109

In addition to a continuous decline in the number of full-time farms, a further reduction in the size of the agricultural labour force can be expected by 1979. The implication of the projections of farm numbers is that the number of farmers and farm managers in England and Wales will fall by almost 20,000 over the 1970s. This would be accompanied by a decline of just over 30,000 in the number of regular agricultural workers. Similar tendencies can be expected in Scotland.

Representative Farm Models
The representative farm models are basically single period linear programming models in which a measure of future profits is maximised, subject to various resource and rotational constraints. Resource constraints were specified as the arithmetic mean of supplies for the group and were estimated initially from census data, but were calculated recursively from the previous year's solution so far as the future was concerned.

The models represent a compromise between a chain of static yearly models in which a solution is obtained for each year, given the initial conditions and assumptions for that year, and a fully dynamic model in which a single optimisation results in a complete solution for the whole period allowing for planned developments over several years to maximise some overall criterion of profitability. The first alternative would not allow sufficiently for farmers' goals beyond the particular year under consideration, while the second involves computational requirements beyond the capacity of the facilities available at the University of Newcastle.

For each year within the period under study, the models are optimised with respect to a single recurrent plan which would be optimal if that year's prices, resources, and so forth, were to continue into the future and livestock numbers could be adjusted as quickly as desired. Since, however, livestock numbers, recent plantings and capital restrictions resulting from past borrowings constrain farmers from adopting such a plan immediately, the current year is considered an adjustment period during which the legacy of past policy decisions is worked out and the recurrent plan phased in. And because each year in practice brings new price expectations and new resource conditions (resulting from the previous year's plan), the models are resolved every year and thus the recurrent plans represent a moving target towards which farmers are continually striving but prevented from reaching immediately because of past decisions.

The successive solution of the models through the years provides a time series of the supply position of each agricultural commodity. The above procedure ensures that these series are consistent with each other so that, for example, the number of dairy cows does not grow outside the limits set by available young stock in the previous year.

Production and technical possibilities

In specifying the individual representative farm models a range of alternative activities was selected which comprised those enterprises which were functioning in the base year, together with any enterprises that might reasonably be considered in the future. Within each enterprise a wide range of technological systems was also specified. For the most part, this was handled by specifying a discrete number of technological packages for the production of each enterprise, which together encompass the major husbandry systems appropriate to the farm. These packages were distinguished by such features as discrete levels of fertiliser use (low, medium or high), length of grass leys (one-year, three-year or permanent pasture), method of feeding and housing livestock, seasonality of production, and type of machinery used. In the case of dairy and beef animals, a discrete number of balanced forage packages were defined to provide adequate grazing and conserved grass products throughout the year. Allowance was also made for rearing or buying breeding livestock, buying or growing cereals for feed, milling and mixing home rations or purchasing balanced concentrates, and buying or producing hay, silage and straw.

The technological alternatives selected for each representative farm model were based on typical technological achievements for the appropriate group in 1969. These data were taken largely from the Ministry of Agriculture's *Farm Management Survey*, although additional information was available from other sources. The models were allowed to select methods of production in an optimal way within the range of technologies offered.

The production and technological alternatives are constrained by the usual resource and husbandry considerations. The resource constraints include seasonal supplies of basic, overtime and casual labour, ploughable land, non-conservable permanent pasture, acreage quotas and building and machinery capacity. The husbandry considerations include rotational constraints and replacement requirements for breeding livestock. In addition, other controls ensure adequate supplies of feed, bedding and purchased animals for the various livestock activities.

A key feature of the models is the handling of technological change. For example, some technological improvements can be attained through capital investment. These opportunities relate mainly to expansion into larger scale sizes for individual enterprises, and the purchase of new and more efficient machinery. In addition, many input/output coefficients are automatically adjusted each year according to forecasts about changes in yields and feed conversion rates. These forecasts are based largely on time series trends and are incorporated into forecasts of gross margins for the various activities.

Capital investment possibilities

Provision is made in the models for considering capital investments in livestock and in machinery and building packages which are specifically associated with individual farm enterprises. Investments in additional land are not considered, although changes in acreage size are forecast independently. Capital requirements for the maintenance of land, buildings and non-specialised equipment are handled as regular components in farm overhead costs.

In order to handle capital investments it was necessary to treat all the farms as though they were owner-occupied. Distinguishing between tenants and owner-occupiers would lead to a number of difficulties, particularly in relation to the problem of identifying the landlord's capital contribution to agriculture. Capital decisions are determined simultaneously with farm production decisions through maximising a measure of future profit each year. This is defined as total gross margin less the sum of established fixed costs, and all additional depreciation costs and interest and principal charges incurred through new investments, determined for the year. The established fixed costs include all interest and principal payments on established loans, together with land and building maintenance expenses. But regular labour, taxes and a rental value for land are not charged.

A working capital constraint is imposed to ensure that the amount of capital tied up in livestock and variable costs each year does not exceed available supply. The major sources of working capital are livestock and crop inventories, the cash and credit assets of the farmer at the beginning of each year, and the available bank overdraft. In addition, provision is made for the purchase of some livestock on hire purchase. The constraint is updated each year as the model is rolled forward on a dynamic basis. In particular, the livestock and crops are valued at the end of each year through an accounting row in the models. The amount of cash the farmer is able to plough back from the previous year's profits is also calculated; this is defined as profit, less family consumption. The sum of the livestock and crop valuation and disposable profit provides the amount of farmer's own capital available for the next year.

The working capital constraints do not take formal account of intra-year cash flows. In specifying the working capital requirements of individual activities, variable costs are partly offset by some proportion of the receipts, the proportion involved depending on the relative timing of costs and returns. For example, in calculating working capital requirements for dairy cows, the variable costs are reduced by 40 per cent of milk receipts.

Longer-term investment opportunities are offered in various machinery and building packages defined for individual enterprises. For simplicity, these are classified into five- and fifteen-year investments. Five-year investments mostly relate to machinery and are constrained to available capital supplies each year. The only source of five-year capital is the transfer of working capital supplies, namely farmers' own capital and a sustained level of bank overdraft. Fifteen-year investments permit expansion of building facilities. They are financed through the transfer of working capital supplies, and through the negotiation of Agricultural Mortgage Corporation loans. Two debt repayment constraints are included to ensure that farmers do not negotiate more loans each year than can be serviced from expected income in both the year of solution and future planning horizons.

Enterprise costs and returns

In principle, enterprise costs and returns should be specified according to farmer expectations in order to obtain predictive results through proper description of the decision environment. This poses particular difficulties when examining the impact on supply of alternative price policies, because the price policies must be translated into the sorts of expectation farmers would hold in making decisions. This requires knowledge of the prices that will be realised and the degree to which different farmers will anticipate these prices.

The models have been specified so that predetermined levels of costs and returns expectations are considered each year. This is consistent with the primary purpose of the model which is to explore the impact of a transition to the CAP, since the latter involves considerable price-fixing arrangements for the important commodities. Yield expectations within each group are assumed to be based on past levels of performance. Typical farm data are used to define the yields in the base year and these coefficients are revised each year on a time-trend basis.

PRICES, COSTS, TECHNICAL PERFORMANCE AND PROFITABILITY

A variety of assumptions about farm prices, the cost of inputs, technical performance levels and the gross profitability of farming activities were incorporated into the farm models. These assumptions are described and the rationale underlying them explained. The assumptions are crucial to analysis in the sense that the farm models are designed to measure the changes in farm organisations – and hence in aggregate supply – that are likely to follow the adoption of the new economic environment of the CAP.

General Comments

Before the turnround in world agricultural markets, following the 1972/73 season, official farm prices in the European Community were markedly above British levels for many products (Table 4.4). From the table it is clear that substantial increases in farm-gate prices were only to be expected in Britain – after the country joined the Community – especially if sterling was devalued against the unit of account (as many predicted). Following the price increases agreed by the European Community for the 1972/73 season, little general increase in Community farm prices was expected during the rest of the 1970s, but few bargained for chronic inflation and for the world-wide shortages discussed in Chapter 1.

TABLE 4.4

Official Farm Prices in the European Community and the
United Kingdom: 1972/73

Product.	Unit	United Kingdom guaranteed price	European Community target price	European Community basic intervention price
Soft wheat	£ per ton	34.40	47.41	43.66
Barley	£ per ton	31.20	43.41	39.90
Sugar beet	£ per ton	8.00	8.31[a]	—
Fat cattle	£ per live cwt	13.20	16.51[b]	—
Pigmeat	£ per score deadweight	2.81	3.10[c]	—
Eggs	p. per dozen	16.00	19.11[d]	—
Milk	p. per gallon	20.6[e]	23.00	—
Sheep	p. per lb. dressed carcass weight	24.3	—	—

[a] Community price free delivered. Minimum ex-farm price £7.31 per ton.
[b] Guide price.
[c] Basic price.
[d] Minimum import price, December 1971.
[e] Pool price.
Note: Community prices converted to sterling assuming £1 equals 2.40 units of account.

Staying with the assumptions of the model, it was deemed unlikely, within the enlarged European Community, that farm prices would rise on average by more than one per cent per annum in money terms. Two constraints were envisaged: the effects of the higher prices on the level of domestic agricultural production in the Community and, hence, on the cost of the CAP; and the interrelationship between the CAP and the expansion of world agricultural trade. But while the general level of farm prices in the Community was expected to show little change over the 1970s, as a whole, it was probable that the price relativities between different commodities would be altered in an attempt to influence the pattern of production. In particular, according to the first results of the Newcastle model, the milk-beef ratio will move in favour of beef; but, for political reasons, a reduction in grain prices relative to livestock prices, whilst desirable, is less probable – at least in the short or medium term.

As well as receiving higher prices for the products they sell, farmers will be faced with higher prices for the inputs they buy. Higher prices for components will push up the price of compound animal feeding-stuffs, despite any change in feed composition in response to changes in the relative prices of the different ingredients and, in particular the increased use of cereal substitutes (such as manioc) due to higher relative prices for feed-grains. Removal of the fertiliser subsidy will lead to increased fertiliser prices, partly offset by freer trade between Britain and the other members of the Community. Agricultural wage rates will rise with inflation and economic growth; in this study an annual rate of wage inflation in agriculture of 8 per cent has been assumed, 4 per cent on account of inflation and 4 per cent representing higher real incomes for agricultural workers. For other cost items – fuel and machinery, agricultural chemicals and so forth – an annual inflation of 6 per cent over the first two years of the supply forecast period and 4 per cent thereafter has been assumed; with hindsight this was probably too modest an assumption.

Since World War II there has been a marked improvement in the productivity of British agriculture. Average yields of both crop and livestock products have increased with the development of improved varieties and breeds. There has been greater efficiency in the conversion by livestock of feed into meat, milk and eggs. Labour productivity has increased as a result of mechanisation and organisational changes. There is no reason to expect that these tendencies will not continue. Not only are agricultural scientists active in developing new technology for application to commercial practice, but there is also great scope for improvements in average performance levels through better management and a wider uptake of techniques currently available. The estimates of technical performance levels for 1979 shown in Table 4.7 were based on the extrapolation of historic trends.

The assumptions about prices, costs and technical performance were used to generate forecasts of gross margins for all the activities specified in the farm models. (The gross margin of an activity is the margin of output over variable costs of production. It should be noted that the gross margins for cattle and sheep make no allowance for the variable costs of forage utilised by the stock.) These forecasts and the underlying assumptions are summarised in Tables 4.5 to 4.8 inclusive. The tables are followed by a commentary on a commodity by commodity basis.

Cereals. Cereal producers can look forward to sizeable increases in gross margins during the transition to the CAP as British grain prices are increased to Community levels. Prices are likely to be around £41 per ton for barley and £44 for wheat by 1979, or some £10 per ton more than guaranteed prices in 1971–72. The main increases in costs will be for fertiliser as the British subsidy scheme is phased out and for seeds because of more stringent Community regulations. With further improvements in yields, gross margins are expected to double

TABLE 4.5

Ex-Farm Prices of Selected Commodities in the United Kingdom:
1970 with Estimates for 1979

Commodity	Unit	1970	1979
Wheat	£ per ton	29.0	44.4
Barley	£ per ton	26.0	41.4
Sugar beet	£ per ton	6.8	8.4
Potatoes	£ per ton	15.2	16.7
Milk	p. per gallon	16.4	21.2
Cull dairy cows	£ per cwt	6.7	15.5
Dairy calf	£ per head	14.1	24.8
In-calf heifer	£ per head	125	161
Beef	£ per live cwt	10.9	19.2
Beef calf	£ per head	23.7	52.5
Beef stores	£ per head	50–65	95–130
Lamb	p./lb dressed carcass weight	18.2	24.2
Eggs	p. per dozen	15.3	18.6
Broilers	p. per lb	7.0	9.8
Pigs	£ per score deadweight	2.5	3.3

TABLE 4.6

Prices of Compound Animal Feeding-Stuffs in the United Kingdom:
1970 with Estimates for 1979 (£ per ton)

Enterprise	1970	1979
Dairy	38.3	53.0
Beef	38.3	52.0
Laying hens	37.0	59.0
Broilers	44.0	70.0
Pigs	37.3	58.6

by 1980, but in the longer term there are likely to be reductions in real cereal prices as the Community takes action to prevent the supply of grains from outstripping demand.

Sugar Beet. Ex-farm prices for beet are expected to be about £8.40 per ton by 1979, equivalent to about £9.90 delivered to the factory. Production costs will probably rise by 40 to 50 per cent, the main increases being for fertilisers and transport. Gross margins are estimated to increase by some 30 per cent; this will be insufficient to keep pace with inflation over the period, although beet will remain an attractive crop in the rotation.

TABLE 4.7

Technical Performance Measures in the United Kingdom:
1970 with Estimates for 1979

Enterprise	Performance measure	1970	1979
Crops			
Winter wheat	Yield (*cwt/acre*)	33.0	37.2
Spring wheat	Yield (*cwt/acre*)	29.0	32.8
Winter barley	Yield (*cwt/acre*)	33.0	37.6
Spring barley	Yield (*cwt/acre*)	29.0	33.0
Sugar beet	Yield (*tons/acre*)	15.5	17.5
Maincrop potatoes	Yield (*tons/acre*)	10.5	12.0
Dairying			
High yield:			
concentrate fed	Yield (*gallons/cow*)	1,000	1,049
bulk fed	Yield (*gallons/cow*)	950	997
Average yield:			
concentrate fed	Yield (*gallons/cow*)	850	892
bulk fed	Yield (*gallons/cow*)	800	832
Sheep			
Early fat lamb	*Lambs/ewe*	1.58	1.64
Late fat lamb	*Lambs/ewe*	1.41	1.51
Store lamb	*Lambs/ewe*	1.34	1.39
Pigs			
Breeding	*Pigs/sow*	16	18
Fattening	Feed conversion (*index*)	100	111
Poultry			
Laying flock	Eggs/bird (*dozen*)	18.9	21.3
	Feed conversion (*index*)	100	105
Broilers	Feed conversion (*index*)	100	109

Potatoes. Returns from the potato crop are also expected to fall in real terms. Prices for main-crop potatoes are only expected to reach around £16.7 per ton by 1979, due to a generally lower level of market protection in the European Community. Costs, on the other hand, will increase rapidly with inflation so that, after allowing for improved yields, gross margins are expected to rise by only 25 per cent over the period.

TABLE 4.8

Gross Margins of Farm Enterprises in the United Kingdom:
1970 with Forecasts for 1979

Crops (£ per acre)

Enterprise	1970	1979
Cereals		
Spring barley	25.9	50.6
Winter barley	30.4	59.0
Spring wheat	28.9	53.3
Winter wheat	35.0	63.5
Sugar beet		
Own harvester	64.9	87.7
Contract harvesting	51.9	68.4
Potatoes		
Maincrop	99.4	123.3

Grassland and Forage Crops: Variable Costs (£ per acre)

System	1970	1979
Grazing		
Intensive 1-year ley	16.4	24.3
Intensive 3-year ley	13.7	20.2
Semi-intensive 1-year ley	10.4	15.4
Semi-intensive 3-year ley	7.6	11.2
Semi-intensive permanent pasture	6.2	9.1
Permanent grassland	0.1	0.2
Silage making		
Intensive grassland	0.9	1.4
Semi-intensive grassland	0.7	1.1
Permanent grassland	0.5	0.7
Haymaking		
Semi-intensive grassland	0.7	1.1
Permanent grassland	0.5	0.8
Kale	10.0	14.8

TABLE 4.8—*continued*

Livestock

System	1970	1979
Dairying (£ per cow)		
High yield, concentrate fed	99.4	143.8
High yield, bulk fed	113.2	166.1
Average yield, concentrate fed	91.9	139.2
Average yield, bulk fed	97.7	146.3
Beef		
Breeding (£ per cow)		
Autumn calving	60	91
Winter/spring calving	63	70
Rearing and fattening (£ per head)		
Suckled calves, winter finished	13	5
Suckled calves, grass finished	19	18
12-month cereal beef	15	4
18-month grass/cereal beef	32	58
Sheep (£ per ewe)		
Early fat lamb production	11.1	13.1
Late fat lamb production	10.3	13.2
Store lamb production	5.3	5.7
Upland ewes: cross bred	7.1	7.5
store production	4.8	4.4
Mountain sheep	3.7	2.4
Pigs (£ per sow)		
Breeding and selling weaners	47.5	59.1
Breeding and fattening: porkers	87.8	100.6
baconers	118.8	135.2
heavy hogs	128.4	123.3
Poultry		
Egg production (£ per hen)	0.63	0.62
Broiler production (£ per bird)	0.03	0.03

Milk. It is anticipated that the economics of milk production will be affected by higher prices for milk, calves and cull dairy stock in the Community. Higher milk prices are expected to be largely a reflection of higher realisation prices for manufacturing milk, whilst prices of dairy calves and other stock will be influenced by conditions in the beef market. Costs of production are also expected to rise, especially for feed-grains, compound feeds and replacement stock. Gross margins per cow, excluding forage costs, are expected to increase by about 50 per cent by 1979, with the advantage moving in favour of systems of production based on grass and bulk feeds.

Beef. It is also expected that fat cattle will realise much higher prices within the Common Market and this will influence the level of prices for other meats. The ex-farm price for fat cattle is expected to reach over £19 per live hundredweight by 1979. The gross margin estimates for the different systems of beef production reflect the impact of higher cereal prices in the Community and highlight the advantages of beef rearing and fattening off grass under Community conditions. In particular, semi-intensive grass cereal beef will remain an attractive system, but the profitability of intensive production will be sorely affected by higher feed-grain prices. Higher end-product prices will be reflected in higher prices for store stock and hence in higher margins for suckler beef cow herds.

Sheep. Only marginal improvements in gross margins from sheep are expected. Much of the increase in gross output from higher lamb prices – estimated to be over 24 pence per pound dressed carcase weight by 1979 – and higher productivity will probably be partially offset by a marginal reduction in wool prices and by increases in costs. Wool is regarded as an industrial product by the Community and does not come within the compass of the CAP. Margins from hill and upland flocks could be reduced further by elimination of the hill sheep subsidies and winter-keep grants in their present form, although some continuing income support to hill sheep farmers is assured.

Pigs. The profitability of pig production depends almost entirely on the relationship between pig prices and the cost of feed. Both will be much higher in the Community, although pig prices are likely to be more unstable than in the past because of the nature of the arrangements for supporting pig prices under the CAP. On average, most of the benefit of higher pigmeat prices is expected to be absorbed by higher feed costs (in spite of improved feed conversion efficiency) and other cost increases. Thus gross margins from the fattening enterprise will probably show little change, but breeding herds and integrated breeding and fattening units are expected to benefit from the improved productivity of breeding stock.

Poultry. So far as poultry is concerned, the enlarged Community will be virtually self-sufficient in eggs and poultry-meat and prices are expected to fluctuate in response to market conditions. As with pigs, the European Community's import restrictions should have little effect on market stability and with no intervention buying prices could fall disastrously when the market is oversupplied. On average, the effect of higher yields and prices will be offset by higher feed costs, even after allowing for more efficient use of feed. Little change in gross margins is expected.

FARM ORGANISATION AND SUPPLY

The above discussion dealt with the research methodology and the assumptions incorporated into the farm models and laid the foundations for a discussion of likely changes in farm organisation, and hence in domestic agricultural production, in the United Kingdom as this country adjusts to the CAP over the period to 1979. Discussion will now focus on the results of the research. First, adjustments at the individual farm level are discussed for five main types of farming; dairy, livestock, pig and poultry, cropping and mixed farms. Secondly, an assessment of probable trends in aggregate crop acreages and livestock populations to 1979 is presented, building up from the adjustments at the farm level. This assessment includes discussion of adjustments in cropping and stocking patterns at both national and regional level. Thirdly, the projections of crop acreages and livestock numbers are converted into forecasts of the total production of the main crop and livestock products in the United Kingdom over the period 1970 to 1979.

Adjustment in Farm Organisation
Farm models are used to predict the adjustments in farm organisation and enterprise structure that will be occurring as farmers respond to the changes in relative profitability implicit in the adoption of European price levels. These farm level changes are discussed in general terms in the following paragraphs for five main types of farming. The intention is to give an overview of the adjustments that will be taking place, rather than provide a detailed description of the changes in organisation predicted for each of the forty-two farm models.

   Dairy farms
   Dairy farms are sub-divided into two categories, *predominantly dairy* farms, which are basically single-enterprise farms; and *mainly dairy* farms, where dairying is the major activity but subsidiary enterprises constitute a significant part of the farming system. Six farm models representing predominantly dairy types and eight mainly dairy models have been developed.
   The main emphasis in *predominantly dairy* farms will be on an expansion of the dairy herd, except on small dairy farms in the Midlands where there will be some diversion of resources from dairying into cereals. No marked changes in systems of milk production are predicted, the advantage continuing to lie with autumn calving herds with an emphasis on winter milk production and maximum utilisation of grazing, hay, silage and forage. The acreage of kale is expected to expand to accommodate the larger dairy herds. Otherwise it is anticipated that little change in cropping patterns will occur on this

type of farm, apart from the increase in cereal acreage already mentioned and a small increase in cereals – mainly barley – on medium to large dairy farms.

Beef cattle and sheep are relatively unimportant on small predominantly dairy farms, but the larger farms frequently have a small subsidiary beef herd or sheep flock. Little change in the overall size of these enterprises is expected, although within the beef herd a marginal shift towards autumn calving beef cows may occur.

So far as trends in farm incomes are concerned, the results of the farm models imply an increase in net farm income on predominantly dairy farms of about one third on average over the period 1970 to 1979. This increase takes account of inflationary increases in agriculture's fixed costs of production.

Similar adjustments are probable on *mainly dairy* farms. In all regions and on all sizes of farms an expansion in the size of the dairy herd is predicted by the models, with but one exception. This is in East Anglia, a relatively unimportant region in England for dairy farming, where a diversion of resources on dairy farms away from milk production and into beef and cash cropping, especially sugar beet, is indicated. Again, little change in systems of milk production is anticipated. Some expansion in the beef breeding herd is forecast on the larger mainly dairy farms, especially in the eastern half of England and Wales, with relatively greater emphasis on autumn calving. Many of these farms rear a proportion of dairy calves for beef and in this connection a virtual disappearance of the intensive barley beef system of production is predicted by 1979; this is a direct consequence of the impact of higher feed-grain prices on the profitability of this activity. It is expected that sheep flocks, an integral part of the farming system in the western and northern parts of England, will remain stable, but that pig herds will expand substantially, particularly in the smaller size groups and in the east.

Few adjustments in cropping patterns are predicted on this type of farm, apart from a general increase in the acreage of kale for the larger dairy herds. Marginal increases in cereal acreages are expected to occur in the south and west of England, but on large dairy farms in the east and south-east a contraction in the acreage of wheat and barley is anticipated to make room for the expansion in the dairy and beef herds.

Income prospects on this type of farm are rather better than for predominantly dairy farms. On average, and after taking account of higher fixed costs, farm incomes are predicted to rise by over 40 per cent between 1970 and 1979.

Livestock farms

Three types of farming are considered below. These are specialist cattle farms, specialist sheep farms and mixed cattle and sheep farms, represented by three, three and five models respectively. The specialist types are less important both in terms of the actual number of farms they represent and of total acreage. In 1970 there were approximately 6000 cattle farms and 3000 sheep farms in England and Wales. By contrast the number of mixed cattle and sheep farms totalled over 12,000.

Given the market situation in the early 1970s for beef in the European Community, and the stimulus likely to be given to beef production throughout the mid-1970s, a marked improvement in both the absolute and relative profitability of beef cattle activities in the United Kingdom is probable. On the face of it, therefore, the medium-term prospects for *cattle* farms under the CAP look particularly promising. This evaluation is confirmed by the results of the cattle farm models. The major adjustments predicted for this type of farm include an expansion of the beef breeding herd, particularly in Wales, the north of England and the east, and a move towards autumn calving. But in the southern and western parts of England a marginal transfer of resources from beef to milk production is anticipated. Some expansion in the acreage of cereals, especially barley, is predicted in the north and east. Income prospects are good with an average increase in net income of over 80 per cent predicted for this type of farm between 1970 and 1979. Where the scope exists for an expansion in grain production, the income trend is likely to be even more favourable.

The situation is more problematical as far as specialist *sheep* farms are concerned. These farms are located mainly in the hill and upland areas of western England and the north of England where the choice of farming system, and the scope for making adjustments to that system, is severely constrained by an unfavourable natural environment. The farming system is a simple one based on the rearing of store sheep and store cattle which are sold off for fattening on other farms, primarily in the lowlands. Membership of the Community is unlikely to lead to many changes in organisation on this type of farm. The only adjustment predicted by the farm models is an expansion of the subsidiary beef suckler herd, with the emphasis remaining on spring calving since natural conditions preclude the move towards autumn calving predicted for other farm types in areas where climate is more favourable. No increase in the sheep flock is expected.

Althought part of any increase in end-product prices for beef and sheepmeat would be reflected back to the store rearer, the income prospects for sheep farms appear uncertain. Wool sales constitute an important element of revenue for the hill sheep farmer and it is probable that higher receipts from the sale of livestock will be offset, at least in part, by lower returns from wool given the Community policy for this commodity. In practice, the income position of this type of farm is dominated by the situation with regard to the special hill farming subsidies. It will be recalled that the forecasts of gross margins presented in Table 4.8 assumed the discontinuation of this form of assistance by 1979. The model results indicate that failure to replace these payments by an alternative form of income support would lead to a reduction of over 40 per cent in the incomes of hill farmers between 1970 and 1979, after allowing for all other price and cost changes. Maintenance of the subsidies at the rates payable in 1970 would lead to an increase in incomes of around one-sixth, whilst increasing the rates with inflation would imply an increase in incomes of rather more than 40 per cent, with the subsidies accounting for a similar proportion of net income as during the early 1970s.

The third sub-type comprises a group of mixed *cattle and sheep* farms. Within the cattle enterprise, the main adjustment predicted on these farms is a marked shift to autumn calving within the beef breeding herd. This is a consequence of the high feed cost policy of the European Community which favours systems of management where cattle are finished on grass in summer, rather than on supplementary feed rations during the winter. Some expansion in the size of beef cow herds is predicted, especially in the Midlands and the east of England. A dairy herd is often an important subsidiary enterprise on the smaller cattle and sheep farms, and an expansion of this enterprise is also predicted. Higher feed-grain prices are expected to bear heavily on intensive beef production from dairy calves and it is predicted that this activity will contract very substantially, but that some expansion in the semi-intensive system of fattening cattle at 18 months of age will occur, particularly on small farms.

Sheep, at a relative disadvantage to beef under Community conditions, are expected to be under pressure on this type of farm. Indeed, there are indications in the models that the ewe flock will be reduced in size to facilitate the expansion of the cattle enterprise.

Little change in cropping patterns is predicted for cattle and sheep farms. There may be an increase in cereal acreages, particularly barley, in the larger size groups, while in the east it is predicted that a larger acreage of potatoes will be grown.

Income prospects for cattle and sheep farms look reasonably promising. On average, it is predicted that net farm incomes will rise by just over one-third between 1970 and 1979, after allowing for the impact of inflation on fixed costs. This makes no provision, however, for the continuation of the hill farming subsidies after entry to the Community. Since over half the cattle and sheep farms in the country are located in the hills and uplands, and given that continuation of some form of income support to farmers in these areas is assured, the estimate probably understates the improvement in incomes that can be expected over the 1970s. It seems more probable that incomes on these farms will rise by between a half and three-quarters over the period, that is within the range of income improvements predicted for specialist cattle and specialist sheep farms.

Pig and poultry farms

The organisation of pig and poultry farms is based on a cereal enterprise, with the grain fed to pigs. A small area of grassland, included for rotational reasons or where land is unploughable, is utilised by a subsidiary grazing livestock enterprise. Three models representing pig and poultry farms have been developed and the results are summarised below.

No change in cereal acreage is predicted on these farms, although it is forecast that grain production will rise with improvements in yields. An expansion in the size of the pig breeding herd is predicted, however, but the most interesting adjustment forecast for the pig enterprise is a change in its structure, particularly so far as the slaughter weight of pigs is concerned. The results of the models show that by 1979, in response to changes in relative profitability, a marked trend towards selling pigs as cutters or at bacon weight will have occurred, with a contraction in the number of pigs slaughtered as porkers. Where a dairy or beef herd exists, some expansion is expected as a result of British membership of the Community, with the emphasis within the beef herd moving towards autumn calving and perhaps a marginal move towards summer milk production within the dairy herd.

Income prospects on pig and poultry farms appear to be quite good, largely on account of the increased margins from cereals. On average, incomes are predicted to rise by about three-quarters over the period 1970 to 1979. Incomes, however, may fluctuate quite widely around the average. This is because of the nature of the price-support system for pigs under the CAP and in particular the ineffectiveness of the arrangements so far as the achievement of market stability is concerned. Pig prices in the Community have shown a marked cyclical trend during the early 1970s. By contrast, mid-1970 British price-support arrangements protect pig producers against the pig cycle. With the British market becoming more unstable as producers are exposed to the full effects of the pig cycle, greater fluctuations in pig prices – and hence in the incomes of pig farmers – are to be expected.

Cropping farms

Two sub-types are identified under the general heading of cropping farms. These are cropping, mostly cereal farms, where wheat and barley are the predominant crops in the rotation, and general cropping farms where sugar beet, potatoes and vegetables also occupy an important role in the cropping plan. Four models representing cereal farms and five models representing cropping farms were specified.

On *cereal* farms, only marginal changes in farm organisation are predicted by the farm models over the period to 1979. In general, marginal increases in cereal acreages are expected to occur, with the bulk of the expansion being in wheat. A small increase in the acreage of potatoes grown on these farms is also predicted. In a few cases, however, the models show that resources will be diverted from cereals and potatoes into grass and forage to accommodate an expansion in dairying; this is an indication of how the CAP could encourage regional specialisation along the lines of comparative advantage. Beef cattle and sheep are relatively unimportant on this type of farm and few adjustments are expected to take place, other than an increase in autumn calving within the beef herd. Similarly, apart from a tendency towards selling the progeny at heavier weights, little change is predicted for the pig enterprise.

On the other hand, a greater degree of change is predicted for *general cropping* farms. In particular, in England a considerable divergence in the pattern of cropping and stocking between cropping farms in different regions is indicated by the models, the east being generally more favourably suited to crop production and the west to livestock. In the east, the results point to a marginal increase in the cereal acreage, and to a rather larger expansion in the acreage of sugar beet, made possible by a reduction in the area of grass and forage crops and a consequent contraction in livestock activities, especially dairying. In this region, a large expansion in pig production on cropping farms is also predicted. On the other hand, developments in the west are expected to be rather different. In this part of the country, less emphasis on cropping and more on livestock is predicted. Dairy herds on cropping farms are expected to expand in size; the models indicate that the area of cereals and potatoes will contract with the land put down to grass to feed the larger dairy herds. Sheep flocks are also expected to come under pressure from competition from dairy cows.

The increase in margins forecast for cereal crops in particular mean that cropping farms have reasonable prospects over the rest of the 1970s so far as the trend in farm incomes is concerned. On average, incomes on cropping farms are predicted to rise by almost half, after allowing for higher fixed costs, over the period 1970 to 1979, with general cropping farms having the more favourable outlook.

Mixed farms

The last main type of farming to be considered comprises those 'mixed' farms where no single activity or enterprise predominates. Four models were developed to represent mixed farming systems.

Little change in cereal acreage is predicted for this type of farm.

The major adjustments in cropping patterns will be in cash roots, namely potatoes and sugar beet. A large increase in sugar beet acreage is predicted for mixed farms in eastern England, but in other regions – and especially the Midlands and the south – any expansion of the arable acreage is expected to be concentrated on potatoes. The indications are that competition for land between cattle and sheep will intensify with sheep flocks likely to contract except in the east of England. Few changes are predicted so far as cattle are concerned. A marginal increase in dairy herds is predicted on small mixed farms in the north and west, whilst in the east the beef suckler herd is expected to expand with a shift towards autumn calving. Intensive beef production is forecast to contract everywhere under the impact of higher feed-grain prices, while an increase in pig production on mixed farms in the east and south is indicated, with a move to finishing pigs at heavier weights.

Income prospects for mixed farms are only moderate. After allowing for higher fixed costs, net farm incomes are predicted to rise by about 25 per cent on average over the period 1970 to 1979.

Supply of Farm Products
The programming results for the forty-two farm models provide the raw material for an analysis of probable trends in the domestic supply of farm products in the United Kingdom over the period from 1970 to 1979. The first stage in the analysis was to raise the individual farm programmes for 1970 and 1979 to the national level using a set of structural weights based on the figures in Table 4.2. This yielded information on trends in crop acreages and livestock populations in England and Wales. Information on adjustments at the regional level was also obtained, using a set of regional weighing factors.

The models developed for use in this study relate only to England and Wales, although models representing agriculture in Scotland and Northern Ireland were being developed. It was necessary, therefore, to devise a procedure for translating the projections for England and Wales to the United Kingdom level. This was accomplished by indexing the figures for crop acreages and livestock populations in England and Wales then applying these indices to the actual acreages and livestock numbers in the United Kingdom, as recorded in the agricultural census for 1970, to obtain an estimate of the overall pattern of cropping and stocking in the United Kingdom in 1979. (England and Wales account for over 80 per cent of aggregate British agricultural output, although the proportion does vary from commodity to commodity.)

The final step in the analysis involved the estimation of trends in British production of the main crop and livestock commodities. The procedure used was similar to the one adopted to forecast cropping and stocking patterns. First, the estimates of crop acreages and livestock populations in England and Wales obtained from the models were converted into production forecasts, using the levels of technical performance – yields, breeding productivity, slaughter weights and so forth – incorporated into the gross margin forecasts for each enterprise and summarised in Table 4.7. The production projections take account, therefore, of the assumed increase in productivity over the period to 1979. The forecasts of production in England and Wales were then put into index number form and the resulting indices applied to the actual British output of crop and livestock products in 1970/71. In this way, projections of British output in 1979/80 were obtained.[3]

Summarised in Tables 4.9, 4.10 and 4.11 are the results of this analysis. Indices of projected crop acreages and livestock populations in England and Wales in 1979 are presented in Table 4.9; this table also includes information for three regions of the country. In Table 4.10 estimates of changes in crop acreages and livestock numbers in the United Kingdom between 1970 and 1979 are given, whilst Table 4.11 shows the projections of production levels in the United Kingdom over the same period.

TABLE 4.9

Indices of 1979 Projected Crop Acreages and Livestock Populations in England and Wales (1970 = 100)

	North[a]	East[a]	West[a]	England and Wales
Crop Acreages				
Wheat	—	—	—	100.2
Barley	—	—	—	102.8
Total cereals	101.4	100.3	102.3	101.0
Sugar beet	125.2	140.0	111.9	137.9
Potatoes	101.3	105.2	100.5	102.3
Forage crops	108.1	101.1	103.5	103.7
Grassland	97.9	93.6	98.9	96.7
Livestock Populations				
Dairy cows	128.1	104.1	105.6	106.1
Beef cows	97.2	105.4	99.6	100.3
Breeding ewes	85.4	70.3	83.7	83.7
Breeding sows	104.8	163.4	119.7	137.6

[a] Ministry of Agriculture, Fisheries and Food administrative regions were allocated to three broad regional groupings as follows:

North: Northern, Yorkshire and Lancashire
East: East Midlands, Eastern and Southeast
West: West Midland, Southwest and Wales

TABLE 4.10

British Crop Acreages and Livestock Populations:
June 1970 with Projections for 1979

	1970 Actual	1979 Projected
Crop Acreages (thousand acres)		
Wheat	2,495	2,500
Barley	5,542	5,697
Total cereals	9,177	9,269
Sugar beet	463	638
Potatoes	669	684
Forage crops	724	751
Grassland	17,917	17,325
Livestock Numbers (thousand head)		
Dairy cows	3,243	3,441
Beef cows	1,300	1,304
Breeding ewes	10,544	8,825
Breeding sows	953	1,311

TABLE 4.11

British Production of Crop and Livestock Products:
1970/71 with Projections for 1979/80

Commodity	Unit	UK actual production 1970/71	Index of production 1979/80 (1970/71 = 100)	UK projected production 1978/79
Wheat	thousand tons	4,169	113.0	4,711
Barley	thousand tons	7,410	117.0	8,670
Total cereals	thousand tons	13,043	109.4	14,269
Potatoes	thousand tons	6,918	118.2	8,177
Sugar	thousand tons	939	155.7	1,462
Milk	million gallons	2,721	111.3	3,028
Beef	thousand tons	987	107.9	1,065
Mutton and lamb	thousand tons	224	85.7	192
Pigmeat	thousand tons	881	173.0	1,524

Cereal supplies

Only a modest expansion of 1 per cent in the British cereal acreage is projected by 1979. The effect would be to enlarge the total acreage of cereals by about 100,000 acres from just under 9.2m acres in 1970 to almost 9.3m acres in 1979. So far as the individual cereal crops are concerned, little change is predicted in the acreage of wheat over the 1970s and any expansion which occurs is likely to be in spring wheat. The acreage of winter wheat during the early 1970s has been largely governed by planting conditions in the autumn. No radical change in cereal husbandry has been assumed in the model. With the advent of chemical cultivation techniques, however, autumn conditions would become less of a constraint. If these techniques were to be widely adopted by farmers during the 1970s, wheat acreage could expand. On the other hand, an expansion of about 150,000 acres in the acreage of barley is projected, the acreage rising from over 5.5m acres in 1970 to 5.7m acres in 1979. Part of this expansion would be the result of a diversion of resources from the oat crop.

The relative stability in cereal acreages predicted by the model confirms the results of earlier work undertaken by the Agricultural Adjustment Unit at the University of Newcastle. Two reasons can be advanced to explain why the cereal acreage is not expected to expand greatly, in spite of the substantial boost to cereal gross margins that will be given by the transition to Community price levels. First, there is the question of rotational constraints which limit the area of cereals which can be grown on any one farm in the interests of good husbandry. This is particularly important in the major arable areas of the country where the upper limit on cereal acreages has already been reached and, in some cases, perhaps, exceeded. It is in these areas, of course, that the bulk of the specialist cropping farms in the country are located.

Secondly, whilst it is true that there is scope for an increase in the cereal acreage in other parts of the country, these regions tend to have a comparative advantage in the production of grazing livestock – cattle and sheep – the profitability of which will also improve under Community conditions. In general, the farm models indicated that only marginal increases in cereal acreages would occur on dairy and livestock farms. In addition, there is a further point to be taken into account. This is that, as a consequence of changes in relative profitability, a change in systems of cattle husbandry is likely to follow entry to the Common Market. With substantially higher feed-grain prices, farmers are likely to rely increasingly on systems of cattle feeding which place more emphasis on grazing, conserved grass products and forage crops. This point will be developed more fully below. All that needs to be said here is that relatively greater use of grass and forage crops in livestock production is a further factor limiting the scope for expanding the cereals acreage.

These arguments are reflected in the regional indices of cereal acreages shown in Table 4.9. Hardly any change in cereal acreage is projected for eastern England, the main area for arable cropping. Whilst some expansion of cereal acreages is projected for the north and west, which are more suited to grass and livestock production, the increases are extremely marginal being of the order of only 1 to 2 per cent over a ten-year period. Of the expected national increase in cereal acreage, about 60 per cent is in the west and a quarter in the north.

In spite of the stability in cereal acreage, grain production in the United Kingdom is projected to expand by almost 10 per cent from 13m tons in 1970/71 to 14.25m tons in 1979/80. This expansion in production would be primarily a consequence of improved yields. Higher yields would push wheat production up by over half a million tons, whilst a combination of better yields and a larger acreage would lead to an increase in barley output from 7.4m tons in 1970/71 to 8.7m tons in 1979/80. Higher yields would be insufficient to compensate for the expected contraction in the oat acreage and production of this crop is expected to decline over the decade.

Beet sugar supplies

Sugar beet is an attractive crop in the rotation and will remain so under Common Market conditions. Overall, the acreage of sugar beet in the United Kingdom is projected to increase by almost 40 per cent over the forecast period, rising from 460,000 acres in 1970 to 638,000 acres in 1979. On a regional basis, the acreage of beet is expected to increase more rapidly in the arable east than in the north and west of England. Indeed, the east should account for almost 90 per cent of the increase in the England and Wales beet acreage with the north accounting for most of the remainder.

In practice, institutional factors will play a major role in determining the acreage of sugar beet grown in the United Kingdom in the future. In particular, a great deal will depend on how far the Government is successful in obtaining an increased national quota for the United Kingdom following the termination of the Commonwealth Sugar Agreement (CSA) at the end of 1974. Under the CSA, Australia had a quota for 335,000 tons of raw sugar, and this will be reallocated between the Common Market countries, including the United Kingdom and certain developing countries.

The Government expects that within the enlarged Community there will be room for an expansion of domestic sugar production in the United Kingdom. The implication of the projected 1979 acreage, assuming an average yield of two tons of white sugar per acre, is that

Britain could expand the beet acreage by 175,000 acres and take up the entire Australian quota. This, however, seems an unlikely outcome.

Turning to sugar production, the projections in Table 4.11 point to an increase of over 50 per cent from 939,000 tons in 1970/71 to almost 1.5m tons in 1979/80. This is a reflection of predictions of both a larger acreage and improved yields of sugar beet. An expansion in production of this order of magnitude has obvious implications for Britain's import requirements for sugar.

Potato supplies

The projections indicate that Britain's potato acreage will increase by 2 per cent between 1970 and 1979. This is equivalent to an expansion of 15,000 acres, so that the total acreage is predicted to rise from 669,000 acres in 1970 to 684,000 acres in 1979. Within this overall trend the model suggests that there will be some contraction in the acreage of early potatoes and greater emphasis on maincrop varieties. In the mid-1970s, the Community's common external tariff should provide a higher level of protection against imports of early potatoes from non-Community countries than British duties did prior to joining the Community. In the early 1970s only about 10 per cent of the United Kingdom's imports of early potatoes were from Community sources. But with harmonisation of plant health regulations in the enlarged Community, more competition from France and Italy is to be expected and as a consequence, British production of early potatoes could decline.

So far as regional adjustments in potato production are concerned, the model points to a greater degree of regional specialisation in future. In eastern England, the acreage of potatoes is projected to expand by 5 per cent over the 1970s, with little or no change in acreage expected in the north and west. As with sugar beet, about 85 per cent of the increase in the national potato acreage will occur in the eastern half of England.

The predicted combination of a marginally higher acreage, improved yields and the switch to relatively greater use of maincrop varieties will result in an increase of almost 20 per cent in total potato production by 1979/80. Production is projected to expand from 6.9m tons in 1970/71 to almost 8.2m tons in 1979/80. This projection is unconstrained by factors operating on the demand side. So far as human consumption is concerned, the demand for potatoes is only likely to increase with population growth. The implication of this is that, with the trend to higher yields, the British potato market could be supplied from a smaller acreage. On the other hand, this could be offset by an increased demand for potatoes for stock-feeding purposes arising partly from increased feed-grain prices.

Milk supplies

It will be recalled that a prominent feature of the dairy farm models was a general expansion in the size of the dairy herd over the 1970s. At the aggregate level, the national dairy herd is projected to increase by 6 per cent between 1970 and 1979. On a regional basis, the most rapid rate of herd expansion is expected to be in the north of England where the number of dairy cows is projected to increase by almost 30 per cent over the period. In the east and west, increases in cow numbers of the order of 4 or 5 per cent are predicted. In terms of absolute cow numbers, it is anticipated that almost half of the increase in the national herd will be in the west with the north accounting for a further third and the east for the remaining 20 per cent.

Overall, the size of the British herd will increase by 200,000 cows, that is from 3.25m cows in 1970 to just under 3.5m cows in 1979. But little change is projected in systems of milk production; under British conditions and with national authorities free to continue the essential features of the current milk marketing arrangements – including seasonal pricing policies – the balance of advantage should continue to lie with autumn calving herds relying heavily on the use of grass and grass products for their source of nutrients. The model does not suggest that there will be any significant shift into systems of producing milk off grass from a herd of spring-calving cows.

With the larger herd and higher yields per cow, total milk production is bound to increase. The model projects an expansion of 11 per cent (300m gallons) over the 1970s, from 2721m gallons in 1970/71 to just over 3000m gallons in 1978/79. When combined with probable developments on the demand side – likely to include relative stability in the consumption of liquid milk and a switch by consumers from butter to margarine in response to relative price changes – the expansion in domestic supply seems likely to lead to a reduction in Britain's import requirements for dairy products.

Beef supplies

The projections arising out of the model indicate that a number of interesting adjustments are likely to occur within the beef sector of British agriculture during the period to 1979. These adjustments can be considered under two sub-headings, namely the size of the beef herd and the consequent level of beef production, and the structure of that herd and of production.

Although the beef breeding herd has been expanding, it is projected that by 1979 the herd will have stabilised at the 1970 level of 1.3m cows. With little change in the size of the beef breeding herd, the bulk of British beef production should continue to rise as meat will be a by-product of the projected 6 per cent increase in the dairy herd, which would result in more calves being available from this source for beef production. Moreover, the combined effect of an expanding dairy herd and a stable beef herd would be to increase the relative contribution of the dairy herd to domestic beef supplies.

After allowing for changes in the size of the breeding herd and in the relative importance of different beef rearing systems, British beef production is projected to expand by 8 per cent over the 1970s from 987,000 tons in 1970/71 to 1,065,000 tons in 1979/80. The main factor holding back a greater expansion in the beef herd would be that, on the basis of the price assumptions incorporated into the model, dairying remains a more attractive enterprise on most farms.

Turning now to the structure of production, the production of beef from the dairy herd is considered first. As was shown in Table 4.8, the profitability of the system of fattening cattle intensively on an almost all-cereal diet for slaughter at 12 months of age will be reduced very substantially in the Community as a direct consequence of the adoption of high Community feed-grain prices. By 1979, it is expected that very few cattle will be reared on this system. On the other hand, with a contraction in barley-beef production, the number and proportion of calves being fed on a cereal/grass mixture is expected to increase as this system becomes relatively more attractive in terms of profitability. The fact that cattle under this system of management are slaughtered at 18 months old and at heavier weights than are barley-beef animals would give a further stimulus to beef production.

Within the beef herd itself, the main change anticipated is a marked shift towards autumn calving. In the model, nearly all the beef cows in the base year of 1970 calved down in the late winter or spring. By 1979, it is projected that over half the cows – within a stable total herd size – will calve in the autumn. This adjustment again reflects the impact of increases in feed costs on the relative profitability of alternative systems of production. A calf from a winter or spring calving beef cow is typically fattened over the following winter on a diet including a relatively high proportion of cereals. Higher feed-grain prices would lower the profitability of this system in the Community, although the impact could be offset, to some degree, by making greater use of conserved grass products. But a calf born to an autumn-calving cow can be weaned in the spring and fattened during the succeeding summer on grass, thereby avoiding much of the impact of higher grain prices.

Both these examples of changes in the structure of beef production provide a clear indication of the stimulus that entry into the Common Market will give to farmers to move out of systems which rely heavily on inputs of concentrate feeding-stuffs, particularly cereals, and into systems where the feeding is based on the use of grass and conserved grass products (hay and silage).

Sheepmeat supplies

The sheep flock is expected to come under considerable pressure through the 1970s due to competition from alternative enterprises. In the country as a whole the number of breeding ewes is projected to decline by one-sixth from 10.5m in 1970 to 8.8m in 1979. This fall in sheep numbers will be partially offset by the improved performance of the breeding ewe which will be reflected in higher lambing percentages. Even so, production of mutton and lamb is projected to contract by 14 per cent over the period, that is from 224,000 tons in 1970/71 to 192,000 tons in 1978/79.

The decline in sheep numbers is not expected to be uniform across the country. The number of ewes in hill and upland areas is projected to remain fairly stable and perhaps even increase marginally over the period. In these areas there are few viable alternatives to sheep. It is in the lowland areas, therefore, that sheep are likely to come under the greatest pressure from alternative enterprises. The results of the model suggest that the number of lowland ewes will fall by almost 50 per cent between 1970 and 1979, thereby continuing a trend which was evident in the late 1960s, but which has been arrested – or even reversed – in the early 1970s.

This decline in the lowland flock is reflected in the regional indices of ewe numbers. The number of ewes is projected to decline by 30 per cent in the east of England, whilst in the west and north numbers are expected to remain relatively more stable. But sheep farmers in the hills and uplands will not be insulated from the decline in the lowland flock, since lowland farms provide the outlet for sheep coming off the hills as cull ewes and store lambs. The implication is that hill sheep farmers will have to fatten a higher proportion of their lambs, or find an alternative outlet for their stock.

Pigmeat supplies

The sheep industry seems likely to go into a decline during the 1970s. The prospects for the pig sector, however, are much more promising. Indeed, this part of the agricultural economy appears to be facing a buoyant future. On the demand side, consumption of pigmeat is expected to be rising with higher per capita incomes and as consumers switch demand from high priced beef to substitute meats. This growth in demand should be matched by developments on the supply side.

The model projections suggest that the British pig breeding herd will expand by almost 40 per cent over the 1970s, the number of sows increasing from just under 1.0m in 1970 to over 1.3m in 1979. The expansion is expected to be most rapid in eastern England where the sow population is projected to grow by almost two-thirds; a 20 per cent expansion is expected in the west. The east will account for nearly 80 per cent of the increase in total numbers, with the west accounting for nearly all of the remainder. This emphasis on the east is a reflection of regional specialisation in pig production, with pigs tending to be located near to the supply of feed-grains, the major input in pigmeat production.

The anticipated increase in the national pig breeding herd and improved productivity, expressed in terms of a larger number of pigs reared per sow per annum, should lead to a rapid expansion in the production of pigmeat. Production is projected to increase by almost 75 per cent from under 900,000 tons in 1970/71 to over 1.5m tons in 1979/80.

Pigmeat output should also be influenced by the expected changes in the structure of production which will lead to an increase in the average slaughter weight of fat pigs. In particular, for the reasons noted earlier, the model projects a decline in the number of light-weight porkers slaughtered at about 100 pounds deadweight. On the other hand, the number of pigs killed as cutters (136 pounds dead-weight) and baconers (150 pounds deadweight) is projected to increase. It is unlikely, however, that many of the additional bacon-weight pigs will find their way to the traditional Wiltshire cure, particularly as harmonisation to Community regulations will require the removal of the Government subsidy paid to British curers. Loss of the subsidy is bound to lead to a radical reorganisation of the British bacon-curing industry. The trend in the future, therefore, will be for pigs to be used for a variety of purposes, carcases being cut up with different parts used for fresh pigmeat, bacon and manufactured products such as sausages and pies.

Total Agricultural Output
In its White Paper on the United Kingdom and the European Community[4] the Government stated that as a result of Britain's entry to the European Community, home agricultural output could be expected to expand more rapidly than would have been the case had Britain remained outside the Community. The Government itself expects additional expansion of some 8 per cent overall between 1971 and 1977 on account of joining the Community. An estimate of total British agricultural output in 1970/71 and 1979/80 at constant prices was obtained by valuing both the individual commodity projections for 1979/80 and actual output in 1970/71 at 1970/71 prices. On this basis it is estimated that agricultural output in the United Kingdom will expand over the 1970s by about 20 per cent – or by rather less than 2 per cent per annum compound. When viewed against the further decline in agriculture's labour force mentioned earlier, this represents a considerable improvement in the productivity of the industry, at least so far as its use of labour resources is concerned.

SUMMARY AND CONCLUSIONS

This chapter has reported on the first results of a model of British
agriculture being developed by the Agricultural Adjustment Unit at
Newcastle University. The research methodology is based on the
mathematical programming of a set of farm models representing different types and sizes of farms in different parts of the country. By using
a set of appropriate structural weights which describe the number of
farms represented by each model, the results for the individual farms
can be raised to the aggregate level. The results of the model thus
permit conclusions to be drawn about probable organisational changes
at the farm level as well as providing information on trends in crop
acreages and livestock populations at regional and national level as
the United Kingdom adapts to the new economic and institutional
environment of the European Community. The projections of crop
acreages and livestock numbers can be converted into estimates of the
production of the major agricultural commodities produced in the
United Kingdom. Moreover, information on future farm income levels
is also generated by the model. Beginning with the base year of 1970,
the model has been used to provide information about changes in
Britain's agricultural economy over the period to 1979 as the country
adopts the CAP. The main conclusions of the research are summarised
below.

The outlook for farm incomes over the rest of the 1970s will vary
according to the type of farming being undertaken. For example, the
model predicts that dairy farms can expect an increase of between one-
third and two-fifths in average net farm incomes between 1970 and
1979 after allowing for inflationary increases in fixed costs. Dairy
farms with subsidiary enterprises, particularly cereals, appear to face
a rather better future than do specialist dairy farms. So far as livestock
farms are concerned, the income prospects for mainly cattle farms
look excellent, but the position of mainly sheep farms appears to be
heavily dependent on the continuation, in some form or other, of the
special assistance presently afforded to hill farming regions. The outlook for pig farms is also good, although more fluctuation in net
incomes must be expected in the future as producers under the CAP
become more fully exposed to the full effects of the pig cycle. The
prospects for cropping farms also seem to be quite reasonable – net
incomes are predicted to increase by one half over the 1970s – but a
more moderate improvement in incomes is predicted for mixed farms.

Turning now to the pattern and structure of domestic agricultural
production in the United Kingdom, the main changes projected in
crop production over the period 1970 to 1979 are as follows. A modest
expansion will take place in the acreage of cereals, mainly in the north
and west of England. The bulk of the increased acreage will be in

barley. With further improvements in yields, cereal production is projected to rise by 10 per cent between 1970 and 1979. A substantial increase in the acreage of sugar beet – and consequently in British domestic sugar production – is projected by the model. The increased acreage will be located almost entirely in the eastern part of England. The models, however, were unconstrained by institutional factors such as acreage quotas which, in practice, will be the main determinant of the future size of Britain's sugar crop; the most important of these is the proportion of the Australian quota under the CSA which is allocated to British growers.

So far as potatoes are concerned a marginal expansion in acreage is projected with greater emphasis on maincrop potato production. As with sugar beet, the bulk of the increased potato acreage will be located in the east. Cereals, sugar beet and potatoes are the chief cash crops produced on British farms. The projected expansion in the acreage of these crops will be made possible by a reduction in the area of grassland and a comcomitant improvement in stocking rates.

A number of adjustments in the livestock sector are also projected by the model. These include a 6 per cent expansion in the size of the national dairy herd over the 1970s. Half of the additional cows will be located in the west, with a third in the north and the remainder in the east. Little change in systems of dairy husbandry is likely however. With higher average yields per cow, milk production is expected to expand by 11 per cent. On the other hand, virtual stability in the size of the beef breeding herd is projected. The main adjustment in the beef herd will be a substantial shift towards autumn calving. It is anticipated that most of Britain's domestic supplies of beef will arise as a by-product of the dairy herd. Fewer dairy calves would be reared for beef under intensive systems of management on virtually all-cereal diets. Instead, indications are that there will be greater emphasis on less intensive systems which make relatively more use of grass and grass products. These anticipated changes are a reflection of higher Community feed-grain prices. With an enlarged dairy herd, more calves would be available for beef rearing and this, in conjunction with the other adjustments, could lead to an increase in domestic beef production of some 8 per cent between 1970 and 1979.

The casualty of the larger cash crop acreage and larger cattle population is likely to be the sheep flock. The size of the national ewe flock is projected to contract by approximately one-sixth over the supply forecast period. The contraction would be entirely in lowland sheep where the competition from alternative enterprises is most severe. The flock in the hill and upland areas of the country is expected to remain stable and perhaps even expand marginally; there are few alternatives to sheep production in these areas.

Finally, a substantial increase in pig numbers is projected by the model. It is anticipated that the size of the pig breeding herd will grow by 40 per cent between 1970 and 1979. The expansion in the pig herd is likely to be concentrated in eastern England close to the source of feed-grain supplies. With greater productivity in the breeding herd, the output of pigmeat is projected to increase by three-quarters through the 1970s. A contribution to the expansion in output is expected to come from an increase in average slaughter weights as light-weight pork production contracts, with an absolute and proportional rise in the number of pigs slaughtered as cutters or at bacon-weight.

NOTES AND REFERENCES

1. The results reported here are the first results of an on-going research project being undertaken in the Agricultural Adjustment Unit at the University of Newcastle upon Tyne. A comprehensive account of the study can be found in T. E. Josling, Brian Davey, Alister McFarquhar, A. C. Hannah and Donna Hamway, *Burdens and Benefits of Farm-Support Policies*, Agricultural Trade Paper No. 1 (London: Trade Policy Research Centre, 1972).

2. It is suggested that readers who are not particularly interested in the methodological aspects of the study should omit this section. The methodology is described in detail in Brian Davey and P. W. H. Weightman, 'A Micro-economic Approach to the Analysis of Supply Response in British Agriculture', *Journal of Agricultural Economics*, Manchester, September 1971.

3. One point of interest is how far the model predictions of the optimum output pattern for the base year differed from the actual situation. A comparison of crop acreages and livestock populations in England and Wales in 1970 predicted by the model and the results of the agricultural census for June 1970 is given below:

		Model	Actual
Cereals	(thousand acres)	8,107	7,859
Cash roots	,,	979	963
Forage crops	,,	604	539
Temporary grass	,,	3,126	3,537
Dairy herd	(thousand head)	3,418	2,714
Beef herd	,,	488	667
Total cattle breeding herd	,,	3,906	3,381
Ewe flock	,,	7,138	8,394
Pig breeding herd	,,	540	764

This comparison suggests that the actual pattern of cropping and stocking in 1970 was reasonably close to the optimum, particularly so far as cropping was concerned. The changes in output projected for the period 1970 to 1979 consist of two elements, namely (i) adjustments as farmers move closer to the optimum and (ii) changes in the optimum pattern itself.

4. *The United Kingdom and the European Communities*, Cmnd 4715 (London: HM Stationery Office, 1971).

Appendix to Chapter 4

NOTES ON NEWCASTLE MODEL

At the most general level, given the volatility of economic conditions in the world over the late 1960s and early 1970s, it is imperative that the kind of econometrics used in policy analysis should lend itself to modification and re-running. Early versions of the Newcastle micro-economic model of British agriculture suffered from a failure to cater for this need and the problem became greater as the model grew in size and complexity. In later versions of the model much work has been done in structuring the input of the technical coefficients and the price coefficients in such a way that they can be presented and easily understood by all, and also easily changed. For example, events in the early 1970s led to considerable uncertainty surrounding the future levels of cereal prices. Thus researchers inevitably wish to explore the sensitivity of supplies of cereals and other products to a range of possible future cereal prices. As there are three major cereal crops whose prices appear in about four matrix constraints (the objective function and cash flow constraints) affecting both cereal-growing and livestock-feeding activities, there may be as many as 50 financial co-efficients to change for each year of the ten-year projection period. In order to cope with such a large number of changes it has been necessary to automate the generation of matrix 'price' coefficients from sets of basic assumptions.

Another consequence of the bout of hyper-inflation since 1972 in agricultural prices has been the need to model in more detail the intra-year cash flows. This mainly affects livestock-rearing activities, where in order to obtain plausible flows of beef animals it has been necessary to define quarterly working capital constraints in addition to a cash constraint for the adjustment period.

Related to these changes, the earlier versions of the working capital borrowing activities have needed further elaboration to keep pace with the changes in interest rates. Similarly the longer-term borrowing activities have been overhauled. For example the fifteen-year borrowing activity has been dropped from the model. This is because new information which has become available on sources and dispositions of such funds (see the Wilson Report for the British Ministry of Agriculture, *Capital Availability to British Agriculture*, HM Stationery Office, 1973) has brought to light some mis-specification of the use of these funds which meant that particular investments were too 'cheap' and others too dear.

Further analysis of the livestock activities has demonstrated the need for greater detail in modelling demographic processes in livestock populations. However, a difficult balance has to be struck here; on the one hand earlier versions of the model imposed too much rigidity in livestock production because of oversimplified age-structure constraints, but a more detailed specification of livestock rearing and trading leads to difficulties in balancing inter-farm trade in the animals.

Finally, high priority has been given to further elaboration of the feeding sub-matrix of the model. As already outlined in this chapter, the early version of the model contained a discrete range of feeding technologies for livestock activities. Thus, for example, substitutability between forage and concentrates could only arise by substitution between the different livestock activities. Furthermore concentrates purchased were of a pre-specified composition. Not surprisingly, given the recent changes in relative costs of animal feeding stuffs, this structure does not give livestock producers sufficient room for manoeuvre within the model. Therefore, work is under way to allow the optimising mechanism more freedom to simulate the actions of producers in substituting between sources of energy and protein.

In addition, because it is so closely related to the agricultural sector for both its raw materials as well as its final products, it has been decided to incorporate a model of the animal feed compounding industry into the supply model. In this way livestock activities within the model will be able to utilise the least-cost feed mixes for any given price regime.

CHAPTER 5

Projected Pattern of British Food Supply and Imports

ALISTER McFARQUHAR and DONALD SILVEY

After the discussion in Chapter 3 of the projected pattern of demand in the United Kingdom following the country's membership of the European Community, and the discussion in Chapter 4 of some of the consequent adjustments in farm organisation, this chapter turns to the projected pattern of British supply and the demand and the effect on imports.

The chapter falls into three parts.[1] First an attempt is made to assess the likely pattern of supply of major agricultural products in 1978. In the second part an input-output table for British agriculture is discussed and its relevance to the estimation of trade patterns is described. In the third part there is a discussion of the likely pattern of trade in the major agricultural products in 1978, taking into account the projections of the demand for food described in Chapter 3, the pattern of supply described below and the relationships expressed in the input-output table, linking supply, demand and trade.

SUPPLY OF AGRICULTURAL PRODUCTS

The early 1970s have been a particularly difficult time to attempt to estimate future trends in the supply of agricultural products in the United Kingdom. Britain has been adjusting to the European Community's common agricultural policy (CAP) with its totally different system of price support (described in Chapter 1, pp. 10–12). Even given economic stability, this major change would have made the assessment of farm adjustment to the import-levy system of farm support an extremely difficult exercise. But farmers had to contend, in the early 1970s, with an increasingly high rate of inflation. Raw material and world food prices increased rapidly and at the same time the energy crisis added its own particular form of uncertainty about the future. Against this background projections of the supply of agricultural products have been made by various institutions and individuals. Over this period, for example, work was progressing in

Cambridge on the development of supply models for the purpose of projecting future trends in British agriculture. But rather than give prominence to any one particular set of supply estimates in circumstances of rapid change and great uncertainty, an attempt has been made to compare and contrast alternative estimates and, as a result, take a view about the likely level of supply in 1978.

Before comparing various estimates of future trends in agricultural production in the United Kingdom some comment on the assumptions and methods of different studies is relevant. Most are based on the analysis of time-series data for the farm sector as a whole. Estimates of future production tend to range between, on the one hand, a forecast which describes the most likely level of output given particular assumptions, often unspecified, about the most probable levels of the factors which affect it and, on the other, projections which are based usually on time-series analysis and are rigorously related to assumptions about price and other relevant variables. At the same time some 'forecasts' are virtually targets, since in fact they represent a planned level of output. These distinctions between targets, forecasts and projections are important, as are differences made in the assumptions. The view is taken here that a projection must follow rigorously and repeatably from the use of a quantitative model applied to specific assumptions about the variables included in the model. A projection which is subsequently adjusted in light of experience and judgement to take account of factors not included in the model is regarded as a forecast. A target subsumes an attempt to reach a certain level of production in the light of other policy objectives such as self-sufficiency or adequate diet.[2] In the discussion below space does not allow a detailed consideration of the methods employed or a detailed comparison of the assumptions made. Indeed, in some cases the assumptions are not stated and in others they vary considerably over time.

For some commodities there are considerable differences in estimates of future production. In general the more rigorous the methodology, the more unlikely the estimate appears. The most plausible estimates are those corresponding with an extended trend line fitted visually to time-series data. Such projections, however, are not necessarily the best estimates of future production. In the circumstances, because of the differences in approach and in assumptions, and because of the particular difficulty in forecasting the United Kingdom's agricultural production at the moment, the various estimates of future production which are available have simply been compared and a best estimate of future production in 1978 made as a result.

A number of detailed supply models have been developed at the University of Cambridge in the late 1960s and early 1970s for estimating the supply of wheat, barley, beef and milk, and sheep; and these commodities cover the major part of farm output. Time-series data are studied in an attempt to quantify the important relationships associated with production. In the case of wheat, for example, the aim of the analysis of time-series data is to account for the supply in terms of the factors, that is to say the independent variables, which affect it. Having made assumptions or predictions about the future level of the independent variables, a process which itself may entail a considerable amount of time-series analysis, a rigorous model is used to estimate future production of wheat. In fact, annual wheat production depends primarily upon two variable factors, namely acreage and yield per acre. Price expectations in turn affect the acreage grown, and both acreage grown and yield are affected by weather conditions. Analyses show that winter wheat and spring wheat are best estimated separately since, apart from the more obvious effects on yield of the weather conditions during the growing and harvesting periods, bad weather in the autumn and winter periods limits the acreage of winter wheat actually sown. In the case of winter wheat the most important factors determining production are found to be the acreage sown, the average earnings by producers for barley (a competitive crop) in the previous year, and the effect of rainfall during the autumn period. The acreage of winter wheat associated with the levels chosen for the latter two variable factors is calculated. This acreage then becomes an independent variable used in estimating the acreage of spring wheat.

The two main factors affecting spring wheat acreage are the expected price for barley in the previous year and rainfall during the sowing period. Consequently total wheat acreage is determined by price and weather factors, and a likely future acreage can be projected for any given assumptions about those two factors. It should be clear, however, that in all the crop projections and forecasts discussed here an attempt is made to produce a medium or long-term forecast which assumes average weather conditions in the year of forecast. That is to say, an attempt is made to estimate for the forecast year the trend level rather than the actual level of production since actual production may fluctuate about the trend as a result of variation in weather and other factors. The work involved in the development of supply models for agriculture is reported elsewhere[3] but, as an illustration of the approach used for wheat, the outline of the multi-stage model is given in Appendix 1 to this chapter (pp. 173–74).

In the case of barley a similar type of approach is used and Appendix 2 gives a brief description of the model. For beef and milk production there is a comprehensive and particularly complex model, described in outline in Appendix 3, which takes account of many factors which affect production, including the effect of imports, supplies and prices and also the effect of changes in the structure of population of beef and milk herds in Britain. Details of the methodology are given elsewhere.[4] The results obtained from the use of these models are discussed below.

Another projection study was carried out by Michigan State University in 1970 and the results are included in the graphical analysis below.[5] This study is based on time-series analysis in which the reactions of producers to changes in farm prices and gross margins are examined for statistically significant relationships. These are found for most commodities with the exception of sheep, eggs and poultry meat. Changes in the technical co-efficients such as crop yields and livestock conversion ratios are also examined and trends are projected. A certain degree of subjective judgement is necessary in making these projections and in interpreting the results. In this study a number of alternative assumptions are made about the future conditions in agriculture in the United Kingdom. Only those results based on the assumption that Britain would be a member of the Common Market with a five-year transitional period ending in 1977/78 are relevant to this study and are quoted below.

A similar study, carried out on behalf of the United States Department of Agriculture (USDA) at the University of Oxford, involved a detailed and rigorous statistical approach leading to projections for 1975.[6] The forecasts of the United Kingdom's Ministry of Agriculture, Fisheries and Food (MAFF) discussed below are included for comparison. They are influenced by judgement and experience, which seems to lead to rather more conservative results particularly in the case of forecasts of cereal production.

At Newcastle two quite different lines of approach are being pursued. First, a model based on linear programming produces estimates of production in 1978.[7] In this case representative farm models are programmed to produce an optimal organisation of enterprises in the light of assumptions made about prices and gross margins. The results from these individual models are then aggregated to produce an estimate of total production for England and Wales. Independently estimated production figures for Scotland and Northern Ireland are added to give an estimate of total production for the United Kingdom. The results are discussed in detail in Chapter 4 and provide a measure of the direction in which farmers might adjust if they were concerned only with maximising profit.

The second study at Newcastle is based on a more conventional time-series analysis and is concerned primarily with the cereal sector in the United Kingdom.[8] This study uses more or less the same assumptions about product prices as the linear programming study. It follows on from previous work such as the Michigan State University study, although of course with many refinements and in more depth, particularly in the sectors associated with cereals. The results from both of the Newcastle studies are examined below.

In the case of projections made by the Food and Agriculture Organization (FAO), time-series analysis is again used and the methodology is fully described in the relevant publication[9] although there is sometimes doubt as to whether estimates of future production are targets, forecasts or projections.

It must be emphasised that one or other of two completely different lines of approach has been employed in the analysis used as a basis for each study. The Cambridge, Michigan, Oxford and FAO studies and one Newcastle study referred to above all depend on variants of time-series analysis. Linear-programming methods form the basis of the other Newcastle study.[10] It is necessary at this point to outline the essential differences between the two approaches since these must be borne in mind while interpreting the results from the studies. Since the two approaches are fundamentally so different, comparison of results from the two types of study is extremely difficult, and not perhaps very fruitful.

In the case of linear programming, it is assumed that farmers are rational in the sense that they allocate their available resources in the optimum economic way, given perfect knowledge. The results are normative, tending to show what farmers ought to do to maximise profits in any particular set of circumstances, rather than positive, showing what they are expected to do on the basis of past reaction and performance. As models become more detailed and take account of more factors, particularly those appertaining to 'non-economic' behaviour, this difference tends to become less well defined. Constraints can effectively be included in the model to limit available resources and to take account of certain other technical factors like the need for a particular balance of crops in the rotation. Constraints to limit the rate of structural adjustment at the farm level can also be included though the rate may well be chosen on the basis of past experience or judgement as to possibilities for future rates of adjustment and not decided within the model itself. Two major problems arise with disaggregated models, first that of dealing realistically with uncertainty and second, the difficulties associated with using one farm to represent a group of farms, each with a different operator having a different balance of fixed resources. On the other hand, the linear programming approach has a considerable advantage if it can provide a basis for estimating farmers' responses to totally new price regimes and technology, which are beyond the bounds of variations in the recent past. In such a case the kind of response to relatively smaller changes in the past as measured by time-series analysis may not be a good guide to adjustment in the future.

In time-series analysis changes in the total supply of a commodity over a given period of time are examined in association with changes in the independent variables which are thought to affect the supply.

Attempts are made to establish statistically significant relationships. These relationships may be complex and it may be necessary to take account of them in a model operated in stages. An example of this approach leading to the formation of a simple multi-stage model was described briefly above for wheat. Once relationships have been quantified, a new set of significant and important independent variables can be postulated for the projection year and the supply projections calculated. Perhaps the main criticism of this approach is that relationships established for a given range of historical conditions, say of price relatives, may not necessarily apply when future conditions are expected to be far outside that range. In order to minimise any potential errors it is desirable that the most recent data be examined particularly carefully so that any changes in trends can be quickly identified and taken into account. It is also necessary at some stage in the operation of a comprehensive model based on time-series analysis to ensure that the resources required for the projected supplies are compatible with those expected to be available though, of course, resource constraints cannot be taken into account at the level of the individual farm.

It is hoped that enough has been said to indicate the difficulties involved in making a comparison of these two alternative approaches and space does not allow more detailed comparison here.[11] The present opinion of professionals appears to be open-minded, the view being taken that all approaches to scientific projection work have a place and may produce useful results.

Wheat Production

Annual wheat production in the United Kingdom since 1961/62 is shown in Figure 5.1. During the 1960s the production trend levelled off though the characteristic wide annual fluctuations due to weather conditions are apparent. At the beginning of the 1970s production increased appreciably and reached record heights. The forecasts discussed above for the 1970s are all consistent with the current high level being maintained until 1980. The longer-term estimates made by the Michigan and FAO studies suggest a crop approaching 5m tons in 1980 in terms of the trend yield for that year. Estimates for 1978 from the two models based on linear-programming and time-series analysis from Newcastle, the latter by Jan Sturgess and probably the more recent, are 4.7 and 5m tons respectively in 1978. The early Cambridge projections confirmed the impression of higher yields in the 1970s, indicating a crop of 4.2m tons in 1975; and the Oxford estimate for that year was very high at 5.6m tons. The average yield for the three years ending 1972/73 is something over 4.5m tons in early 1974 and the MAFF forecast for 1973/74 was nearly 5m tons. In view of the subsequent changes in international conditions and prices, particularly for food, and balance-of-payments difficulties, and with the likelihood of a steady improvement in technology, it may well be that wheat production in the later 1970s will tend to increase rather than stabilise. The best estimate of wheat production in 1978 has therefore been taken as 5.5m tons. It must be emphasised that this is an estimate of the trend and that actual crop production in that year might be appreciably higher or lower depending on weather conditions. This estimate

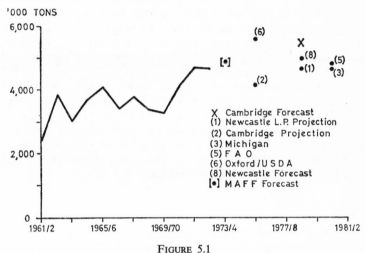

FIGURE 5.1

United Kingdom Wheat Production

of 5.5m tons in 1978 is only 10 per cent above the independent estimate in the Sturgess study[12] of 5m tons for the same year. If the line joining average wheat production over the three years centred on 1971/72 to the forecast of 5.5m tons in 1978 is taken as the trend in production, then output in 1973/74 would be 4.8m tons, just below the early 1974 MAFF forecast for that year. The Sturgess forecast is related to an expected ex-farm price of wheat in 1978/79 of £56 per ton. This price may appear unrealistically low in view of the high rate of inflation expected over the period. It must be emphasised, however, that deflated prices have been used throughout this study so that if, for example, the United Kingdom experiences a 100 per cent rate of inflation over the period until 1978 the money price of wheat would in fact be £112 per ton ex-farm.

In general, with cereals, the critical problem is that of forecasting future yields. As a result of a special study made by Sturgess it was estimated that overall cereal yield would rise by about 7 per cent over the period 1970 to 1978. This is a conservative figure compared with other studies where, in some cases, yields are expected to rise by much higher amounts. Discussions with the trade suggest that there is considerable support for the opinion that the increase in cereal yield over the next ten years may be moderate rather than high. The cereal yield trend, rising rapidly in the 1950s, did level off in the 1960s when, to a considerable degree, advantage had been taken of the potential to increase yields by increased fertiliser use, the development and use of better varieties and improvements in husbandry. In addition yield increases tended to be offset in some measure by the deleterious effects arising from intensification of cereal growing.[18] The high-yielding variety Maris Huntsman was expected to raise the national average wheat yield appreciably and proved very popular with growers. But disease is becoming a problem and may well limit the acreage of this variety that can be grown. A moderate rather than a very great improvement in yield therefore seems likely over the next few years. It should be added that our estimate of 5.5m tons of wheat has been considered in relation to the estimated production of each of the other temperate cereals. Barley, the most important in quantitative terms, is discussed below. Our estimate of total cereal production of 16.5m tons is in line with other forecasts for 1978.

Barley Production

As in the case of wheat, barley production rose rapidly in the 1960s to a peak in 1967/68 of over 9m tons (see Figure 5.2). For the next four years production was lower but in 1972/73 a new peak was established at a slightly higher level. The basic problem is to determine whether a new plateau has been established or whether the trend will rise again, albeit at a more modest rate than in the 1960s. Production in 1970/71 was particularly low at 7.4m tons but despite this the average production over the period 1970/71 to 1972/73 was about 8.3m tons. The Newcastle linear-programming study suggests that production in 1978 will approach 8.7m tons, something above the recent three-year average. On the other hand, time-series analysis at Cambridge produced an estimate of 10.8m tons by 1975/76. The tendency of time-series analysis to produce estimates which project a continuing and rising trend is reflected also in the Oxford study. Our own independent investigations suggest that a more likely figure for 1978 would be of the order of 9.7m tons. This provides for a steady expansion in production to 1978 of about 17 per cent on the three-year mean from 1970/71, or approximately 3 per cent per annum, and gives an estimated production very little below the Newcastle time-series study figure of about 9.9m tons in 1978 – a figure very much in line with general thinking in the industry as a whole. Again, as in the case of wheat, the MAFF forecast for the year 1973/74 of about 8.9m tons lay close to the trend line joining the three-year average centred on 1971/72 to our estimated 1978 production.

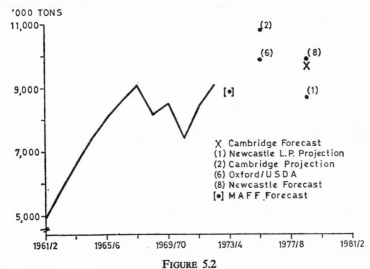

FIGURE 5.2
United Kingdom Barley Production

Total Cereal Production

Production estimates derived from the different studies of wheat, coarse grain and total cereal production are shown in Table 5.1 for appropriate years between 1975 and 1980. In some cases variation in estimated production is reduced if total cereals are considered together. This is reasonable when some of the variation in wheat and barley estimates is due to a difference in emphasis between the two crops. For 1975 estimates of total cereal production are 16.35 and 16.0m tons for Cambridge and Oxford respectively, although the contributions made by wheat and coarse grains differ appreciably in the two cases. In 1978, on the other hand, estimates of total cereal production in the two Newcastle studies are 14.3 and 16.5m tons but the difference lies mainly in the estimates for coarse grains. Our own forecast for total cereals is in line with the larger estimate of 16.5m tons although a somewhat different view is taken of the balance between wheat and barley. The Michigan estimate for 1980 of 22.5m tons for total cereals seems too optimistic. It should perhaps be added that the contribution of wheat to total production of cereals in the United Kingdom varies from something over 20 percent to 35 per cent. The proportion of wheat is expected to remain at the higher level during the 1970s.

TABLE 5.1

Future Production of Cereals in the United Kingdom:
a Comparison of Studies[a]

Forecasts and projections			Wheat m tons	Coarse grains m tons	Total m tons
Study[b]		Date			
Cambridge Projection	(2)	1975	4.20	12.15[c]	16.35
Oxford	(6)	1975	5.6	10.4	16.0
Newcastle L.P. Projection	(1)	1978/79	4.7	9.6	14.3
Newcastle Forecast	(8)	1978	5.0	11.5	16.5
Michigan	(3)	1980	4.8	17.7	22.5
FAO	(5)	1980	4.9	12.1	17.0
Forecast for this study		1978	5.5	11.0	16.5

[a] For complete studies see Notes 2–9.
[b] Numbers in brackets correspond to numbers in Figs 5.1–5.10.
[c] Projection is actually for barley (10.80 m tons) to which an estimate of 1.35 m tons has been added for other coarse grains.

Beef and Veal Production

Nothing causes more difficulty to those concerned with the projection of future trends in the United Kingdom's agriculture than the beef cycle. Over the period from 1961/62 shown in Figure 5.3 this cycle was clearly established with peaks in production in 1963, 1967 and 1970. The cycle has followed the traditional process, which involves a period of shortage of supplies from home or overseas sources leading to high prices and, in turn, to high investment by farmers. The subsequent high level of production is associated with low farm prices but often with insufficient decline in retail prices to clear the additional supplies. Surpluses are then put into store or imports reduced, or both.

Against this background of cyclical production in the United Kingdom is a strong upward trend clearly illustrated in Figure 5.3 which led to an average level of production over the period 1970/71 to 1972/1973 of 943,000 tons. Forecasts and projections for the period until 1980 seem to indicate a continuation of this upward trend, though the swings in cyclical production make the estimation of the actual level of production in any future year extremely difficult. The various projections which are set out in Figure 5.3 seem to indicate upper and lower bounds for the likely production trend. A conservative estimate of production is indicated by the projections and forecasts by Oxford for 1975, by Newcastle for 1978 and by Michigan for 1980. These three forecasts, consistent with a linear trend, indicate a continuation of the rise in beef production, though at a slightly lower rate than in the past, with production in 1978/79 reaching the level of about 1.015m tons. The early 1974 MAFF forecast for 1973/74 of 924,000 tons suggested that that year would be one of the troughs of the cycle. This latter projection, however, is not strictly comparable, since it was an estimate of actual production in that year taking account of cycles whereas the other figures tend to be forecasts of the average or trend level of production in the years to which they refer. In this case, a period of

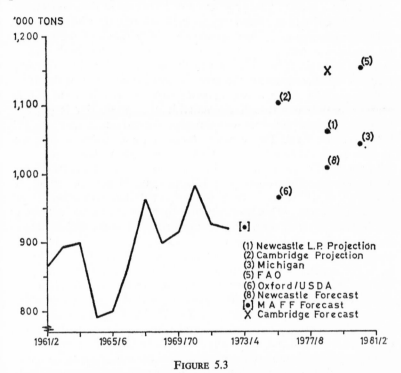

FIGURE 5.3

United Kingdom Beef and Veal Production

very low farm prices beginning early in 1974, in spite of continued high retail prices, led to a considerable amount of stock disposal because of high feed costs. This was bound to have an effect on production in 1975 and 1976. The question is whether or not the trend will have recovered its previous level and rate of increase by 1978.

Among the more optimistic forecasts, the FAO sees beef production reaching a level of 1.157m tons by 1980, and an early Cambridge projection for 1975 based on a very detailed model of the livestock sector estimated that production would reach the level of 1.105m tons by 1975. The projection of the Newcastle linear-programming model, the result from which is also consistent with an upward trend in production, lies between the two extreme estimates and it should be borne

in mind that this model includes constraints, both technical and financial, which operate at the individual farm level. Detailed work at
Aberdeen University[14] concerned primarily with very short-term forecasting produces two projections for 1975, the lower being 1.061m tons
and the higher 1.105m tons. The less conservative estimates are consistent with a level of beef production of 1.1m tons or thereabouts. The
view of the writers midway through 1974 was that the difficulties then
being experienced in the beef industry would be followed in due course
by production falling 20 per cent or more from the peak and an
increase in retail prices. This, it was thought, would lead to a cyclical
recovery fluctuating about the continuous upward trend of the 1960s
and early 1970s. Since it is anticipated that by 1978 the cycle will be
nearer a peak than a trough, the actual level of production is expected
to be of the order of 1.15m tons though the trend line in that year will
be at a lower level. This estimate takes account of the various projections discussed above plus the views of interested parties.

In early 1974 the Meat and Livestock Commission estimated that
production in 1974 would reach 1.025m tons, 20 per cent above the
low level of 1973. In 1975 it was expected that production could
exceed 1.08m tons. This assumed that there would be no increase in
the imports of Irish stores but slaughterings of steers and heifers in
the second half of 1974 were expected to be 21 per cent above those
of the previous year. Cow and bull slaughterings were expected to rise
by 6 per cent compared with July-December 1973. These estimates
are not inconsistent with our forecasts for 1978. They do, however,
almost certainly reflect the likelihood at the time of the estimate that
production would peak around 1975. The low level estimated by
the MAFF probably subsumed a much lower sale of stock in 1974
than actually occurred. Typically, conditions of over-supply lead to
a very rapid weakening of farm prices, loss of confidence and a reduction in stock numbers; a situation which was well established in the
spring of 1974. Clearly, however, following the past trends, with the
reduction of supplies prices will increase further, confidence will be
restored, supply will be increased and a new cycle will be established.
The reasons given by the farming organisations for the unexpectedly
high rate of slaughterings in 1974 include shortage of grass due to the
dry season and the high cost of concentrate feed which would normally
substitute for grass. Presumably very high interest rates and the cash
flow problems associated with higher costs all round, plus the expectation of a further fall in farm prices for beef, have also played a major
role in the decision to slaughter stock.

Political pressure from farmers' organisations is another factor
which had to be taken into account. For example, farmer pressure for
high beef prices was relayed by the British Government to the Commission of the European Community and resulted in an 11 per cent

increase in the intervention price, followed by a 5 per cent increase 'across the board' in autumn 1974, and thus at that time it would have been reasonable for farmers to expect some recovery in beef prices.

Even in a season when grass is short it seems doubtful that the added cost of keeping beef for a few months would exceed the additional return. Traditionally, however, a large proportion of farmers are unwilling to feed alternatives to grass in the summer. In late 1974 it was likely that beef production would have been considered unprofitable when the price fell below £19 to £20 per live hundredweight, and the economics of production at any precise stage in the process would have been ignored. In this situation the debts of farmers would also have to be taken into account. If most farmers had large overdrafts the sale of beef cattle to reduce this debt would be tempting. Thus, a high rate of slaughtering was expected in the second half of 1974, subject to the influence of grain sales which may have gone towards reducing the overdraft.

Unfortunately, low farm prices are not closely associated with low retail prices since butchers seem to take the view that lower retail prices following lower farm and wholesale prices will not encourage consumption and that consequently retail margins have to be kept high to maintain their returns. By mid-June 1974, however, prices of beef had fallen in the shops and there was considerable fear of surplus supplies. The European Community had been unloading supplies out of store to the United Kingdom and this had further reduced long-term confidence, which tends to be a function of current prices and feed costs, among British farmers. Expectations of producers are another factor which had to be taken into account.

The length of the beef cycle seems to have been shortening as a result of more intensive methods of production so that the period between peaks of the cycle has been reducing from seven years in the pre-1960 period to four, and perhaps even three, years in the late 1960s with peaks in 1963, 1967 and 1970. Accordingly a fall in production following the probable, slightly late, peak of 1975 is likely to be followed by a recovery leading to a level of production in the region of our forecast of 1.15m tons by 1978 (Figure 5.3).

Mutton and Lamb Production
As can be seen from Figure 5.4, mutton and lamb production remained at much the same level, about 250,000 tons, from 1961/62 until 1966/67. It then declined to 215,000 tons, partly due to the marketing price uncertainties of the European Community arrangements. Since 1970/71 production appears to have levelled off at about 224,000 tons and the early 1974 MAFF forecast for 1973/74 was only slightly higher than that at 235,000 tons. Forecasts from other studies are

consistent with production levels of between 200,000 and 300,000 tons in 1978. The extreme projections are given by the Cambridge and Oxford models which produced figures of 265,000 and 267,000 tons respectively by 1975 on the one hand and by the Newcastle linear programme model on the other with a prediction of only 192,000 tons in 1978/79. Of the two forecasts for mutton and lamb production in 1980, that of the FAO is the most optimistic at 285,000 tons. However,

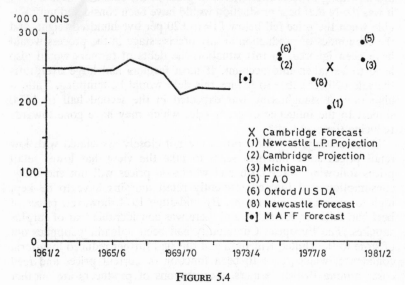

FIGURE 5.4

United Kingdom Mutton Production

until world trends in the trade for mutton and lamb assert themselves in a more definite way, perhaps resulting in a reduction of supplies from Australia and New Zealand due to increased demand in other parts of the world, any forecast of production in 1978 is difficult to make. General pressure on the livestock industry due to high feed, fertiliser and labour costs does not suggest that mutton and lamb production will expand very quickly even in response to a considerable improvement in farm prices, should this result from an increase of substantial proportions in retail prices. Appreciable increases in lamb production in the United Kingdom seems likely only to follow technological breakthroughs in breeding and systems of fattening after these have been established in the field. It seems unlikely therefore that much change will take place in the industry before 1978 and the general opinion appears to be that production is likely to level off at something around 250,000 tons.

Pigmeat Production[15]

Pigmeat production in the United Kingdom expanded rapidly during the 1960s. Figure 5.5 shows that after reaching a peak in 1965/66 it fell sharply in 1966/67 and again in 1967/68. By 1968/69 production was again rising and expansion continued until 1971/72, the previous peak level of production being surpassed in 1970. In 1972/73 production fell a little but early 1974 the MAFF forecast for 1973/74 suggested that output in that year would exceed slightly the 1971/72 peak.

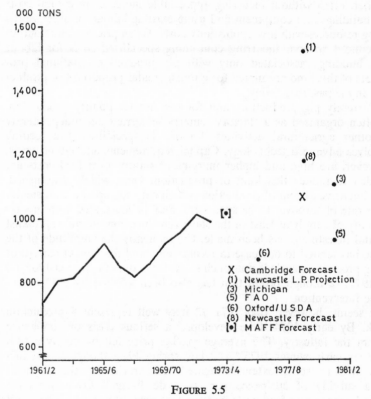

FIGURE 5.5

United Kingdom Pigmeat Production
(including bacon and ham as pigmeat equivalents)

Projections from various sources show that pigmeat production is difficult to forecast. The pig breeding herd has, in the past, expanded and contracted quite rapidly depending upon expectations within the industry. The pig cycle is traditionally even more pronounced than the cattle cycle and its length is shorter because less time is needed to breed and fatten a pig. This means that the level of pigmeat production has fluctuated widely in a comparatively short time about the long-term trend, though for reasons explained below the amplitude of the cycle has tended to decrease.

Other factors are associated with this fluctuation. Land is necessary only as a site for production units and is not needed to produce feed, especially grass, as is normally the case with grazing livestock. Concentrates necessary for feeding can easily be bought in. Consequently, given attractive margins of returns over feed costs, small producers can be encouraged to start producing pigs or to expand production further, often without incurring appreciable increases in capital costs for buildings and equipment and using existing labour, in other words using resources with low opportunity costs. When prices decline output is reduced without incurring continuing specialised costs for labour and buildings associated only with pig production. Marginal producers of this kind accounted for a much greater proportion of production in the past than today.

Currently pig production, and for that matter poultry production, is often organised as a 'factory' enterprise carried out independently of other agricultural activities. Labour is specialised and feeding involves advanced technology. Capital requirements and labour costs, however, are high and higher margins of returns over feed costs are needed to induce this kind of production. Once widely established, this intensive system of production, which depends upon a consistently high rate of turnover to be successful, may be associated with greater stability of supply at least in the short run since considerable specialist capital investment has been made. Consequently the amplitude of the cycle has tended to decrease in recent years and the typical pattern of a pig production cycle is not much in evidence over the period 1967/68 to 1971/72 though production has also been affected by government price intervention.

It seems, however, that 1971/72 may well represent a production peak. By early 1974 there developed a serious crisis of confidence within the industry. The average market price fell by nearly a fifth between early winter 1973[16] and late spring 1974, though this reduction was to some extent mitigated temporarily by the payment of a subsidy of 50 pence per score deadweight. Over the same period concentrate feed costs increased by over 80 per cent. The result was that by April 1974 the margin of total returns, including subsidy, over all costs, other than interest charges, had fallen to near zero.[17] Coincident with this, capital costs had been very high and bank interest rates were around 16 to 18 per cent. Given this situation it appeared that production would probably fall for a while before conditions changed. It was assumed that measures would be taken to encourage production and our forecast for 1978 is 1.07m tons. This figure is rather more conservative than some of the possibilities suggested by the various supply studies, the results of which are consistent with a level of production in the range of 900,000 to over 1.5m tons.

So far attention has been concentrated on production of pigmeat as a whole and not its two component parts – pork, and bacon and ham – these are better discussed as distinct and separate commodities.

Pork. The greater part of pigmeat production in this country is marketed in the form of pork. The pattern of production is therefore to some extent similar to that already discussed for pigmeat. Production cycles for pork are, if anything, rather more evident though since 1967/68 their amplitude has been reduced. Production increased appreciably over the period from 1961/62 to 1972/73 shown in Figure 5.6 and a further increase was expected in 1973/74 according ot the MAFF forecast. Cambridge do not have a model for pigmeat production and only limited information on the production of pork or bacon and ham as separate commodities exists in other supply studies. However, this information and our own forecast of weighted bacon and ham production, derived as described below, was discussed with experts in the industry. The opinion was that the most rapid expansion of pork production considered feasible would raise production to a level of 800,000 tons in 1978. Conditions within the industry in early 1974 suggested that production would probably decline in the immediate future but recover again fairly quickly. It seems unlikely however that it will reach the 800,000-ton level by 1978 and our forecast of pork production is therefore 710,000 tons for that year.

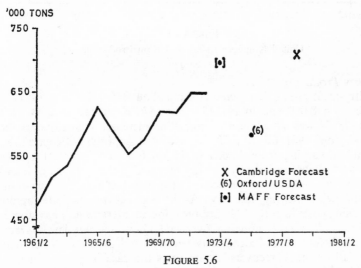

FIGURE 5.6
United Kingdom Pork Production

Bacon and Ham. Bacon and ham production in the United Kingdom has shown a slight upward trend since 1961/62 as shown in Figure 5.7. Experts in the industry feel that expansion in bacon and ham production will probably be limited by industrial capacity to about 280,000 tons in 1978. An increase in capacity seems unlikely in the United Kingdom since some of our partners in the European Community are especially competitive in this field and the industry in the United Kingdom has experienced particular difficulties in recent years. This figure of 280,000 tons is, therefore, our forecast for 1978.

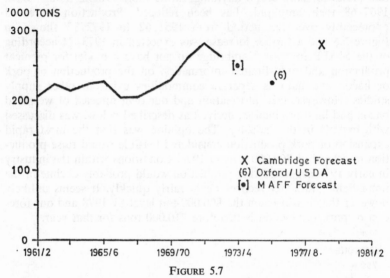

FIGURE 5.7

United Kingdom Bacon and Ham Production

Poultry Production

Poultry-meat production increased from about 346,000 tons in 1961/62 to nearly 658,000 tons in 1972/73. The MAFF forecast in early 1974 for 1973/74 was 674,000 tons. Production increased annually over the period from 1961/62 to 1972/73, with one important exception, by quantities varying from 16,000 to 65,000 tons. Poultry-meat is now produced almost entirely by 'factory farming' and the spread of intensive rearing systems has proceeded at a very fast rate even by comparison with the pig industry. As in pigmeat production, rapidly increasing costs in early 1974 put pressures on margins and any appreciable increase in production over and above current levels seems unlikely before 1978. Indeed, between 1974 and 1978 production may even fall before it recovers. Again as is the case in pig production, considerable capital has already been committeed to poultry production. In the short run this will tend to have something of a stabilising effect on production. Our production forecast for 1978 of 700,000 tons can, in the circumstances, however, only be regarded as very tentative. The Michigan study offered a production forecast of 710,000 tons for 1980 and the estimate made at Newcastle by Sturgess is 690,000 tons for 1978. This latter figure is on an appreciably higher trend than that suggested in the Oxford study namely 558,000 tons in 1975.

In general, the production of poultry-meat in the United Kingdom is now more difficult to estimate than the production of almost any other commodity. There is usually a tendency to believe that a rapidly rising trend will level off and the forecasts for the period 1975 to 1978 discussed above reflect this prejudice. However, with the recent dramatic increase in beef, mutton and lamb prices poultry-meat has more than held its competitive position. Much depends on how demand responds and whether or not poultry-meat consumption has reached a saturation point in the United Kingdom. The evidence is that it has not. Consequently if the recent feed cost increases level off, poultry may experience a new surge of production which will emerge during the period from 1976 to 1978. On balance, however, the more conservative view, related to a continuation of high feed costs, prevails and this leads to an estimate of 1978 production at not much above the 1973 level.

Milk Production
Milk production rose over the period shown in Figure 5.8 by nearly 20 per cent and the early 1974 MAFF forecast for 1973/74 suggested that the annual increase seen over the last few years may have been levelling off. Supply study estimates are broadly consistent with a level of production in 1978 within the range 2800m to 3150m gallons, though the Cambridge macro-model predicts a falling trend until 1975. Opinions from the milk industry suggest that production is likely to be towards the upper rather than the lower end of the range. This suggests some reduction in the linear trend apparent over the period 1966/67 to 1974.

Increases in concentrate feed costs and the consequent squeeze on margins are likely to have their effect on production. Particular attention has to be given to grassland management, an area where there is often room for improvement, and to the efficient utilisation of any available by-products. This would almost certainly be accompanied by some increase in the demand for expensive 'primary' inputs the most significant being fuel and fertilisers, especially nitrogen. Yield per cow is likely to remain more or less constant with the shift to increased use of forage in the diet. The net effect may well be to reduce the recent quite high average rate of increase in production to a more modest level. It appears that production could easily reach

3000m gallons plus or minus 10 per cent by 1978 but in view of the comments of the industry our forecast has been set at the slightly more optimistic level of 3100m gallons, an annual average increase in the MAFF forecast for 1973/74 of only something over one-half of 1 per cent per annum.

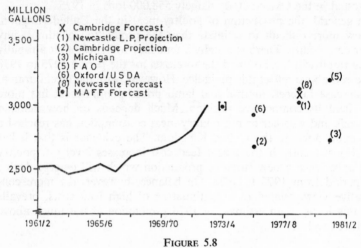

FIGURE 5.8

United Kingdom Milk Production

Beet Sugar Production

Production of raw sugar has been rising rapidly in the United Kingdom over the period shown in Figure 5.9 though there are considerable fluctuations in yield per acre from year to year due mainly to variations in weather conditions. Average production in the three years centred on 1962/63 was 767,000 tons and rose to an average of 994,000 tons in the three years centred on 1971/72. The early 1974 MAFF forecast for 1973/74 was 1.075m tons. The projections shown in Figure 5.9 are in line with production of 1.05 to 1.5m tons. It must be borne in mind, however, that this latter figure is from the Newcastle linear programming model in which it was assumed that the national quota would be appreciably increased, in fact to 638,000 acres in 1978/79, not impossible in view of the shortages which have emerged in mid-1974.

Details of future community policy on sugar will vitally affect British and Commonwealth producers. Commonwealth sugar had access to British markets until the end of 1974 when the British Commonwealth Sugar Agreement (CSA) ended. Terms were to be renegotiated and the common sugar regulations themselves were to be revised

Considerable competition from producers in the European Community is likely in the medium run though the effect of this competition was reduced during 1974 as world conditions and a poor 1974 crop in the United Kingdom switched the Community balance from an expected surplus of about 5 per cent to a deficit.[18]

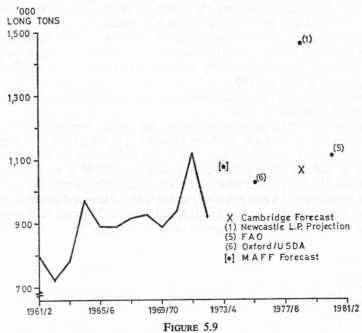

FIGURE 5.9

United Kingdom Raw Sugar Production

We have assumed that by 1978 British producers will supply the same average amount of raw sugar as over the past few years, that is around 1m tons, plus about one-fifth of the Australian quota, and that the developing Commonwealth countries will retain their market in this country at the present level. Our production forecast for 1978 is therefore 1.065m tons of raw sugar. This may well be a conservative estimate. Results from the Newcastle linear-programming model suggest that constraints at the farm level are no barrier to considerable expansion of sugar beet acreage in this country since, under the price conditions stipulated, production of raw sugar rose to nearly 1.5m tons in 1978/79.

The situation with regard to the logistics of the distribution and processing sector of the British sugar industry is, perhaps, more contentious. Some published data are used to suggest that British raw sugar production might be increased by a quantity even greater than the Australian quota,[19] others suggest that any increase above current levels of production would require Government subsidies.[20] However prices have changed considerably since these studies were made. For example the latter study assumed a CSA basic price of £50 per ton but estimates in mid-1974 suggested that the world price could reach much higher levels following the shortages in the United Kingdom and the world as a whole. There seems little doubt that some increase in domestic production can be expected by 1978, though its likely size is as yet by no means clear. Our forecast for 1978/79 however, is very much on the trend indicated by alternative forecasts and projections for the period 1973 to 1980.

Potato Production
Total production of potatoes, maincrop and earlies, fluctuated widely from year to year in the 1960s as shown in Figure 5.10. Production fell, for example, from 7.5m tons in 1965/66 to 6.5m tons in the following year and rose from just over 6.1m tons in 1969/70 to nearly 7.4m in 1970/71. Over the period, however, production expressed as a moving average was comparatively stable with perhaps a slight upward trend. Over the four-year period 1969/70 to 1972/73 production averaged about 6.8m tons compared with 6.6m tons for 1961/62 to

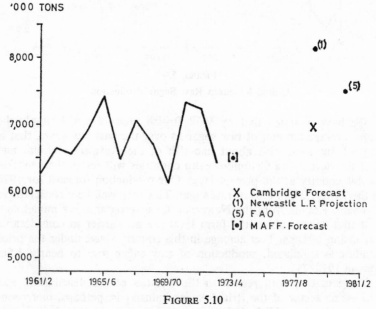

FIGURE 5.10
United Kingdom Potato Production

1964/65. The MAFF forecast for 1973/74 was something over 6.5m tons. Yield increased over the period, the average for the last four years shown in Figure 5.10 being some 23 per cent higher than for the first four, but this can fluctuate from year to year by over 10 per cent as a result of disease and changes in weather.

The increase in yield over time has been more or less matched by a drop in the acreage planted. There is no reason to suppose that the broad policy on potatoes current in 1974, namely that domestic production should cover domestic demand with the exception of that portion of the demand for earlies which cannot be produced at home, will be changed. This assumes that expansion of potato production for purposes other than domestic human consumption is unlikely to be encouraged. The forecasts from the supply studies shown in Figure 5.10 suggest an increase in 'normalised' production by the end of the decade. Our own forecast figure of 7m tons, based on discussions with experts, is a more conservative estimate incorporating only a very modest increase on production in the early 1970s.

EFFECT OF INFLATION ON FARM INCOMES
AND SUPPLIES

The real value of farm income is obviously affected by the rate of inflation in the United Kingdom, which has increased appreciably since 1970 as shown in Table 5.2. Over the decade 1960/61 to 1969/70

TABLE 5.2
United Kingdom Retail Price Index – All Items (1972/73 = 100)

1960/61	61/62	62/63	63/64	64/65	65/66	66/67
57.4	59.3	61.8	63.1	65.1	68.2	70.9

67/68	68/69	69/70	70/71	71/72	72/73	73/74
72.7	76.1	80.2	85.3	93.4	100.0	109.2

Source: *Annual Abstract of Statistics* (series, HM Stationery Office).

the retail price index increased by 40 per cent from 57.4 to 80.2, taking prices equal to 100 in the base year 1972/73. In the following four years alone prices increased by 36 per cent from 80.2 in 1969/70 to 109.2 in 1973/74. During 1974 a good deal of discussion was centred on the effects of inflation on British agriculture. Input prices had increased and were said to have resulted in the so-called cost-price squeeze. It was claimed that these pressures on margins would result in reductions in the supply of agricultural commodities by 1975. Before commenting on the likely effect on supply adjustment within the agricultural industry it is necessary to ascertain the extent of the cost-price squeeze on net incomes. Farming net income is defined as the return to farmers and their wives for manual and managerial labour and for the use of tenants' capital after provision has been made for depreciation.[21] Published estimates of farming net incomes merit consideration.

Annual net farm income for the national farm sector since 1960/61 is shown in Figure 5.11 in index form, the base year being 1972/73. Three-year averages based on the current and previous two years are used in order to reduce random annual fluctuations due, for example, to weather. The index is constructed to measure annual net income at constant (1972/73) prices in order to discount the effect of inflation.[22] Between 1960/61 and 1962/63 the index rose from 89.4 to 96.6, subsequently fell consistently over an eight-year period until 1970/71 when, at 90.8, it was only 1 per cent above the 1960/61 level. From the peak in 1962/63 to the trough in 1970/71 the purchasing power of total farm income fell by about 6 per cent in spite of considerable increases in productivity. Surprisingly less complaints were heard over this period from farmers and farm organisations than in the early 1970s.

In the following two years, however, real farming net income increased rapidly and by 1972/73 it was 3 per cent higher than the previous peak of 1962/63. For the following year, 1973/74, it was calculated that the index, on the basis of income forecasts, could be as high as 118.3. This estimate, not shown in Figure 5.11, was based on the highly tentative forecast for 1973/74 of a net farm income of £1224m. In fact, in 'real' terms, that is to say discounting changes in the value of money as measured by the retail price index, average farming net income increased rapidly after 1970/71. In the first year of the period, that is to say 1970/71 to 1971/72, the increase is nearly 3 per cent, in the second 7 per cent and in the last, if the 1973/74 forecast is accepted, it is 18 per cent, giving some 30 per cent overall. This averages a 10 per cent per annum increase in real farm income compared with a 6 per cent fall over the previous eight years.

These increases must have been sufficient to cover the rise in interest rates over the period, high though these were. This does not necessarily mean, however, that the return accruing to farmers and their wives for their labour and management[23] has increased since investment of tenant's capital might have increased. The data necessary for an accurate and detailed analysis of tenant's capital are not available. However, published estimates of gross annual investments in new plant, machinery and vehicles by the agricultural industry[24] can be taken as roughly representing new investments of capital by tenants.[25] If these are converted to new investments at constant (1972/73) prices, appropriate interest charged at progressively higher interest rates can be deducted from real net income in each year leaving a residual to cover interest on previous investments, that is those made before 1970/71, plus a return to the farmers and their wives for their labour and management.

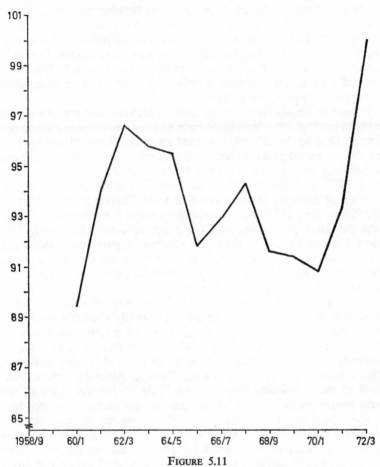

FIGURE 5.11

United Kingdom Farming Net Income at Constant Prices (1972/73 = 100)

This analysis shows that the increase in the real residual income as defined above from 1970/71 is zero in the first year, 4 per cent in the second and a further 15 per cent in the third, that is about 20 per cent overall. In making the estimate for the third year, 1972/73 to 1973/74, it is of course again necessary to accept the high forecast of net income for 1973/74. Even if this latter forecast is considered too high it seems likely that the increase has been more than sufficient to enable producers to cover the increases in interest charges and maintain the return on their manual labour and management. This is not to say that this was the case in mid-summer 1974, since at that time input-output price ratios appeared to have moved strongly against producers. Some fluctuations, however, in farming net income from year to year is to be expected as is shown by the pattern since 1960/61 in Figure 5.11 and discussed above. The crucial point is whether the trend in real income had levelled off or had turned down. Certainly the indications were that the appreciable rise of the early 1970s had reached a peak and government action on a considerable scale could be necessary to prevent a decline.

It must be emphasised that the above discussion concentrates on the measurement of total farming income and not the average income per farmer. Despite the difficulties caused by inflation and higher rates of interest of recent years, agricultural producers as a whole have been maintaining the reward for their labour and management, at least until 1974, and covering their increases in capital costs. Since the number of full-time farmers declined from 230,000 in June 1971 to 222,000 in June 1973 and of part-time farmers from 68,000 to 66,000 over the same period, incomes per head must have improved. This effect has not yet been taken into account. If part-time farmers are given a 50 per cent weighting, the increase is 3.5 per cent between 1971 and 1973, in itself an appreciable contribution towards the increase in interest charges on capital.

Aggregate figures for the whole industry may, of course, obscure difficulties in specific sectors. In times of rapidly changing conditions the relative profitability of different types of farming may also be changing quickly. The only available comprehensive and detailed financial information for each of the major types of farming in Britain comes from the Farm Management Surveys. Attention here is confined to those covering England and Wales.[26] The definition of net farm income in the Farm Management Surveys corresponds with that used in the departmental calculation of farming net income discussed above for the agricultural industry as a whole except that no deduction is made for interest on commercial debt for current purposes. This deduction has, in recent years, been equal to about 7 per cent of farming net income per annum. The income margins in the Farm Management Surveys are thus by definition about 7 per cent higher on average than they would be if the departmental definition were used.

The eight major types of farming groups which will be discussed are: specialist dairy, mainly dairy, mainly sheep, cattle and sheep, cereals, general cropping, mixed, and pigs and poultry.[27] However, a number of important factors in the Farm Management Survey must be remembered. Though all types of farm are covered, attention is confined only to those providing a full-time occupation. The sample is not completely random though improvements are being made in this respect. Certain farms are under-represented, those producing pigs and poultry for example and very small and very large farms. In 1972/73 2326 farm accounts were analysed and the resulting data are weighted according to the size distribution of holdings indicated in the Agricultural Census for the particular type of farming group.

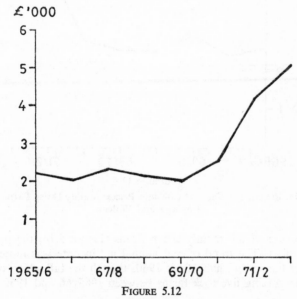

FIGURE 5.12

Net Income per Farm at Constant Prices: Specialist Dairy Farms
(England and Wales)

Figures 5.12 to 5.19 show the net income per annum in pounds per farm for each of the types of farming groups for the period 1965/66 to 1972/73 at constant (1972/73) prices. Over the period some farm size adjustment was, of course, taking place. Over the second half of the 1960s real net income per annum for the specialist dairy farms (Figure 5.12) was more or less constant, though with some annual fluctuation, and within the range of £2000 to £2300. In the three years between 1969/70 and 1972/73 it increased sharply by 150 per cent to nearly £5100 per farm per annum. The pattern of real net income for the mainly dairy group (Figure 5.13) is broadly similar, with a more or less horizontal trend over the period 1965/66 to 1969/70 and an annual figure somewhere in the range £2400 to £3000 per farm. In the following three years there was a sharp rise of 131 per cent to nearly £6000 per farm per annum.

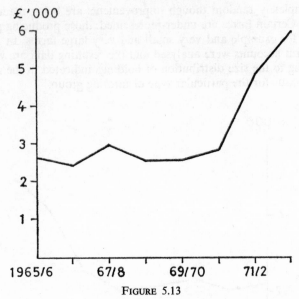

FIGURE 5.13

Net Income per Farm at Constant Prices: Mainly Dairy Farms
(England and Wales)

In the case of the mainly sheep farms (Figure 5.14) the pattern is
not dissimilar. The trend of real annual net income was more or less
level over the second half of the 1960s though the fall which occurred
on all the grazing livestock farms between 1965/66 and 1966/67 was

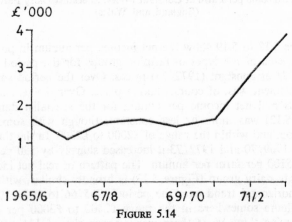

FIGURE 5.14

Net Income per Farm at Constant Prices: Mainly Sheep Farms
(England and Wales)

rather more pronounced, dropping from nearly £1650 to something over £1100 per farm. Between 1969/70 and 1972/73 real annual net income rose by 167 per cent to about £3900 per farm, the greatest percentage increase for any of the eight major farm types discussed. The cattle and sheep farms (Figure 5.15) show an increase in real net income per annum of 164 per cent to nearly £5300 per farm between 1969/70 and 1972/73.

FIGURE 5.15

Net Income per Farm at Constant Prices: Cattle and Sheep Farms
(England and Wales)

Some interesting differences in real net income per annum are shown in Figure 5.16 for the cereal farms. The trend over the period 1965/66 to 1968/69 was definitely downward, falling from nearly £4500 to nearly £3100 per farm. However, after 1968/69 the trend recovered and over the four-year period until 1972/73 the total increase in real net income was 114 per cent to £6600 per farm per annum. This is of course a lower percentage increase than for livestock farms and is over a period longer by one year (for livestock the percentage increase was discussed for the period 1969/70 to 1971/72). Real net farm income for the general cropping group fluctuated more over the period 1965/66 to 1970/71 than those incomes discussed above though as for cereal farms, the trend was downward (Figure 5.17). After 1970/71 real net income rose to about £5800 in 1972/73.

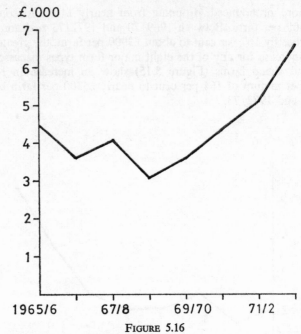

FIGURE 5.16

Net Income per Farm at Constant Prices: Cereal Farms
(England and Wales)

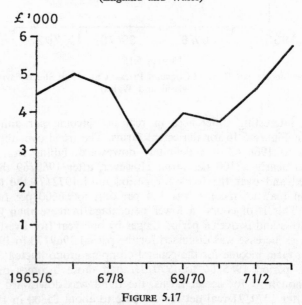

FIGURE 5.17

Net Income per Farm at Constant Prices: General Cropping Farms
(England and Wales)

an increase of 54 per cent in two years. Although this percentage rise was one of the lowest for all farm types it is still spectacular.

As might be expected the mixed farms show a pattern in real net income influenced by both cropping and livestock enterprises. There was a slight downward trend over the period 1965/66 to 1969/70 (Figure 5.18). Over the following four years until 1972/73, however,

£ '000

FIGURE 5.18

Net Income per Farm at Constant Prices: Mixed Farms
(England and Wales)

the trend was strongly upward. Real net income increased over the period by 139 per cent to nearly £6300 per farm. In the case of pig and poultry farms, after an initial rise between 1965/66 and 1966/67, real net income per farm shows a steady downward trend until 1970/1971 (Figure 5.19). Over the following two years it rose by 89 per cent to something over £4800 per farm.

To summarise, over the period from 1965/66 to 1972/73, all of the eight type-of-farming groups exhibit a spectacular increase in real net income per farm. During the second half of the 1960s, the livestock farms maintained real net incomes at much the same level, thought in the case of pigs and poultry farms there was some decline. On cropping farms real net incomes fell slightly during the same period. In the early 1970s all types of farm show appreciable percentage increases in real net income; particularly the grazing livestock farms. Percentage increases were lower in the case of cropping farms but, since levels of income at the beginning of the 1970s were higher, absolute increases were also substantial. In fact between 1969/70 and 1972/73 the increase in real net income on specialist dairy, mainly dairy, cattle and sheep, cereal and mixed types of farm was near or above £3000 per farm. For mainly sheep and pigs and poultry the increase was about £2400 and £2100 per farm respectively and for general cropping about £1800 per farm.

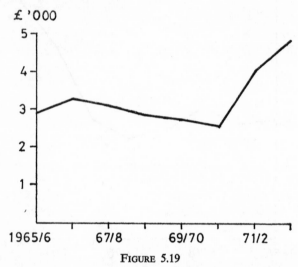

FIGURE 5.19

Net Income per Farm at Constant Prices: Pig and Poultry Farms
(England and Wales)

For purposes of comparison net incomes for the eight farming types are shown in Table 5.3 for 1972/73. The weighted average farm size in acres of crops and grass and standard man days is also shown. Those types with an important arable sector, cereals, general cropping and mixed farms, tended to have higher net incomes and larger acreages of crops and grass (see Table 5.3). The highest net income was about £6600 for cereal farms, followed by mixed and mainly dairy at nearly £6300 and £6000 respectively. General cropping net income was about £5800 and cattle and sheep and specialist dairy farms had net incomes well above £5000. The lowest figures are for pig and poultry farms at something over £4800 and mainly sheep farms at below £4000. Unfortunately details on investments of tenant's capital are not available and therefore estimates of returns to the operators for their manual labour and management cannot be made for each type of farm. There is no evidence, however, to suggest that the supply of agricultural commodities is likely to be seriously threatened by a squeeze on margins over the period ending 1972/73. In fact, in the early 1970s real margins on all types of farm increased.

TABLE 5.3

Specimen Net Incomes for Different Types of Farm, 1972/73

Type of farm	Acres of crops and grass[a]	Weighted average net income per farm (£)
Specialist dairy	106	5090
Mainly dairy	162	5979
Mainly sheep	121	3907
Cattle and sheep	184	5284
Cereals	346	6604
General cropping	215	5805
Mixed	211	6294
Pigs and poultry	71	4849
All types[b]	167	5522

Source: Ministry of Agriculture, Fisheries and Food, *Annual Review of Agriculture* (series, HM Stationery Office).

[a] Weighted average.
[b] Excluding horticulture.

The published forecasts for net incomes on full-time farms in England and Wales are 'sufficiently reliable only to indicate the direction and approximate size of changes in average farm incomes'.[28] For 1973/74 they are based partly on changes between 1972 and 1973 recorded in the Agricultural Census and partly on the projections of production, prices and costs made for the 1973/74 departmental estimate of aggregate farm incomes. As has been discussed above, however, they suggest that farm incomes as a whole will rise appreciably in both money and real terms. Variation is, of course, expected between farm types. Cropping farms, particularly cereal farms, are expected to do well in comparison with livestock farms, and dairy farms are likely to experience a drop in net income. Details are given in the MAFF publication *Farm Incomes in England and Wales.*[29]

As has been indicated above, it would appear that the forecasts are over-optimistic particularly in terms of concentrate feed costs. Though difficulties will be experienced in the livestock sectors, perhaps much greater difficulties than were envisaged at the time of publication, it would appear that overall net income in many sectors of the agricultural industry will rise appreciably in real terms.

One further point is relevant. In the departmental estimates of aggregate real net income for the agricultural industry the increase between 1970/71 and 1972/73 is 10 per cent. It is evident that this increase is very much less than the increases measured by the Farm Management Surveys in any of the type-of-farming groups discussed above. In fact the smallest increase in real net income over the 1969/70 to 1972/73 period is 46 per cent for general cropping farms. Only a very small part, about one-seventh, of the difference between the two estimates of increases in net income can be accounted for by the difference in definition of net income discussed above concerning interest charges on commercial debt for current purposes. Even if this interest charge is added to aggregate net income, so that both the definitions correspond, the increase is only something over 15 per cent; still considerably less than any of the increases estimated for the individual farm sectors.

A detailed examination of the possible reasons for these apparent discrepancies cannot be made here but would seem to lie in the nature of the Farm Management Survey samples since the definitions and objectives of measurement are similar. Perhaps the sample holdings are managed more efficiently and are better able to adapt quickly to changing circumstances. Also it must be remembered that net income represents the difference between gross output and all inputs (other than the manual and managerial labour of the occupier and his wife and interest on tenant's capital). Any errors in calculation of input or output factors will have a disproportionate effect on the net income since it is the residual.

Input-Output Model
The input-output model specifies the input of primary products from the agricultural sector required to produce commodities consumed as food. It summarises all the commodity flows which take place between the various sectors of the food production industry and is used to estimate the quantities of primary products necessary to satisfy a given level of consumer demand.

A few primary products need little or no processing other than grading and packing before distribution to retail outlets, for example potatoes or eggs, and supply requirements of these products are indicated directly in consumer demand analysis. In most cases, however, direct demand, if it exists at all, is only a part of total demand for a commodity and considerable processing is usually necessary before a primary product can be retailed or used as a raw material by another section of the food production industry.

Relationships between retail food items and their constituent primary products can be complex and several distinct processing stages may be involved. Retail demand for flour confectionery, for example, induces intermediate demands for flour, refined sugar and processed fruit in addition to any direct retail demands for these commodities. These intermediate demands in turn create demands from the primary sector for cereals, raw sugar and fresh fruit. Total demand for a particular primary product may, at the same time, be derived from several different retail commodities. In the case of barley, for example, total demand is influenced by the demand for beer as well as for livestock products.

The input-output model takes account of all these relationships, including the intermediate stages, so that a projected level of consumer demand can be accurately translated into total requirements of primary products from the agricultural sector. Any difference between total requirement and domestic supply is made up by imports or exports.

As well as estimating total derived demand for primary farm products, the level of production needed from ancillary agricultural industries, in particular the animal feedingstuffs and fertiliser industries, can be calculated since the table which derives from the model specifies requirements of feed and fertiliser per unit of output in the grain and livestock sectors. In this way the effect of a specific policy, for example British membership of the European Community, on these industries supplying the agricultural sector can be assessed.

The input-output model has forty-one commodity groups. Some contain a single item, others, a group of relatively homogeneous commodities. The commodity groups are selected to be compatible with those of the demand model modified to some extent by the form in which data are available. Some of the groups are for 'finished' retail products, some for intermediate products and others for the primary agricultural commodities.

Five of the groups are for straight cereals, namely wheat, barley, oats, maize and 'other cereals', and a sixth for cereal products. Cereals are essentially primary products and undergo considerable processing, appearing at the retail level in a completely different form. It is estimated for 1978 for example that some 50 per cent of total consumption of the main temperate cereals, wheat, barley and oats, will be for livestock feed. Of the remainder, most of the wheat will be milled for flour and the barley used for brewing and distilling. 'Other cereals' is a comparatively unimportant group containing rye as well as exotic cereals like rice and sorghum. Home production of maize, currently averaging about 6000 tons per annum may increase in future. Maize is an important animal feed but is also widely imported to be used with other cereals and farina as a raw material in the starch and glucose industries. The products of this latter industry, which is included in the cereal products commodity group, are used by many sectors of the food industry, for example, in confectionery, jams and preserves, and soft drinks; and indeed are sometimes used by firms producing non-food commodities.

As far as possible these and other similar complex manufacturing chains have to be quantified and taken into account in the relationships expressed between the various commodity groups of the input-output model. The cereal products group also contains a number of other commodities, some very important, for example cakes, biscuits and breakfast cereals, and is especially hard to quantify.

Information on output and to some extent on input-output relationships was obtained from the Census of Production for some commodities. Sometimes, however, the Census of Production, which is confined to firms employing a certain minimum-sized labour force, covers only part of total output. This is so in the case of cakes and bread since a good deal of output is from small bakeries. In addition, some of the input-output data are available only in cost terms. Consequently it is necessary to estimate weights by using a conversion factor such as unit cost. Data are supplemented by information from manufacturers wherever possible. In addition to these six commodity groups covering cereals and cereal products there are two other associated groups in the input-output model, flour and bread.

There are six commodity groups for meat; beef and veal, mutton and lamb, pork, poultry, bacon and ham, and meat products. The latter group unavoidably contains a number of rather heterogeneous commodities like pork and beef sausages, meat pies and processed cold meats. However, a number of manufacturers supplied information which enabled estimates to be made of total production of all the items of major importance and the necessary inputs of meat, rusk filler, flour, fat, and so on were estimated by using 'typical' recipes obtained from the trade in conjunction with information on statutory minimum requirements for various products. This information was supplemented by data from the Census of Production.

The five commodity groups covering the milk and dairy sector are milk, butter, cheese, cream and 'other milk products'. Information on flows between these groups is more easily obtained than is the case for many of the commodities discussed above, particularly from the publications of the Milk Marketing Boards. For example, technical relationships like the conversion rate of milk to butter are well documented and information on consumption of liquid milk is readily available. Details, however, of the utilisation of milk products by the various sectors of the food production industry are difficult to establish. The approach used has been outlined above for cereal and meat products.

The remaining groups cover all the other food and drink commodities except tea and coffee. Among the more important are eggs, margarine and shortening, other fats, raw sugar, refined sugar, potatoes, fresh vegetables, fresh fruit and fish. Collection of data is comparatively straightforward for some items of most commodity groups but difficult for others, particularly the rather more heterogeneous groups like fresh vegetables, fresh fruit and fish. But various authorities were approached for information which enabled estimates to be made. The remaining groups which give particular difficulty are, as is the case with cereals and meat, those for 'products', that is to say fruit, vegetable and, especially sugar products. Since there are extremely important commodity flows between the food and drink sectors discussed above and the rest of the economy and since the input-output model is comprehensive, as is the demand model, there is a final commodity group which represents the whole non-food and drink complex.

Provision is also made in the input-output model for inclusion of intermediate sectors for cereals for livestock feed and for fertilisers. Inputs flow into the livestock feed sector from the various cereal commodity groups. Output is defined in starch equivalent terms and is imputed to the different livestock groups according to their level of output. Analyses of concentrate usage by the different classes of livestock made by the MAFF are a particularly useful starting point in this section. Estimates are also made of usage of nitrogen, phosphate and potash for the individual crops and grassland and these are included in the input-output model. More details of these two intermediate sectors, particularly of modifications to input-output relationships to take account of expected technological changes are given below.

In the first stage of development of the input-output model the quantitative relationships are those appertaining in the 1967–69 period, a three-year rather than a one-year period being used to reduce the effect of short-term deviations. Some of these technical relationships will change in the future, others will remain static. For instance, feed conversion ratios in the livestock fattening sector have changed rapidly in the past and some improvements are to be expected in the future. On the other hand, no great changes are likely in certain production techniques incorporated in the model. For example, in converting raw to refined sugar or milk to butter substantial further improvements in the 'extraction' rate are unlikely, though there may be changes in the quality of the raw materials which will alter the input-output ratios. Adjustments have been made to the projections of demand for primary commodities obtained from the model to take account of expected improvements in input-output ratios when these are significant and when a reasonable estimate can be made of their magnitude.

Some input-output relationships are closely affected by changes in relative prices. Within certain technical limits, for example, the components of animal feedingstuffs will depend upon their relative prices and feeding values. Currently the input-output model does not take the effects of expected price changes into account. Adjustments can, however, easily be made in the projections of demand for cereals for feeding, derived from consumer demand projections by means of the input-output model, in the light of information available, for example, from the feedingstuffs trade.

Since imports and exports affect supply they have to be incorporated in the model. Exports increase the demand for a domestically produced commodity while imports reduce it. These imports may be substituted for primary, intermediate or retail products. To take account of these effects several types of commodity are distinguished in the input-output model when calculating future domestic production. Home production of wheat, barley, and beef and veal, for example, is considered to be independently determined, that is to say determined by factors outside the model, projected supply being deducted from total demand to give an estimate of imports or exports. Very early potatoes on the other hand cannot be produced in this country and a certain quantity is normally imported. In this case future imports, which represent only a small percentage of the total supply of potatoes, are independently specified and home production is the residual from total demand. Some commodities are non-competitive imports, like tropical fruit, which are not produced domestically at all.

Considerable effort has been expended in collecting data for the model and many sources have been used.[30] In addition to published statistics, information has been sought, with varying degrees of success, from the food-processing trades. Sometimes, where such information exists, it has most generously been made available. In other cases the comments of the trade have been of considerable assistance in helping to trace commodity flows through the food sector and forming opinions on likely future developments.

TECHNOLOGICAL CHANGE 1968–78

As examples of the projection of technological change the cases of fertiliser and cereals for feed are now discussed in some detail. The consumption of inorganic fertilisers increased over the period 1965 to 1972 by over 50 per cent in the case of nitrogen and by 10 and 6 per cent respectively for phosphate and potash (Figure 5.20). Many factors affect consumption of these nutrients and projections are particularly difficult to make. As a starting point the consumption by each primary commodity of each of the three nutrients was estimated for the base period 1967 to 1969. Total supply, information on which is published by the Fertilizer Manufacturers Association Ltd, was allocated on the basis of the Rothamsted Experimental Station surveys of fertiliser practice supplemented by technical recommendations where data on rates of application to specific crops were unavailable. This is a time-consuming procedure but ensures that total supply corresponds with total utilisation in the base period used for the input-output table.

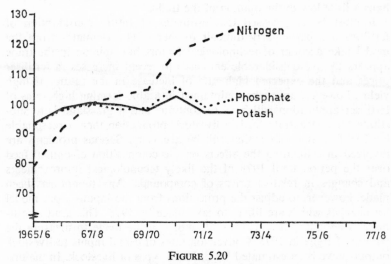

FIGURE 5.20

Consumption of Inorganic Nitrogen, Phosphate and Potash in the United Kingdom (1967/68=100)

As a first step in the projection of demand for these nutrients the base year input-output figures were examined in conjunction with information on trends in fertiliser application. These figures, with adjustments to take account of the trends, were then applied to the expected pattern of agricultural production in 1978 and the estimates obtained were discussed with representatives of the trade. Opinion was that the projections were high for phosphate and potash but low for nitrogen. For phosphate an increase in total consumption of about 2 per cent per annum is predicted by the model over the period until 1978 but the trade estimate is more conservative at around 1 per cent per annum. The predicted increase for potash is something over 2 per cent per annum but again 1 per cent maximum is suggested by the trade.

The future consumption of nitrogen is perhaps the most difficult prediction to make. Applications to crops other than grassland appear already to be near the economic limit on many farms, leaving little scope for increased national use. In fact this may also quite possibly be the case for the other two fertilisers. There is still, however, considerable room for improvement of grassland yields through the increased use of nitrogen though a very high standard of grassland management would be necessary to reap the full benefit of greater output. It seems unlikely that the rapid increase in the consumption of nitrogen in the early 1970s will continue but an increase of about $1\frac{1}{2}$ per cent per annum until 1978 is a reasonable estimate, though perhaps a little low in the opinion of the trade.

It must be emphasised that estimates of future consumption of fertiliser are particularly difficult to make. The estimates from the model take account of technological factors but opinion in the trade appears to give considerable emphasis to recent increases in fertiliser prices and the expected high rate of increase in the future. If high yields, however, are to be maintained in arable farming high rates of fertiliser application will have to continue and if grassland is to substitute for concentrate feed in livestock production then a reasonable level of fertiliser application will be necessary. Serious problems are involved in estimating the effects on the composition of animal feed over the period until 1978 of the likely technological improvements and changes in relative prices of compounds. An attempt has been made, however, to adjust the projections from the input-output model for changes which are likely to take place by 1978. This kind of estimate is necessary if a realistic attempt is to be made to measure the pattern of trade in 1978. Conversion rates of cereal inputs to livestock outputs have been estimated for different types of livestock. In making these calculations particular reference has been made to the work done recently at Newcastle by Ian Sturgess.[31] On average, for the livestock sector as a whole, the improvement in conversion rate is expected to be about 9 per cent. At the same time, it is assumed that the cereal content of concentrate feed will be reduced by about a third between 1968 and 1978 since cereals will be replaced by cheaper forms of carbohydrate energy, for example sugar beet pulp and potato products, as cereals become more expensive. It is assumed, though, that the proportions of wheat, barley and maize used in the base period of livestock feed will be similar in 1978. It is clear that there may be substitution between the various cereals, as discussed below, particularly in response to short-term changes in price relatives.

TRADE PATTERNS

The future pattern of trade in British agricultural products depends on the difference between the projections of demand and domestic supply. Demand projections depend primarily on population growth, income (or rather expenditure) growth and the price effects determined by the demand model discussed in Chapter 3. The population projections used in the demand model are based on official estimates,[32] but the likely growth in income is largely a matter of judgement at the present time. In the early part of the projection period, which covers 1975 to 1978 inclusive, the growth of consumers' real expenditure per capita (that is to say consumers' real disposable income net of savings, the definition of income used for projections of the demand model) was negative and was expected to remain so for the first half of the projection period. For the remainder of the period positive growth was anticipated. The actual growth rates forecast were −3 per cent in 1975, −5 per cent in 1976, 3 per cent in 1977 and 5 per cent in 1978.[33] On average, therefore, the annual rate of growth is zero. The projections of final demand at the 0.0 per cent income growth rate were included in the input-output model with the estimates of future agricultural supply discussed above to obtain the projected intermediate demand and trade pattern for the United Kingdom in 1978. The resulting demand for primary agricultural commodities (projected consumption) and the associated trade pattern is shown in Table 5.4.

TABLE 5.4

United Kingdom Agricultural Trade in 1972 and 1978 with a Growth Rate for 1975 to 1978 of 0.0 per cent per annum (thousand tons)

Commodity	1972[a]	1978[b]			
	Imports	Domestic production	Con-sumption	Imports	Exports
Beef/veal	274	1150	1107	Nil	43
Mutton/lamb	326	250	524	274	—
Bacon/ham	345	280	634	354	—
Pork	46	710	710	—	—
Poultry	9	700	700	—	—
Wheat hard		—	2599	2599	—
soft	4127	5500	4308	—	1192
net		5500	6907	1407	—
Barley	729	9674	6704	—	2970
Maize	3095	—	3043	3043	—
Raw sugar equivalent	2031	1065	2442	1377	—
Cheese	149	189	303	114	—
Butter	350	63	323	260	—
Fats and oils	1222[b]	132	1354	1222	—
Fresh fruit	1476	546	2052	1506	—

[a] *Annual Abstract of Statistics 1973.*
[b] estimated

Meats

In 1978 beef is projected to be in surplus by 43,000 tons, an appreciable reversal of the shortfalls of the late 1960s and early 1970s. An increase in domestic supply has been consistently projected by Cambridge and is now on the market, accentuated by short-term pressures. Final demand is expected to reduce as a result of the rise in the retail price of beef associated with British membership of the European Community. This rise would be accentuated by the shortage of supplies likely to occur in the projection period before the upswing of production in the new cycle. In a normal, reasonably free, market it might be expected that as the supply position improved, under the initial stimulus of rising farm prices, retail prices would level off causing the fall in demand to be halted. Equilibrium would be restored at some price and quantity involving less movement from the original position than at first envisaged. The Commission of the European Community used high farm prices in the early 1970s in an effort to correct the deficit in the Community supply.[34] An 11 per cent increase in the intervention price to maintain returns to farmers in a period of surplus beef and low farm prices was followed by the 'across the board' increase of 5 per cent in autumn 1974. However, despite price increases, the fall in producer prices combined with rapid increases in feed and other costs resulted in panic sales of young stock in the summer and autumn of 1974. This led to unexpectedly high surpluses and overflowing cold stores in mid-1974 with forecast shortages to follow. The resulting high farm prices likely to occur in the future encourage an upswing in production by 1978 to a level approaching 1.15m tons.

Mutton and lamb imports, after falling in the early 1970s, are expected to increase by 1978 and level off at 274,000 tons. The situation, however, could change if the Community decides to bring lamb under the common agricultural policy (CAP) regulations, thus fixing a price and enforcing the payment of import levies. It is not likely that this will occur, because Britain is the only major importer of lamb and also the only major producer in the Community. British-produced lamb does not compete with imported lamb quite as much as might be expected because the two products have different selling seasons. There is therefore likely to be less demand for protection on the grounds of unfair foreign competition. Further, the fat lamb price would seem sufficient to provide the British farmer with an adequate return at least until the early part of 1974. It is assumed therefore that the government of the United Kingdom would be unwilling to support the introduction of a common agricultural policy on lamb.

Bacon and ham imports are projected to remain at the 1972 level due to the projected increase in consumption and the fact that bacon production in the United Kingdom has been set at a maximum 280,000 tons, about 25 per cent above present production. This increase in production is reckoned to exhaust existing capacity, but is unlikely to emerge much before 1977/78 in view of the hard times and subsequent cutback in the pig industry likely in 1976. The favourable position of Denmark from the point of view of both supply and marketing plus the price-cost squeeze in 1974 is likely to preclude the possibility of a further increase in productive capacity. The increase in costs in pig production had, by mid-1974, reduced profit to near zero on average and this is expected to increase the pressure towards further cycling in pig production in Britain heralding, as in the case of beef shortages discussed above, a return to surplus by 1978.

Grains

Wheat production in the United Kingdom is expected to remain at a high level under a Community price regime but the pattern of demand is expected to change, as shown in Table 5.5, with the result that the net deficit of wheat will be substantially reduced from 4.127m tons in 1972 to 1.407m in 1978 (Table 5.4). However, the situation is rather more complex than these figures suggest since the United Kingdom produces only soft wheat while imported hard wheat is necessary in the grist for all kinds of flour although its proportion in bread is being steadily reduced. The exact proportion depends upon the foodstuff to be manufactured from the flour. It may be as low as 10 per cent for biscuit manufacture or as high as 70 per cent for bread manufacture. Ian Sturgess[35] calculated that in 1969 the maximum proportion of British wheat which could be used in flour was, on average, as high as 47 per cent although, in fact, for the five years ending December 1970 the actual proportion averaged only 32 per cent. Applying a factor of 48 per cent[36] to the projected input of wheat for flour in 1978 gives a minimum requirement of 2.505m tons of hard wheat for flour manufacture.

It must be emphasised that this figure assumes that the potential use of British wheat is exploited to the full. This seems a fair assumption since import levies under the CAP ought in normal circumstances to discourage the purchase of wheat at world prices (assuming that world prices are lower than Community prices by 1978). This substitution of British for imported wheat is occurring because millers are tending to increase the proportion of soft wheat in flour intended for making bread.

In addition to hard wheat for milling, 94,000 tons is required for breakfast cereals giving a total import requirement of 2.599m tons of hard wheat, a substantial reduction from present levels. If the utilisation of British wheat for milling does not change but remains at its average 1965–70 level of 32 per cent, the import requirement of hard wheat becomes 3.37m tons in 1978, a figure well below the 1972 import of 4.127m tons, and the surplus of soft wheat increases by 771,000 tons. It should, however, be remembered that the figures shown in Table 5.5 for animal feed assume that the cereal mix fed to livestock in 1978 contains the same proportions of cereals, that is to say barley, maize, wheat, and so on, as the base period 1967 to 1969.

After the demands for wheat input have been satisfied there is therefore a surplus of 1.192m tons of soft wheat projected for 1978. European Commission figures for the 1972/73 season show a surplus to requirements of 12.8m metric tons for the Six, two-thirds of which was exported and the rest denatured.

TABLE 5.5

Utilisation of Wheat in the United Kingdom (thousand tons)

	Average 1967/68/69[a]	*1978*
Wheat for		
Seed	175	274
Flour	5000	4818
Breakfast cereals	96	94
Miscellaneous	57	56
Sub-total	5328	5242
Animal feed	2386	1665
Total demand	7714	6907

[a] Figures from Ministry of Agriculture, Fisheries and Food, *Output and Utilization of Farm Produce in the United Kingdom* (various years. HM Stationery Office).

The picture changed in 1973/74 with the disappearance of wheat stocks in North America, heavy purchasing by Russia and poor crops in the Third World. This was followed by a period of very high prices and the promise of continued yield increases which created conditions for a surplus of production over domestic requirements by 1978. The presence of a surplus of wheat in the United Kingdom would curtail any need to import wheat for stock feeding purposes, a trade which averaged 600,000 tons per annum in the late 1960s. Of course any surplus may be substituted for maize depending largely on relative prices. Maize imports are forecast at 3.043m tons in 1978.

Total demand for wheat in 1978 is expected to decrease by 10 per cent compared with the period 1967 to 1969 due mainly to the substitution of cereals by lower-priced concentrates like dried sugar beet pulp in the concentrate mix fed to livestock as discussed in the section above. The quantity milled for flour, by far the most important use, remains virtually unchanged.

An increase in the supply of barley is also forecast resulting in a surplus of 2.970m tons. There is some evidence to suggest that the Community maize price will be above that of barley in 1978,[37] which may result in a substitution of barley for maize in animal feed. If this happens it would provide a use for the barley surplus and reduce the imports of maize below the 3.043m tons projected for 1978. Of this amount of maize just over half is used by the animal feed industry and half by the manufacturing industries for the production of starch and glucose and so on.

Dairy Products
Butter imports are projected to fall below 1972 levels by one-quarter to 260,000 tons in 1978. This does not take account of the British butter subsidies which should slightly delay the expected fall in consumption in the United Kingdom resulting from the high Community price. Under the agreement on British entry negotiated with the Community, New Zealand was guaranteed exports to the United Kingdom of approximately 128,000 tons of butter and 14,000 tons of cheese, leaving a market of 132,000 tons of butter and 100,000 tons of cheese to be filled in 1978, presumably from Community sources. Domestic production of cheese in 1978 is forecast at 189,000 tons. This would mean that the United Kingdom supplies 61 per cent of the home market leaving an import requirement of 114,000 tons in 1978; 24 per cent down compared with 1972 imports.

NOTES AND REFERENCES

1. Acknowledgement is made of the contribution by A. C. Hannah, while a TPRC Fellow in the Department of Land Economy, University of Cambridge, to the preparation of the input-output model for British agriculture. Debt is also expressed to G. B. Aneuryn Evans, of the Faculty of Economics, University of Cambridge, for assistance in developing and programming the input-output model.
2. For a more detailed discussion of the importance of the distinction between targets, projections and forecasts, see Alister McFarquhar (ed.), *Europe's Future Food and Agriculture* (Amsterdam: North-Holland, for the Association Scientifique Européenne pour la Prévision Economique à Moyen et à Long Terme, 1971), pp. xiv–xv.
3. Descriptions of the work involved in the development of supply models for agriculture in the United Kingdom are given in McFarquhar, *op. cit.*, pp. 420–51 and 466–9; McFarquhar and Martin Evans, 'Projection Models for Food and Agriculture', *Journal of Agricultural Economics*, Vol. XXII, No. 3, 1971; and Evans, 'Growth Models of Cattle Production under the Guaranteed Price System', *The Farm Economist*, September, 1971.

4. Martin Evans, *op. cit.*

5. John N. Ferris *et al.*, *The Impact on US Agricultural Trade of the Accession of the United Kingdom, Ireland, Denmark and Norway to the European Community* (East Lansing: Institute of International Agriculture, Michigan State University, 1971).

6. George T. Jones, *United Kingdom: Projected Level of Demand Supply and Imports of Agricultural Products 1970, 1975, 1980* (Oxford: Institute for Research in Agricultural Economics, 1969).

7. Brian Davey, of the Agricultural Adjustment Unit (AAU), Department of Agricultural Economics, University of Newcastle upon Tyne, supplied information on the projections from the AAU's model of supply response in British agriculture.

8. Ian Sturgess, Agricultural Adjustment Unit, University of Newcastle upon Tyne, private communication; Sturgess and Robin Reeves, *The Potential Market for British Cereals* (London: Home Grown Cereals Authority, 1962); and Sturgess, *Price and Marketing Prospects for UK Cereal Growers within the EEC* (London: Home Grown Cereals Authority, 1973).

9. *Supplementary working paper to main agricultural commodity projections: Working paper no. 6: Implications of the possible enlargement of the EEC for the agricultural commodity projections* (Rome: FAO, 1971).

10. Davey, *op. cit.*

11. For a more detailed comparison of linear-programming and time-series analysis, see McFarquhar, *op. cit.*, p. xviii; C. S. Barnard, 'Farm Models, Management Objectives and the Bounded Planning Environment' (and discussion, *Journal of Agricultural Economics*, Vol. xv, Vol. 4, 1963.

12. See note 8 above.

13. E. E. H. Fiddian, 'The Difference between National and Regional Yields and the Potential Yield from Present Recommended Varieties', *Proceedings of the 12th NIAB Crop Conference, 1972.*

14. G. R. Allen (ed.), *The Outlook for Beef in the United Kingdom, 1974 and 1975* (Aberdeen: School of Agriculture, University of Aberdeen, 1974).

15. In some of the supply studies data are available for pigmeat only and not for pork or for bacon and ham separately. In order to compare projections of total pigmeat production, bacon and ham has been converted to 'pigmeat equivalents' and added to pork. The pigmeat supplies shown in Figure 5.5 for the United Kingdom have been estimated in a similar way. Because of the method of estimation the figures must be interpreted with caution.

16. Average market price in November 1973 was £4.6 per score d.c.w. and no subsidy was paid.

17. The margin in 1972 was about £0.4 per score and in 1973 £0.5 per score and no subsidies were paid. By April 1974 the margin on the 'instant' pig was zero despite the subsidy. It should be borne in mind, however, that these are 'full costs' and that the pig enterprise makes a contribution to the fixed costs of the farm even when the margin is zero. Information on pig returns, costs and margins was supplied by R. F. Ridgeon, of the Agricultural Economics Unit, Department of Land Economy, Cambridge.

18. Ian Smith, 'Britain's Sugar Dilemma', *Journal of Agricultural Economics*, Vol. xxv, No. 1, 1974.

19. F. G. Sturrock and M. C. Thompson, *Sugar Beet: A Study of Sugar Production in the UK and the Feasibility of Expansion*, Agricultural Enterprise Studies in England and Wales, Economic Report No. 7 (Cambridge: Agricultural Economics Unit, Department of Land Economy, University of Cambridge, 1972).

20. Smith, *op. cit.*

21. In estimating farming net income, farmers are treated as tenants. A rental charge on landlord's capital is imputed to owner-occupiers.

22. The three-year mean for each year is multiplied by the 1972/73 retail price index for all items and the product divided by the retail price index for that year.

23. That is to say the residual after all interest charges on tenant's capital have been deducted (actual and imputed).

24. *National Income and Expenditure*, series, HM Stationery Office.

25. Government grants are ignored. These would in any case apply mainly to other categories of investment.

26. *Farm Incomes in England and Wales*, Ministry of Agriculture, Food and Fisheries, London, series.

27. For details of the classification used, see *ibid.*

28. *Ibid.*

29. *Ibid.*

30. The major sources of information are as follows: (i) Ministry of Agriculture, *Output and Utilisation of Farm Produce in the United Kingdom*, for various years; (ii) Department of Trade and Industry, *Reports on Census of Production* (especially 1968); (iii) Monopolies Commission, various reports; (iv) Food and Drug Acts, Statutory Minimum Requirements of Ingredients for Certain Types of Food Commodities; (v) Department of Trade and Industry, *Business Monitor*, production series; (vi) Department of Trade and Industry, *Overseas Trade Statistics*; (vii) various agricultural commodity reports of the Commonwealth Secretariat; (viii) various agricultural commodity reports, National Economic Development Office; (ix) Home-Grown Cereals Authority, annual reports; (x) White Fish Authority, annual reports; (xi) various reports, reviews and statistics published by bodies associated with specific sectors of agricultural trade, for example *Dairy Facts and Figures*, a series of United Kingdom Milk Marketing Board Publications, the Eggs Authority *Quarterly Reviews*; and so on. In addition many specialists, particularly in the food processing industries, were approached for information and comments. The authors are extremely grateful for their assistance.

31. See note 8 above.

32. *Annual Abstract of Statistics*, series, HM Stationery Office.

33. For a detailed discussion of the expected rates of growth, see Chapter 10 below.

34. In negotiations on the 1972–73 Community farm price levels, the Commission argued that differentials should favour beef at the expense of the grains. Because a large proportion of beef calves come from the dairy herd, however, they did not at that time favour the development of a differential between beef and milk prices, which would favour beef production. See Jacques van Lierde, Recent EEC Decisions on Price and Structural

Policy', paper given at a conference on the common agricultural policy at the University of Newcastle upon Tyne, July 1974, p. 4.

The European Community's Commission does seem to be aware of the possibility of a reaction on the part of the consumer similar to the one projected here. Professor van Lierde states that the Commission was unwilling to increase its original offer of a 9 per cent increase in the price of beef for 1972–73 because a higher price might depress beef consumption to an undesirable extent. See van Lierde, *op. cit.*

35. See note 8 above.
36. After discussions with milling trade specialists, this was considered a reasonable percentage to assume for 1978, in view of current trends at the time of writing.
37. See note 8 above.

Appendix 1 to Chapter 5

CAMBRIDGE WHEAT MODEL

The following notes need to be borne in mind when reading the Cambridge wheat supply model and also the supply models set out in the other appendices to this chapter.

1. The four figures printed beneath each equation are, from left to right: the coefficient of multiple determination, adjusted for degrees of freedom (R^2); the Durbin-Watson statistic (d); the modulus of the highest correlation coefficient (r) between any pair of independent variables in the equation; and the number of observations in the sample (n).

2. The figures in brackets beneath each estimated coefficient are Student's t ratios.

3. In the *crop* models, the subscript t means the variable refers to the crop year June $(t-1)$/May (t), either as a point in time (e.g. June or December Census) or as the average value for the period between June $(t-1)$ and May (t). In the *livestock* models, the subscript t means the variable is observed at the December Census, and the subscript $t/t-1$ means it refers to average values or accumulated quantities for the calendar year between time $t-1$ and time t, unless otherwise stated.

4. Unless otherwise stated all price variables are deflated by the Agricultural Price Index (1954/55–56/57 = 100) for the same period.

Predetermined endogenous variables:
Aww   acreage of wheat at the December Census ('000 acres)

Current endogenous variables:
Asw   acreage of 'spring' wheat, i.e. difference between June and December wheat acreage ('000 acres)
Yw   average yield of all wheat (cwt/acre)

Exogenous variables:
GPb   guaranteed price for barley (£/ton)
PRb   average producer returns for barley (£/ton)
Www   total England and Wales rainfall during September, October, and November (inches)
Wsw   total England and Wales rainfall during February, March, and April

DM   De Martonne Index, June–August
TIME   time in years (1950 = 1, 1951 = 2 . . .)

(1.1) $Aww_t = 1180 + 14.92PRb_{t-1}^{-1} - 84.95Www_t$
                 (1.4)   (1.4)   (4.1)
      0.50   1.9   0.04   18

(1.2) $Asw_t = 2806 - 1.19Aww_t - 59819GPb_{t-1} + 60.85Wsw_t$
                 (5.5)   (10.5)   (2.0)   (2.2)
      0.86   1.9   0.28   19

(1.3)   Log $Yw = 3.238 - 1.356DM + 0.023\ TIME$
                   (42.7)   (2.5)   (8.5)
      0.82   1.3   0.13   20

Appendix 2 to Chapter 5

CAMBRIDGE BARLEY MODEL

In reading the model below, regard should be paid to the notes set out at the beginning of Appendix 1 to this chapter.

Predetermined endogenous variables:
Ab   acreage of barley at the June Census ('000 acres)

Current endogenous variables:
Yb   average yield of barley (cwt/acre)

(2.1)   Log $Ab_t = 2.112 + 0.9776$ Log $Ab_{t-1} + 0.4326$ Log PRb_{t-1}
                 (2.2)   (24.6)   (2.0)
      0.97   —   0.09   18

(2.2)   Log $Yb = 3.114 - 0.914DM + 0.021\ TIME$
                   (30.0)   (2.0)   (9.7)
      0.84   1.1   0.13   20

Appendix 3 to Chapter 5

CAMBRIDGE CATTLE MODEL

Regard should be paid, in reading the model below, to the notes set out at the beginning of Appendix 1 to this chapter.

Unless otherwise stated, variables refer to calendar years. Those marked with a § denote that the raw data refer to April/March years and have been put on a calendar-year basis by appropriate weighting.

Predetermined endogenous variables:

M	male calves ($<$ 1 year old) at December ('000s)
F	female calves ($<$ 1 year old) at December ('000s)
H	heifers in first calf at December ('000s)
BH	total cows in calf and in milk at December ('000s)
PDC	proportion of dairy cows in the total cow herd at December
PRM§	(both deflated and undeflated) average producer returns for milk (d/gallon)
PRB§	(undeflated) average producer returns for clean fat cattle (s/live cwt)

Current endogenous variables:

SS	home-fed steer slaughterings ('000s)
HS	home-fed clean heifer slaughterings ('000s)
CBS	cow and bull slaughterings ('000s)
VS	calf slaughterings ('000s)
O	outflow of cows from cow herd ($= CBS +$ live cow exports)
CC	'calving coefficient' $= (M_t + F_t + VS_{t/t-1})/(BH + H)_{t-1}$
MK§	milk production ex-farm (m gallons)
YB	beef production from steer and clean heifer slaughterings ('000 tons)
CB	beef production from cow and bull slaughterings ('000 tons)
V	veal production from calf slaughterings ('000 tons)
BV	total beef and veal production from domestic slaughterings ('000 tons)
MPB	average market price for clean fat cattle (index: 1954/55–56/7 = 100)

Exogenous variables:

GPB§	average guaranteed price for clean fat cattle (s/live cwt)
GPM§	average guaranteed price for milk (d/gallon)
FP	average price of compound cattle feed (index: 1954/55–56/57 = 100; harvest years)
CRS	[calf rearing subsidy (£/head) $\div$ retail price index (1958 = 100)] $-$ 1.722[a]
HCS	[hill cow subsidy (£/head) $\div$ retail price index (1958 = 100)] $-$ 2.1826[a]
$IMPS$	imports of steers as stores from Eire ('000)
$IMPH$	imports of heifers as stores from Eire ('000)
$IMPF$	imports of steers and heifers as fatstock from Eire ('000)
I	national disposable income (£ million)
SQ§	national standard quantity for milk
YD§	average milk yield per dairy cow
$TIME$	time in years (1954 = 0, 1955 = 1, . . . 1968 = 14)
D	dummy variable for TB clearance (1954–59 = 1, 1960–68 = 0)

3.1 Calf retentions and slaughtering

(3.1.1) $M_t = (0.09 + 0.31 \text{ Log } GPB_{t/t-1}$
$\qquad (2.8) \quad\ (4.8)$
$\qquad\quad + 0.19 (\text{Log } MPB_{t/t-1})(BH + H)_{t-1}$
$\qquad\quad (4.1)$

$\quad 0.87 \qquad 1.5 \qquad 0.55 \qquad 14$

(3.1.2) $F_t = (0.67 + 0.33 \text{ Log } PRM_{t/t-1} + 0.05 \text{ Log } MPB_{t/t-1}$
$\qquad (7.2) \quad\ (3.7) \qquad\qquad\qquad (2.0)$
$\qquad\quad + 0.03 (CRS_{t-1/t-2})(BH + H)_{t-1}$
$\qquad\qquad\qquad\qquad\qquad\qquad (1.8)$

$\quad 0.79 \qquad 2.1 \qquad 0.68 \qquad 14$

(3.1.3) $VS_{t/t-1} = \{CC_{t/t-1}(BH + H)_{t-1}\} - (M_t + F_t)$
$\qquad$ where $CC_{t/t-1} = 0.7198 + 0.0045 \, TIME$
$\qquad\qquad\qquad d = 1.78 \qquad n = 13$

3.2 Retention of replacements for the cow herd

(3.2.1) $H_t = (0.95 - 0.08 \left(\dfrac{GPB}{GPM} \right)_{t/t-1} - 0.002 \, FP_{t-\frac{1}{2}/t-1\frac{1}{2}}$
$\qquad (5.8) \quad\ (3.1) \qquad\qquad\qquad (2.6)$
$\qquad\quad + 0.08 \, HCS_{t/t-1} + 0.04 \, D)F_{t-1}$
$\qquad\quad (2.6) \qquad\qquad (2.9)$

$\quad 0.87 \qquad 2.4 \qquad 0.76 \qquad\quad 14$

3.3 Net investment in the cow herd

(3.3.1)[b] $H_{t-1} - O_{t/t-1} = 4694 \, PRM_{t-1/t-2} + 373.3 \, HCS_{t-1/t-2}$
$\qquad\qquad\qquad\qquad (9.0) \qquad\qquad\qquad (5.4)$
$\qquad\qquad\qquad - 0.43 \, BH_{t-1}$
$\qquad\qquad\qquad (9.7)$

$\quad 0.89 \qquad 1.4 \qquad 0.50 \qquad 12$

(3.3.2) $BH_t - (H_{t-1} - O_{t/t} = 1.18 \, BH_{t-1} - 568.5$
$\qquad\qquad\qquad\qquad (14.9) \qquad\quad (1.7)$

$\quad 0.94 \qquad 2.5 \qquad\ — \qquad 14$

3.4 Proportion of dairy cows in the cow herd

(3.4.1) $PDC_t = 1.017 - 0.002 \, PRB_{t-1/t-2} + 0.005 \, PRM_{t-1/t-2}$
$\qquad\qquad (30.6) \quad (6.7) \qquad\qquad\qquad (2.5)$

$\quad 0.91 \qquad 1.8 \qquad 0.87 \qquad$ (Prices are not deflated)

3.5 Slaughterings

(3.5.1) $(SS - IMPS)_{t/t-1} = 448.5 + 0.66 \, M_{t-2}$
$\qquad\qquad\qquad\qquad (4.3) \quad (7.8)$

$\quad 0.83 \qquad 1.5 \qquad\ — \qquad 13$

(3.5.2) $(HS - IMPH)_{t/t-1} = 624.9 + 0.50\,F_{t-2} - 1.16\,H_t$
$\qquad\qquad\qquad\quad (1.9)\qquad (4.3)\qquad\quad (2.4)$
$\quad\ 0.64\qquad 1.7\qquad 0.15\qquad 13$

(3.5.3)^c $CBS_{t/t-1} = 0.92\,O_{t/t-1}$
$\qquad$ where $O_{t/t-1} = 1.18\,BH_{t-1} - BH_t + H_{t-1} - 568.5$ (see
$\qquad\qquad\qquad\qquad\qquad\qquad\qquad\qquad\qquad$ equation (3.3.2))

3.6   Price formation

None of the price variables are deflated.

(3.6.1) $PRM_{t/t-1} = 0.975\,GPM_{t/t-1} - 0.01(MK - SQ)_{t/t-1}$
$\qquad\qquad\qquad\qquad (247)\qquad\qquad\quad (17.7)$
$\quad\ 0.99\qquad 1.6\qquad 0.46\qquad 15$

(3.6.2) $MPB_{t/t} = 139.5 + 0.005\,I_{t/t-1}$
$\qquad\qquad\qquad (11.4)\quad (9.7)$
$\qquad\qquad\qquad - 0.055(SS + HS + IMPF)_{t/t-1}$
$\qquad\qquad\qquad (6.7)$
$\quad\ 0.98\qquad 2.1\qquad 0.86\qquad 14$

(3.6.3) $\mathrm{Log}\,PRB_{t/t-1} = 0.313 + 0.795\,\mathrm{Log}\,GPB_{t/t-1}$
$\qquad\qquad\qquad\qquad (1.7)\qquad (17.2)$
$\qquad\qquad\qquad\quad + 0.159\,\mathrm{Log}\,MPB_{t/t-1}$
$\qquad\qquad\qquad\quad (4.9)$
$\quad\ 0.98\qquad 1.4\qquad 0.61\qquad 14$

3.7   Yields of meat or milk per animal

(3.7.1) $V_{t/t-1} = 0.022\,VS_{t/t-1}$

(3.7.2) $YB_{t/t-1} = (SS + HS)/(3.58 + 0.034\,TIME)$
$\qquad\qquad\qquad\qquad\qquad (209)\quad (17.3)$

(3.7.3) $CB_{t/t-1} = 0.261\,CBS_{t/t-1}$

(3.7.4) PROJECTION MODEL:
$\qquad YD_{t/t-1} = \tfrac{1}{2}(666.8 + 9.797\,TIME) + \tfrac{1}{2}(618.7$
$\qquad\qquad\qquad (67.4)\quad\ (8.7)\qquad\qquad (52.0)$
$\qquad\qquad + 65.279\,\mathrm{Log}\,TIME)$
$\qquad\qquad (11.1)$

3.8   Meat and milk production

(3.8.1) $BV_{t/t-1} \equiv (YB + CB + V)_{t/t-1}$

(3.8.2) $MK_{t/t-1} = 1.080\,[(YD_{t/t-1})(BH + H)_{t-1}(PDC)_{t-1} \times 10^{-3}]$
$\qquad\qquad\quad (9.7)$
$\qquad\qquad\quad - 774.0$
$\qquad\qquad\quad (2.4)$
$\quad\ 0.92\qquad 1.2\qquad\ -\qquad\ 9$

NOTES

ᵃ 1.722 and 2.1826 represent the mean (static) values of the calf and hill cow sub-sidies (deflated by the retail price index) respectively for the period 1955–67.

ᵇ The parameters of this equation were estimated by applying least squares to the transformed equation $Y_t - \rho Y_{t-1} = \Sigma\beta_i'(X_{it} - \rho X_{it-1})$, where ρ is the first order serial correlation coefficient for the residuals $\hat{u}_t$ of the original equation $Y_t = \Sigma\beta_i X_{it}$. This gave the value of ρ as -0.6660.

ᶜ In 1970, cow and bull slaughterings comprised 92.3 per cent of total cullings, the remainder being exported live. In the projections, this same proportion is assumed for each year. It should be noted however, that historically, some of the variation in cow and bull slaughtering, about a normal level of 20 per cent of the cow herd per year, can be explained by changes in the milk price, viz.

$$CBS_{t/t-1} = 1135 + 0.21\, BH_{t-1} - 3644\, PRM_{t-1/t-2}$$

$$\begin{array}{ccc} (3.2) & (2.8) & (3.6) \\ 0.52 & 2.4 & 0.45 \qquad 13 \end{array}$$

This milk price is the variable which determines most of the net growth in cow numbers in the cattle model (see equation (3.3.1)).

Appendix 4 to Chapter 5

CAMBRIDGE SHEEP MODEL

In reading the model below, regard should be paid to the notes at the beginning of Appendix 1.

Pre-determined endogenous variables:
BF   'Breeding flock': breeding ewes (U.K.) + tupped shearlings (G.B.) at December ('000s)

Current endogenous variables:
SLS   sheep and lamb slaughter ('000s)
ERS   ewe and ram slaughter ('000s)
L   'lamb' production ('000 tons)
M   'mutton' production ('000 tons)
ML   total mutton and lamb production ('000 tons)

Exogenous variables:
GPFS   guaranteed price for fat sheep, April $(t - 1)$/March (t) (d/lb est dcw)
GPW   guaranteed price for wool, April/March (d/lb)
TP   mean monthly temperature, January–March, of England and

Wales, Scotland, and N. Ireland weighted according to total sheep numbers in each country (°C)

PN   mean monthly rainfall calculated in the same manner as *TP* above (cm)

(4.1) $BF_t = 0.784\, BF_{t-1} + 5358(GPFS_{t+1/t} + GPFS_{t/t-1})$
$$\qquad\qquad (15.6) \qquad\qquad (3.7)$$
$$\qquad\qquad + 4581(GPW_{t+1/t} + GPW_{t/t-1}) - 6374$$
$$\qquad\qquad (3.5) \qquad\qquad\qquad\qquad (3.3)$$

     0.98   —   0.61   14

(4.2) $SLS_{t/t-1} = 9444 + 1.130\, BF_{t-1} - 20793\, GPW_{t+1/t}$
$$\qquad\qquad (1.7) \quad (9.5) \qquad\quad (2.7)$$
$$\qquad\qquad + 517.5\, TP_{t/t-1} - 460.9\, PN_{t/t-1}$$
$$\qquad\qquad (5.1) \qquad\qquad (4.4)$$

     0.93   2.3   0.59   14

(4.3) $ERS_{t/t-1} = 3702 + 0.238\, BF_{t-1} - 2981(GPF_{t+1/t} + GPF_{t/t-1})$
$$\qquad\qquad (2.8) \quad (6.9) \qquad\qquad (3.0)$$
$$\qquad\qquad - 2929(GPW_{t+1/t} + GPW_{t/t-1})$$
$$\qquad\qquad (3.2)$$

     0.90   2.5   0.61   14

(4.4) $L_{t/t-1} = (SLS_{t/t-1})/(50.29 + 0.299\, TIME)$
$$\qquad\qquad\qquad\qquad (102) \quad (4.8)$$

     $d = 1.55 \qquad n = 13$

(4.5) $M_{t/t-1} = ERS_{t/t-1}/35.76$

(4.6) $ML_{t/t-1} \equiv (L + M)_{t/t-1}$

CHAPTER 6

Income Transfer Effects of the Common Agricultural Policy

T. E. JOSLING and DONNA HAMWAY

The European Community's common agricultural policy (CAP) can be considered as *either* a set of regulations governing the marketing of farm products in the Common Market together with some associated measures relating to the structure of the farm business, *or* as an inter-governmental pact which seeks to coordinate the actions of national governments taken in response to common problems. This latter view has gained ground in the 1970s as the European Community has been shaken both from without, by commodity price increases and by the oil crisis, and from within as the economies of the Community struggle to control inflation and maintain employment. But it is still an elusive concept and one which is not responsive to normal analytical methods. In this chapter, then, will be considered the more concrete manifestation of the CAP, namely the set of instruments which have been tried and tested as a means of regulating European farm markets.[1] The aspect of the CAP that is to be explored is the way in which a particular set of price-support instruments distributes incomes, both within the farm sector and between farmers and their ultimate customers, the consumers.

Any attempt at an empirical study of such income transfer effects runs the risk of being quickly dated by events. Just as policies change to accommodate new situations, so informed views about the reasonableness of assumptions are modified with experience. Since any study of this type, which makes assumptions about policy instruments and price levels, is in a sense 'self-contained', what can change is the applicability of the conclusions to the actual situation in the European Community rather than the accuracy of the results as such. As with the previous chapters in the empirical part of the volume, this chapter should not be regarded as a set of forecasts, but as an illustration of the types and magnitudes of income transfers generated by agricultural price policies within the context of the CAP.

To put the point another way, consider four possible broad developments of the CAP, in the rest of the 1970s.

180

1. The policy could be radically altered by the frustration of the various governments in the Community, by the collapse of an economy or by some major political *volte-face*. In this case the results presented here will have only a nostalgic value, relating to a particular policy and period unlikely to re-emerge.

2. Then again, world prices could resume their sharp upward movement of the period 1972 to 1974, turning the policy into a defence of consumer living standards and a guarantee of the security of the European Community's food supplies. Such an event is not entirely improbable. The world food situation remains precarious and a slowdown in agricultural technology, or a climatic shift, could precipitate such a crisis. But the evidence is not enough to warrant the construction of elaborate hypotheses regarding prices and policies under such conditions. The prophets are still in the wilderness.

3. Somewhat more probable is a situation whereby the average level of prices in the European Community stays closely in line with those on world markets. In this case the instruments of the CAP would become much less important and the impact of the policy on income distribution would be rather small.

4. Such a benign outcome, although desirable as an economic and political objective (in terms of the management of the policy), is again too early to assume. As remarked in Chapter 1, the protective pressures which led to the establishment of a high-price regime in European agriculture, relative to other producing areas, are still extant.[2]

The study is therefore intended to explore the fourth possibility: that the CAP will emerge from the period of high world prices in a form not too different from that which existed up to 1972. For it is assumed that a significant gap will reopen between import prices and those in the Community for the major temperate-zone commodities, and the instruments will remain the variable levy and the export subsidy backed up by intervention buying on the domestic market. It is in this kind of situation that major income transfers are implemented through the market both within countries and among member states.

If the CAP were to retain its present instruments until the 1980s, and if import prices were to fall back to a level below that guaranteed to Community farmers, an important transfers of purchasing power would be effected to the farm sector at the expense largely of the European Community's consumers. This has been, after all, a major objective of the policy.

The goal of the Treaty of Rome to free the impediments to agricultural trade within the European Community could have been achieved merely by removing obstacles to the movement of such goods. No interventionist policy was needed. Surety of supply to consumers could have been achieved by long-term contracts with overseas producers. But the original imperative behind the CAP was the building of a preferential and protected Common Market for the benefit of the Community's farmers and to the economic advantage of those countries within the Community which had export interests in the agricultural sector.

Explored below are the income-transfer effects of the CAP within the United Kingdom and among member countries. This is not to imply that all such transfers are misguided. Those who favour such a policy to transfer income are as likely to wish to know its success as those who criticise are to assess its folly. The chapter is divided into two parts.

Attention is first given to the probable impact of the European Community's price levels on the British farm sector and on domestic consumers. The material was given in more detail in a previous report, on the Trade Policy Research Centre's programme,[3] in the context of the implications of a change from a deficiency-payments system to one of support through levies either within or outside the Community. This particular comparison seems now somewhat out of place and is thus not pursued further. Should a future British Government attempt to withdraw from the Community then such questions as the relative merits of different farm programmes might once again be of interest. There continues to be a need, however, to understand the implications of a set of policies that the United Kingdom has adopted since 1973 and which are continuously undergoing examination at the Community level as well as within national administrations. Consequently there is included below an abbreviated restatement of some of the conclusions of the earlier paper on the internal income-distribution implications of the CAP for the United Kingdom.[4]

Secondly, the transfers set up by the CAP among the European Community's member countries – and among producers and consumers in those countries as a whole – are examined. For comparison an alternative situation is needed and the most convenient is the absence of the price provisions of the CAP. Once again it should be emphasised that the choice of an open trade policy as a base for assessment of income transfers is not to be taken as an inherent judgement of the superiority of such a system. Those who consider that a liberal trade stance would spell disaster for the European Community's agriculture can take comfort from the level of income support generated by the policy. To those who consider such transfers misplaced the costs are additional thorns in the flesh. By taking free trade as a comparison one is merely saying that the best way to judge a policy is to compare the situation with and without that policy.

INCOME-DISTRIBUTION EFFECTS IN BRITAIN

The adoption by Britain of the European Community's CAP can be expected to have a significant effect on the distribution of income within the farm sector of the British economy. Prices of certain products, for example cereals and dairy and to a certain extent beef, are still expected to rise significantly with the full implementation of Community farm rules. As in the earlier paper, the results reported below must be interpreted as the initial change which would come about if the prices of the CAP were applied immediately, to which farmers would respond by changing production patterns. In practice, the actual change in the distribution of incomes during the period of transition, from the beginning of 1973 to the end of 1978, is a gradual one.

The earlier paper suggests that the benefits from the adoption of the CAP are not evenly distributed either among commodity classes or by farm-size groups. In general, the benefits received, expressed as a percentage of net farm income, are expected to increase with farm size as measured by standard man-day units. Cattle and cereal farms, the paper shows, would benefit by a very large increase in their net farm incomes. Cereal farmers, for instance, might find their final incomes doubled, whereas the increase in income on small dairy farms is only 40 per cent.

Two types of farming appeared likely to benefit less than the average. Sheep farms, the paper indicated, might find their incomes increasing by between 17 per cent and 49 per cent, whereas pig and poultry farms, under the new set of prices, suffer a serious decline in net farm income and might even be left with no surplus of farm receipts over costs. An explanation for this, the paper suggests, is that those enterprises which rely heavily on cereal-based feeds find the increased price of this input not recompensed by higher prices for their output.

The distribution of income by quartiles is a convenient way to summarise the effect of the adoption of the CAP. This is shown in Table 6.1 together with the corresponding distributions for income without a farm-support policy. Compared with the distribution which would prevail with no agricultural support policy, the CAP is expected to increase income disparity within the farm sector, with the inequality coefficient on net farm incomes rising from 0.22 to 0.32.

TABLE 6.1

Comparison of the Distribution of Farm Incomes among Farmers
Ranked by Income Quartiles (percentages)

	First Quartile	Second Quartile	Third Quartile	Fourth Quartile	Inequality Coefficient
No farm support	13	25	21	41	0.215
Common agricultural policy	15	10	25	50	0.318

Referring to the income quartiles, the study shows that the poorest 25 per cent of farmers could expect to receive some 15 per cent of income under the Community's support system, compared with 13 per cent if there were no support policy. The highest income quartile receives 50 per cent of income compared with 41 per cent with no agricultural price support policy. The second lowest quartile fares less well under the European Community's CAP, with their share of support benefits decreasing from 25 per cent to 10 per cent. While the Community policy tends, on the whole, to increase disparity of farm incomes, it does appear marginally to benefit the poorest section of the industry.

Implications of the CAP for Households

The implications of agricultural policy for consumers and taxpayers in different income groups is also investigated in the earlier paper. The Family Expenditure Survey[5] of the United Kingdom was used since it identifies – for families of different composition types and income groups – original income, tax payments, receipts from government programmes (such as pensions and family allowances) and major consumption items.[6] The level of income before taxes paid to the government, and before benefits received from the government, is called 'original income'. Income after tax payments, both direct and indirect, and after including state benefits, is referred to as 'final income'. Since people presumably identify more easily with their earned income, the distribution of households by original income was used as the underlying classification. When the paper was prepared the latest available data were for 1969.

Table 6.2 shows the impact of the costs of the CAP on households as consumers relative to a situation where there is no agricultural support policy. The burden of farm-support costs was expected to increase with the size of family at higher levels of income. Anticipated costs ranged from £19 per year for one-adult low-income families to over £60 a year for high-income families.

As a proportion of income (see Table 6.3), the incidence of support costs declines sharply as incomes increased. Two-adult families with no children in the lowest income bracket bear costs equivalent to 5.75 per cent of final income, whilst the same type of household within the high-income range pays only 0.137 per cent of income in higher consumer prices. The proportion of costs to income also increases slightly with family size.

Although most categories of families in the United Kingdom are represented in the preceding cost-distribution tables, three types of household were singled out for separate consideration. These families were (i) pensioner households with original income of less than £216; (ii) two-adult households with one to four children and original income

TABLE 6.2

Average Cost of CAP per Household, by Income and Composition: United Kingdom (£ per year)

| Household Composition | Original income (£ per year) | | | | | | | |
	At least 216 / Less than 315	315 / 559	559 / 816	816 / 1,196	1,196 / 1,752	1,752 / 2,566	2,566 / 3,770	3,770 / 5,503
1 Adult	19.39	20.56	20.89	23.31	20.60	14.61	21.66	—
2 Adults	33.02	35.16	36.24	37.23	38.81	36.50	36.23	46.52
2 Adults and 1 child	—	—	41.20	37.45	40.54	44.39	53.13	—
2 Adults and 2 children	—	—	43.70	44.35	46.31	53.15	58.83	58.18
2 Adults and 3 children	—	—	52.59	47.09	52.95	56.55	56.08	—
2 Adults and 4 children	—	—	—	58.38	62.63	55.84	—	—
3–4 Adults	—	—	51.02	48.90	68.63	61.01	60.63	61.74
3 Adults and 1–2 children	—	—	—	52.27	59.45	66.57	63.42	—

TABLE 6.3

Cost of CAP as a Proportion of Final Income: United Kingdom (percentage)

Original income (£ per year)									
House Composition	*At least* *Less than*	*216* *315*	*315* *559*	*559* *816*	*816* *1,196*	*1,196* *1,752*	*1,752* *2,566*	*2,566* *3,770*	*3,770* *5,502*
1 Adult		4.60	3.90	3.65	3.36	2.12	1.11	1.23	—
2 Adults		5.75	4.97	4.67	4.57	3.77	2.51	1.75	1.37
2 Adults and 1 child		—	—	5.67	4.27	3.60	2.82	2.42	—
2 Adults and 2 children		—	—	4.60	4.30	3.60	3.15	2.40	1.70
2 Adults and 3 children		—	—	4.09	4.80	4.10	3.35	2.75	—
2 Adults and 4 children		—	—	—	4.71	4.52	3.48	—	—
3–4 Adults		—	—	4.80	4.33	4.17	3.59	3.26	2.51
3 Adults and 1–2 children		—	—	—	3.98	4.15	3.75	2.75	—

of less than £559 (referred to hereafter as the child-poverty group); and (iii) households with original incomes greater than £5502. Table 6.4 presents the corresponding data for these households. (The income figures, it should be remembered, relate to 1969.)

TABLE 6.4

Incidence of CAP Agricultural Support Costs
for Pensioners and Low- and High-Income Households
(£ per year with percentages of final income in brackets)

	One-adult pensioner	Two-adult pensioners	Two-adults, 1–4 children 'low-income'	High-income
Original income	less than 216	less than 216	less than 559	greater than 5502
Total food expenditure	107 (30.1)	206 (38.7)	294 (36.5)	512 (10.1)
CAP costs	17.91 (5.01)	32.67 (6.08)	37.67 (4.7)	67.16 (1.3)

The study shows the increase in costs borne by pensioners under the European Community's support system to be quite dramatic. A two-adult pensioner family pays nearly £33 a year for agricultural support, and a child-poverty family almost £38 a year. The burden on very high-income families was calculated at £67 a year. Expressed as a proportion of income, poverty families and pensioners might spend about 5 per cent of final income on farm support, whilst high-income households pay as little as 1.3 per cent.

The distribution effect can again be shown by examining the effect on income quartiles. It was calculated that the lowest income quartile pays 13 per cent of price support costs, while receiving only 6 per cent of original income (see Table 6.5). The highest income quartile pays 32 per cent of costs and receives 48 per cent of original income. Taking the first and second quartiles together, those households with below average incomes pays 38 per cent of all support cost, although they only receive 27 per cent of original income.

TABLE 6.5

Share of Agricultural Support Costs by Household Income Quartile
Compared to Original and Final Income Shares (percentages)

	First Quartile	Second Quartile	Third Quartile	Fourth Quartile	Inequality Coefficient
Original income	6	21	26	48	0.385
Final income	11	19	27	43	0.282
CAP costs	13	25	30	32	0.156

The second and third quartiles taken together (that 50 per cent of all households which fall neither in the lowest nor the highest income group) receive 47 per cent of original income and 46 per cent of final income. For these two groups it appears that the incidence of tax and government policies is roughly neutral. Under the CAP these groups together might bear 55 per cent of programme costs. Since the first quartile also pays a higher share of support costs than it receives as income, the main burden of support falls most heavily on the bottom 75 per cent of the population ranked by income.

Significance of Income Distribution
By their nature, support systems that raise farm prices favour those farmers with relatively high incomes. This is not unexpected. High-income farms generally have superior management or abundant resources. A farmer with a considerable amount of capital (irrespective of the physical size of the farm) would expect to receive a net farm income larger than a farmer with more limited capital. Similarly farms with the same endowment of capital and of family labour have different net incomes depending on their efficiency. If the distribution of capital among farms is unequal then it would be expected that net farm income would also show variation. In particular, one would expect the highest 50 per cent of farms ranked by income to obtain more than 50 per cent of the total income of all farms. This would hold in the absence of support programmes and also under any policy which operated on farm prices. According to the study, price policy will, over time, tend to exaggerate the effect of any dispersion of asset ownership among farms.

To report that a set of farm-support policies distorts the distribution of income among British farmers is not in itself to condemn those policies. For one thing, it might be an objective of policy to reward large and efficient farms. But this justification would have to rest on the assumption that the distribution of income without any farm-support policies is unduly favourable to the small and inefficient units. It is not obvious why this should be the case. The figures in Table 6.1 suggest that in the absence of any policy, the highest quartile receives 41 per cent of farm income; the lowest quartile, only 13 per cent.

The same point can be made in a somewhat different way by referring to the situation under the previous British policy based on deficiency payments.[7] Of the total payments of £218m made to the farm sector of the United Kingdom in 1969, £129m went as price support. Of this, £122m was distributed in a manner which increased the inequality of income distribution. Not only did higher-income farmers get a higher proportion of such payments, but that proportion was higher than their share of income. Of the £89m spent on production grants and subsidies, about one-half (£43m) tended to increase income inequality, whilt the rest tended to reduce it. Thus in total £165m was spent on policies which increased inequality and only £54m on programmes that reduced this inequality. Clearly any switch in emphasis away from the payment of production grants towards support through product prices alone will even further benefit higher income farmers. In the European Community it has come to be widely recognised that price methods alone do not eliminate the incidence of poverty in rural areas.[8] The results cited in the earlier paper indicate that low-income farmers in the United Kingdom can expect only a marginal benefit from the adoption of the CAP.

Moreover, a change from a deficiency-payments policy to a policy based on import restrictions is bound to affect the distribution of the costs of farm support among the non-farm population. The detailed incidence of costs under the various schemes was discussed in the earlier study. As was shown in Table 6.5, under the Community's import-levy system, the highest income quartile pays 16 percentage points less of farm-support costs than they receive as their income shares, while the lowest quartile pays 7 or 8 points more than their income share.

Although the total tax system imposes costs roughly proportional to income, the effect of crediting households with benefits from government spending evens out considerably the distribution of final income. As shown in the earlier paper, when compared with shares of final income, the previous deficiency-payments policy bore somewhat less heavily on low-income households. The top income quartiles paid a slightly higher proportion of farm-support costs than they received of final income. But again, an import-levy policy might result in high-income families paying considerably less (11 percentage points) of the costs than their share in income. The CAP is clearly regressive with respect to income.

Farm programmes involve a transfer from households as consumers and taxpayers to farm households. The benefit of the CAP, as has been seen, are likely to accrue disproportionately to high-income farmers. The costs are paid in proportion to income under a policy which pays farmers from tax receipts, but fall more heavily on low-income households when the transfer is effected through higher food prices. But it could still be the case that this transfer tends to make incomes more equal if farmers are among the lowest income groups. To examine the net effect of the transfer between these groups, it is necessary to rank farmers and other households within the same income classes. Table 6.6 attempts this for the CAP, defining – in 1969 income terms – the transfer relative to a situation where farm policy existed. The results are instructive: households with an income below £1850 per year (£36 per week) pay more for farm support as taxpayers and consumers than the farmers in that income group receive. The reverse

TABLE 6.6

Net Transfers among Income Groups under the CAP (£m)

Range of Income £ per year	< 500	501–1,100	1,101–1,300	1,301–1,850	1,851–2,350	2,351–2,800	2,801–3,400	3,401–5,000	5,000+
Farm households	−9.86	24.42	21.09	41.37	71.12	26.49	63.17	64.55	140.76
Other households	47.58	200.54	100.13	233.24	67.17	12.95	2.40	3.30	20.15
Net transfer	−57.44	−175.82	−79.04	−191.87	3.95	13.54	60.77	61.25	120.61

might be true of households with income above £1850 per year. In other words, there is the possibility of a transfer from families earning below £36 per week to those earning more.

The full implication of the European Community's system of price-supports, at the assumed levels of Common Market prices, is a possible net transfer of £504m from those earning less than £36 per week. But not all of this accrues to higher-income families in the United Kingdom. The study estimated the possible payment abroad (as levies paid into the European Community's Agricultural Guidance and Guarantee Fund (FEOGA) on imports from third countries or as a transfer to member-country farmers exporting to Britain at higher prices) to be £250m. Thus high-income families receive about £254 more than they would in the absence of any support policy for agriculture.

The aim of the study was to illustrate the effect on income distribution of farm-support schemes. This discussion was limited to the immediate effect which would be felt by farmers and other households if the policy towards agriculture were to change suddenly. In practice producers react to price changes by altering their farming patterns, and consumers change their food purchasing habits. Moreover, the government reacts, over time, to political forces and alters the tax-and-benefit system to offset undesirable effects on particular income groups. But knowledge of the impact on income distribution is useful in order to appreciate the extent of producer and consumer reaction to higher prices. By hypothesising a sudden change in policy under the present production and consumption patterns one measures the full extent of the economic forces to which households will react.

The discussion above, of the effect on low-income families of Britain adopting the CAP, illustrates the distinction between the 'impact' effect of a policy change and a projection of the final effect of that change after adjustment. These families have to reduce their level of food consumption unless compensated by other government measures. The results of this study focus on the necessary amount of such compensation and by implication on the method of raising the money required to pay the increased benefits.

TRANSFERS WITHIN THE EUROPEAN COMMUNITY

The discussion so far has concentrated on the possible direct income-distribution effects of the adoption of the CAP on groups within the United Kingdom. The influence of the CAP, though, is not only on the direction of internal transfers, however important these might be to individual governments, but on the pattern of trade and on resource and financial flows within the European Community. The previous study was developed to examine these implications following the adoption of the CAP by the United Kingdom, Denmark and Ireland.

This section will consider the resulting intra-Community income transfers.

Calculating Intra-Community Transfers

To quantify the potential transfers of income among member countries of the European Community arising from the CAP it is necessary to form a view both about the future structure of production, consumption and trade within the Common Market and also to attempt a guess at what the situation might be in the absence of the CAP. Both estimates are hazardous. In particular, world prices – or rather the prices at which agricultural products are available to the European Community and at which Community goods can be sold abroad – are notoriously difficult to predict. In the mid-1970s, world prices for cereals and for sugar were at about the same level as that prevailing in the Common Market. Should this state of affairs continue to the end of the 1970s there would be little point to looking at the CAP in the way which has been done in this study: the policy itself would be either inoperative or of a different character. But few people have expected the high prices to continue for the rest of the 1970s. There has been a feeling that, although prices are unlikely to return to the low levels of the mid-1960s, they may fall to a level consistent with a rising trend since 1970. The trend in this study is taken to be 5 per cent per year in sterling terms: European Community prices are also expected to rise in a manner consistent with the projections used elsewhere in the Trade Policy Research Centre's research programme, as reported in this volume.

Production, consumption and trade patterns are less variable and hence slightly easier to predict. The picture for the United Kingdom is taken from the projections for 1978 in Chapters 3 and 5. For other Community countries the estimates derived in an earlier study were updated and modified in the light of recent experience.[9] To establish the trade flows to and from each country and the outside world it was necessary to make some simplifying assumptions – basically that internal needs were satisfied first and that neighbouring countries had easiest access to each other's markets. To arrive at an estimate of patterns of production, consumption and trade in the absence of a Community price policy for agricultural goods, it is necessary to use values for the elasticity of supply and consumption. Although these are not available on a consistent basis for the European Community, the rough order of magnitude is likely to be similar across countries.

Briefly, the method of calculating the transfers is to value production, consumption and trade at both world and Community price levels. The extra producer receipts are then divided between producer income and extra production cost on the assumption that the supply curve represents the marginal private cost of expansion. The extra consumer expenditure is deemed to replace expenditure on other goods of the same value to the consumer, and the value of expenditure on agricultural goods is taken as being reflected in how much consumers are willing to pay for various amounts of the products concerned. The change in consumer valuation on agricultural goods adjusted by expenditure changes gives a measure of real consumer gain or loss. This is commonly referred to as a change in 'consumer surplus'. All import levies are taken as being paid to the FEOGA and all costs of export subsidy programmes come from that fund.

The steps can be summarised, and the terms defined, as follows.

1. *Economic costs and benefits for each country.* Producer net benefit is taken as the producer price change multiplied by the *average* level of production. Consumer surplus calculations are similarly based on the *average* consumption level and the price change, on the assumption that farm price increases are passed on (in absolute rather than percentage terms) to the final consumer. In the case of feed-grain costs, the 'consumer surplus' change is subtracted from producer gains in the livestock sector.

2. *Transfer among countries.* Since it is assumed that domestic consumers buy domestic production when available, the breakdown of national consumer costs and producer benefits can be calculated for each country. Excess consumer cost over domestic producer benefit implies payments to FEOGA on third country imports and to other European producers on intra-Community trade. Similar calculations are performed on producer benefits. The resulting picture represents the transfers across borders. Per capita transfers are derived from projections of population for each country and the percentage employed in agriculture. The calculations of proportionate income benefit and consumption cost are derived from an extrapolation of GNP, spending patterns, and the proportion of GNP accounted for by agriculture in the various countries.

The European Community's agricultural policy is designed to transfer income directly from consumers to producers and their suppliers within the preference area. A member state's contribution to the Community's agricultural sector is in this sense related to its food consumption. The potential gain of the CAP to a community member depends upon its agricultural production. In other words, income is transferred from net importers of agricultural commodities within the Community to net producers.

Results of Enquiry

Following the steps outlined above, on the basis of the price and policy assumptions, the net position of consumers and producers within each member state in 1980 was calculated relative to a situation where there was no protection for the European Community's agriculture. The results are shown in Table 6.7. The main beneficiary countries are shown to be those which produce for export the commoties included in the study – cereals, beef, pigmeat, mutton and lamb, and dairy products. Ireland, Denmark, France and the Netherlands show net economic benefits from the operation of the policy, with the other countries registering a net loss. Clearly, a different set of price assumptions would change the size of the gains and losses, but the pattern of the results is predictable for a situation where agricultural prices are supported above world levels. The net loss to the Community as a whole indicates that there must be a transfer from another source – such as members' contributions to FEOGA from value-added tax receipts or duties on other imports.

TABLE 6.7

Burden and Benefits of the CAP for Community Members
Relative to World Prices: 1980[a]
Relative to World Prices: 1980[a] (£m)

	Producer Benefit	Consumer Burden	Net
United Kingdom	616	896	−280
Ireland	267	64	203
Denmark	218	126	92
France	1678	990	688
West Germany	1116	1257	−141
Belgium–Lux	173	250	−77
Italy	614	1002	−388
Netherlands	288	283	5
Total	4970	4868	−102

[a] Note that in this table the extra cost of feed grains used in livestock production has been subtracted from producer benefit rather than being included as a consumer burden. Consumers bear the burden indirectly through higher livestock prices.

As would be expected from an agricultural price-support system, by far the largest part of the farm-income transfers come from extra food costs to consumers. This consumer burden can be divided into three parts: that which is a benefit to domestic producers (such as was discussed for the United Kingdom in the previous section of this chapter), that which goes to other farmers, through higher input prices on intra-Community trade, and that which is paid into the agricultural fund as levies on imports from third countries. Table 6.8 shows the distribution of contributions for each member state in 1978. It costs British consumers, for example, £896m under the study's price assumptions.

Only £546m of this cost is a direct transfer to domestic producers. The remaining £350m represents a contribution of £208m to producers in the rest of the Community and a £142m transfer of levy revenue to the Agricultural Fund.

TABLE 6.8

Breakdown of Burden on Consumers by Beneficiary: 1980 (£m)

	Domestic producer	Community producer	FEOGA	Total burden
United Kingdom	546	208	142	896
Ireland	52	3	9	64
Denmark	87	14	25	126
France	970	15	5	990
West Germany	959	90	208	1257
Belgium–Lux	168	36	46	250
Italy	546	155	301	1002
Netherlands	204	22	57	283
Total for the Nine	3532	543	793	4868

Italy and West Germany also appear to be major potential contributors. West Germany, which bears the heaviest burden of all member states, contributes £208m in levies and in support of Community farm incomes. Italy's contribution to the rest of the Community is largest. Nearly 16 per cent of the burden on Italian consumers represents a direct benefit to Community producers. The pattern which emerges for the remainder of the Community suggests that benefits to domestic producers represent a significant share of the total consumer burden. France, for instance, transfers to French producers about 98 per cent of the total cost which she incurs by operating the CAP. The transfer in Ireland and Holland to domestic producers represents 81 per cent and 72 per cent, respectively, of consumer costs.

The extent to which producers in member countries stand to benefit from the European Community's farm policy is indicated above. Table 6.9 shows the sources of these benefits. Transfers from domestic consumers represent the largest share of produced benefits in all countries except Ireland and Denmark. As a proportion of total gains, Irish, Danish and French producers appear to benefit most from higher prices received on intra-Community sales and from subsidies paid on third country exports. Transfers from domestic consumers represent only 19 per cent of the total benefit of the CAP to Irish producers. For the major portion of their support, Irish producers rely on higher priced exports. Whilst French producers depend proportionately less on transfers from Community consumers and from FEOGA than do the

Irish, in absolute terms France is the major recipient of FEOGA payments. Total outgoings of FEOGA are £895m of which nearly 51 per cent is a direct transfer to French producers for subsidies on third-country exports.

TABLE 6.9

Breakdown of Producer Benefits by Source: 1980 (£m)

	Domestic consumer	Community consumer	FEOGA	Total benefit
United Kingdom	546	44	26	616
Ireland	52	114	101	267
Denmark	87	60	71	218
France	970	253	455	1678
West Germany	959	36	121	1116
Belgium–Lux	168	—	5	173
Italy	546	5	63	614
Netherlands	204	31	53	288
Total for the Nine	3532	543	895	4,970

On average, 71 per cent of total benefits accrue to producers through transfers from domestic consumers and 18 per cent through payments from FEOGA. The remaining 11 per cent represents a transfer from Community producers to domestic producers.

In order to assess further the effect of the European Community's farm policy, it is useful to examine the relationship between the burden of farm-support costs and expenditure on the one hand, and support payments and farm incomes on the other. The implied distribution of support costs and payments per head is shown in Table 6.10. At the

TABLE 6.10

Estimated per capita Consumer Cost of the CAP by Country: 1980
(£ per head)

Country	Total consumer cost	Of which	
		To nationals	To other members
Denmark	23.64	16.42	7.22
Belgium–Lux	23.62	16.00	7.62
West Germany	20.59	15.76	4.83
Ireland	19.57	15.89	3.68
Netherlands	19.56	14.11	5.45
France	17.90	17.52	0.38
Italy	17.32	9.80	7.52
United Kingdom	15.05	9.31	5.74

lower end of the cost scale, British consumers might expect to pay approximately £15 per year while Danish consumers contribute over £23 annually to support agricultural incomes. Within this range, German and Belgian consumers bear higher than average costs.

Table 6.11 gives more information about support benefits to Community producers. Average support payments range from nearly £134 in Italy to approximately £1098 per year in Denmark. Not only do Italian farmers gain least from operating the CAP but they also gain the smallest proportion of net farm income from support payments compared with producers in the rest of the European Community. Next to Italy, Ireland benefits her producers least by operating the Community's farm policy for these products.

TABLE 6.11

Producer Benefit per Farmer by Country from the CAP: 1980
(£ per head)

| | | Of which | |
| | | --- | --- |
Country	Total benefit	From nationals	From other members
Denmark	1,097.55	712.13	385.42
West Germany	842.81	751.86	90.95
United Kingdpm	797.58	734.01	63.57
Belgium–Lux	793.42	775.42	18.00
Netherlands	686.64	565.84	120.80
France	573.22	395.34	177.88
Ireland	469.43	152.18	317.25
Italy	133.92	121.18	12.74

The support as a proportion of net farm income is shown in Table 6.12. Apart from West Germany, it appears that producers in the new member countries are the most dependent on support benefits. The average Irish farmer depends on benefits from farm policy for more than 69 per cent of his income. British and Danish producers rely on support payments for 59.4 per cent and 55.7 per cent, respectively, For the United Kingdom this figure can be compared with an average of 59 per cent of net farm income which in 1969 was directly attributable to farm-support payments.

It is also interesting to note that Irish and Italian consumers pay support costs which are lower than average, but which represent the highest proportions of total consumer expenditure. French consumers also pay less than average support costs. These costs, however, expressed as a proportion of total expenditure, are smaller than for all other Community members.

The figures in Table 6.12 can be interpreted in another way. The first column is an approximation of the equivalent general sales tax that would impose the same burden on consumers. Thus a tax of 2.5 per cent (France) to 5.2 per cent (Ireland) would place a burden of the same order of magnitude as might the price provisions of the CAP by 1980. Alternatively (column 2) the same burden could be expressed as a tax on food consumption expenditure of between 8.5 per cent and 18.4 per cent depending on the member country. For Britain, these tax-equivalents are 2.7 and 10.9 per cent on general spending and on food respectively. The disparity indicates the selective impact which the CAP appears to have on Community consumers.

TABLE 6.12

Proportionate Costs and Benefits of Community Farm Policy: 1980

	Consumer cost		Producer benefit
Country	Percentage of consumer expenditure	Percentage of food expenditure	Percentage of income
United Kingdom	2.72	10.89	59.39
Ireland	5.18	18.37	69.24
Denmark	2.94	13.99	55.71
France	2.50	8.52	35.15
West Germany	3.10	11.15	64.63
Belgium–Lux	3.90	13.81	49.59
Italy	4.03	11.10	17.67
Netherlands	3.49	14.37	38.66

The disparity is even more marked in the case of benefits to farmers as a proportion of their income. This measure is approximately equivalent to the 'effective rate of protection' used by economists. Although it is unwise to draw too much from international comparisons of such effective rates, it does suggest that the CAP can act as a strong pull for resources to enter, or remain in, agriculture in countries where the support level is highest. The low figure for Italy (17.7 per cent) reflects the fact that specifically Mediterranean goods – such as olive oil, durum wheat, wine, and citrus fruits – are not included in the calculations, but the range between say, France (35.2 per cent) and Germany (64.6 per cent), is significant.

The analysis has enabled a separation of the two major forms of transfer among member countries arising from the full operation of the CAP at a time when world prices are below those guaranteed to Community farmers: the payment of higher prices for Community imports (and higher receipts for exports), and the gain or loss on the

FEOGA account with respect to third country trade. The total net gains and losses by country were given in the last column of Table 6.7: Table 6.13 shows the surpluses and deficits with FEOGA implied by the above calculations, and Table 6.14 gives the corresponding gains and losses arising from intra-Community trade flows. In the case of FEOGA payments, the largest (net) proportion accrues to France (£450m) followed by Ireland (£92m) and Denmark (£46m). Italy (£238m) and the United Kingdom (£116m) are calculated to have the highest deficit with FEOGA under these conditions. The same countries have the greatest interest in transfers through intra-European trade, with the United Kingdom losing slightly more than Italy. West Germany and Belgium-Luxemburg also lose both through the FEOGA and the European terms of trade for farm goods, although by a smaller amount: for the Netherlands, the policy has little net impact.

TABLE 6.13

Gains and Losses from FEOGA Receipts and Expenditure arising from CAP

Gains		Losses	
Country	£m	Country	£m
France	450	Italy	238
Ireland	92	United Kingdom	116
Denmark	46	West Germany	87
		Belgium–Lux	41
		Netherlands	4

TABLE 6.14

Gains and Losses from Increased Prices of Traded Agricultural Goods within Europe arising from CAP

Gains		Losses	
Country	£m	Country	£m
France	238	United Kingdom	164
Ireland	111	Italy	150
Denmark	46	West Germany	54
Netherlands	9	Belgium–Lux	36

What interpretation should one put on such results? First, it should be emphasised that they illustrate only one possible outcome in terms of price levels and production, and are subject to the qualification that policies can change rapidly. But they indicate orders of magnitude which are potentially important both in political and in strictly economic terms. The CAP has arisen as a set of responses to pressures to protect farmers from outside competition. In spite of modifications during the 1972–75 period of high world prices, these pressures still exist. The forces acting on the European Community's agricultural policy, however, are more complex than the traditional desire for 'remunerative' prices by those who are engaged in farming and for liberal access to the cheapest source of food for those whose only interest in agriculture is as consumers. Governments are aware of the way in which international policies have an impact on domestic objectives and the development of the CAP has effects on national economies unrelated to farm income or consumer price levels. It is in this context that the international transfers are significant. Unless or until payments, either direct or indirect, between member states of the Community become of no political significance, the income income transfer effects of the CAP will remain important.

NOTES AND REFERENCES

1. The instruments of the CAP are briefly described in Chapter 1, pp. 10–12.
2. See pp. 16 and 17 above.
3. T. E. Josling and Donna Hamway, 'Distribution of the Costs and Benefits of Farm Policy', in Josling *et al.*, *Burdens and Benefits of Farm-Support Policies*, Agricultural Trade Paper No. 1 (London: Trade Policy Research Centre, 1972) pp. 50–85.
4. The method employed in the study is described in an appendix to the initial report, *ibid.*, pp. 83–5.

    For a more detailed discussion of the problems of measurement of income distribution, the reader is referred to the contributions by James T. Bonnen, 'The Distribution of Benefits from Selected US Farm Programs', and Vernon C. McKee and Lee M. Day, 'Measuring the Effects of US Department of Agriculture Programs on Income Distribution', in the President's National Advisory Commission on Rural Poverty, *Rural Poverty in the United States*, Report (Washington: US Government Printing Office, 1968) pp. 461–505 and 506–21.

    More academic discussions can be found in Mary Jean Bowman, 'A Graphical Analysis of Personal Income Distribution in the United States', *American Economic Review*, New York, September 1956, and in James Morgan, 'The Anatomy of Income Distribution', *Review of Economics and Statistics*, Cambridge, Massachusetts, August 1962.
5. *Family Expenditure Survey*, Department of Employment, London, various issues.
6. For a full description of the Family Expenditure Survey, see W. F. F. Kemsley, *Family Expenditure Survey: Handbook of the Sample, Fieldwork and Coding Procedures*, Government Social Survey (London: HM Stationery Office, 1969).
7. Briefly, this policy was based on the liberal importation of agricultural products, subject to certain restrictions, and on an annual price review which determined 'guaranteed prices' to domestic farmers, who then re-

cieved 'deficiency payments' from the Exchequer that made up the difference between import prices and the higher guaranteed prices. The policy was thus designed to place the burden of support on taxpayers rather than on consumers. Food prices in the shops were thereby meant to stay in line with 'world prices'.

For a short analysis of the deficiency-payments system, compared with the import-levy system of the European Community, see Josling, *Agriculture and Britain's Trade Policy Dilemma*, Thames Essay No. 2 (London: Trade Policy Research Centre, 1970).

8. See, for example, Group of European Agricultural Economists, *Reform of the European Community's Common Agricultural Policy*, Wageningen Memorandum (London: Trade Policy Research Centre, 1973), reproduced in *European Review of Agricultural Economics*, Amsterdam, No. 1, 1973.

9. Josling, *Agriculture and Britain's Trade Policy Dilemma, op. cit.*

Appendix to Chapter 6

DATA ON FARM AND HOUSEHOLD INCOMES

Data used in the study for farm incomes and support payments is based on the Farm Management Surveys carried out in England and Wales, Scotland and Northern Ireland. It is not always possible to arrive at particular support figures from published sources. For example, in the Farm Management Survey, deficiency payments, except for cereals, are included in the total receipts for each commodity. For commodities where support figures are not recorded separately, it has been necessary to impute a value of payments from the relationship between deficiency payments and total receipts used for the United Kingdom. All estimates are restricted to identifiable items of direct Exchequer support. For example, they do not include the effect on returns of indirect support methods; such as the regulations of marketing boards (with the exception of the estimates of an implicit milk subsidy) or minimum import prices. Support which accrues to landlords in the form of grants has also been excluded.

Since income-support estimates for Scotland and Northern Ireland were received too late to be included in the first section of the study, the main emphasis has been on the distribution of farm incomes and support payments in England and Wales. A reliability check was carried out for the entire United Kingdom farm population by including support and income figures for Scotland and Northern Ireland. The results suggested that the distributions based on England and Wales were representative of the United Kingdom as a whole. The Farm Management Surveys cover approximately 2600 full-time farms in England and Wales. That is to say, the survey covers all types of farming, but is confined to farms providing a farmer with a full-time occupation. The main analysis is confined to the middle range of full-time farms (275–4177 standard man-days) since neither very large nor very small farms are adequately represented in the survey.

Farms are classified according to type of farming and size of business using a classification based on standard man-days.[a] A standard man-day represents eight hours of manual labour for an adult male, working under average conditions. In other words, by calculating the standard labour required for cropping and stocking individual farms, the standard man-day size classification reduces to a common unit of measurement for all farms in the country irrespective of enterprise type and acreage, the unit being based on average labour input.

It is possible to make some comparisons between the sample and farms in the country as a whole. The distribution of farms by enterprise type within the 275–4199 standard man-days covered in the sample appear to represent reasonably well the Census distribution of farms.[b] Comparing the distribution of the sample with the Census by size groups, the sample is found to contain somewhat more larger farms (1200–4199 standard man-days) and fewer small farms (275–955) than the actual farm population. The main deficiency among types of farming and enterprise size in the sample is an inadequate representation of pig and poultry farms.

TABLE 6.15

Comparison of 1969 British Producer Prices with Community Equivalents
(as used in the calculations for Tables 6.1 to 6.6 above)

	Unit	UK farm price 1969	Community equivalent	Percentage difference
Wheat	£ cwt	1.37	1.83	33.0
Barley	£ cwt	1.26	1.70	35.0
Oats	£ cwt	1.39	1.65	19.0
Fat cattle	£ live cwt	10.00	14.35	43.0
Fat sheep	p lb	17.6	20.10	14.0
Fat pigs	£ sc dwt	2.39	—	—
Milk (pool price)	p gall	16.35	19.5	19.3
Sugar beet	£ ton	6.83	7.19	5.3

The data related to household incomes, expenditure and taxes used in the report is collected by the Family Expenditure Survey. The survey covers a total sample of over 10,000 British households, including farm families, and has an average response rate of 70 per cent.[c] The main deficiency in the sample is a lower response rate among high-income households than would accurately represent the distribution of incomes in the country. There is also evidence to suggest that the data relating to high-income households may be less accurate than data for low-income groups.

The survey classifies households according to composition and to original income; that is, income before any taxes are paid to the government and before any state benefits are received. To simplify interpretation of the support-cost tables, some aggregation of income groups and family types has been done. The survey, in fact, classifies households within 17 different composition types and 27 ranges of income. Hence a random household can fall into one of 459 cells. Typically, there is not an even distribution of households among cells. Many cells are likely to be either empty or to contain less than 10 households. No result is published for cells containing less than 10 observations, since one unrepresentative family could seriously bias the results. While there are good reasons for not reporting figures for

TABLE 6.16

Comparison of 1969 British Average Consumer Prices with Community Equivalents (as used in the calculations for Tables 6.1 to 6.6 above)

	Unit	UK price (average 1969)	Community equivalent	Percentage difference
Beef and veal	p lb	32.8	42.2	29
Pork	p lb	27.1	27.1	—
Mutton and lamb	p lb	24.19	27.7	15
Bacon and ham	p lb	26.1	28.7	10
Liquid milk	p pt	4.5	5.2	17
Butter	p lb	17.0	47.5	179
Cheese	p lb	19.1	30.9	62
Flour	p lb	3.2	4.2	29
Bread	p lb	4.5	4.9	10
Cream	p pt	30.0	44.07	47

Source: Average retail prices in 1969 from National Food Survey in *Annual Expenditure by Households on Food*, Ministry of Agriculture (London, 1969). Community equivalents assume full cost increases are passed on to consumers.

these cells, the result is that estimates for non-pensioner households with very high or very low incomes are excluded.

In order to correct for this deficiency, two composite cells have been included.[d] One cell relates to the problem of child poverty. All families in the sample with original incomes under £559 a year and with two adults and one to four children have been amalgamated. The other composite cell relates to very high-income households. As mentioned earlier, families at the top end of the income scale are seriously under-represented in the sample. To correct for this, all households with original incomes over £5502 have been combined. Lastly, the term 'pensioner households' needs some explanation. The study follows the Central Statistical Office in defining a pensioner household as one which receives at least three-quarters of its income from state retirement or some similar pension.

NOTES AND REFERENCES

[a] A detailed description of the classification procedure used in the survey is given in *Farm Classification in England and Wales*, 1963 (London: Ministry of Agriculture, 1964). Also see *The Northern Ireland Farm Management Survey*, 1969–70, *Studies in Farm Economics* (Belfast: Northern Ireland Ministry of Agriculture, 1971) and *Farm Incomes in England and Wales*, (London: Ministry of Agriculture, various years), as well as *The Changing Structure of Agriculture* (London: HM Stationery Office, 1970).

[b] *The Changing Structure of Agriculture, op. cit.*

[c] For a full description of the Family Expenditure Survey, see W. F. F. Kems-

ley, *Family Expenditure Survey: Handbook of the Sample, Fieldwork and Coding Procedures*, Government Social Survey (London: HM Stationery Office, 1969).

[d] This follows the approach used in C. V. Brown, *Impact of Tax Changes on Income Distribution*, Broadsheet 525 (London: Political and Economic Planning, 1971).

Action at National and International Level

CHAPTER 7

Interrelationship of Agricultural and General Economic Policies

T. E. JOSLING

It has been fundamental to the objective of the studies reported in this volume that agricultural policy should be seen, not in isolation as a set of farm prices and marketing measures, but in the context of economic policy as a whole. Clearly, in any analysis of agricultural policy the effect on the output and income of the farm sector must be fully explored, as must the implications for food supplies and the consequent trade balance. Similarly the method of financing farm support has to be examined with its associated implications for income distribution. These were the topics of the empirical chapters in Part II. But a complete view requires the result of these investigations to be put in a wider perspective. In Part I, particularly in Chapter 1, a number of questions were raised regarding the place of agriculture in the political and economic decisions facing governments in the industrialised democracies. This chapter seeks to answer some of those questions from the standpoint of the United Kingdom. Since the solution to problems often requires international consultation and action, the discussion ranges over a wider field than specifically British concerns, so that the proposals in the concluding chapter in Part III should be of general interest.

It is useful to have a framework within which to consider the place of agricultural policy in economic strategy. Such a framework might be established by identifying the major objectives of economic policy and relating the performance of agricultural measures to those aims. But the picture is not complete unless general economic policy measures are also related to the objectives set for the agricultural sector. The remainder of this chapter deals with these two topics.

AGRICULTURAL POLICY AND GENERAL ECONOMIC OBJECTIVES

Agricultural policies have had varying importance in terms of economic management. At the time of the Great Depression, these policies assumed a role over and above that of supporting rural business; they were seen as part of general economic stabilisation policy. During World War II, farm policies ensured food supplies for military and civilian populations and later played a part in the economic strategy of post-war reconstruction. As affluence overtook Western Europe, and as traditional trading patterns in temperate foods were re-established, the profile of agricultural policies was reduced. Departments and ministries of agriculture ran these policies within increasingly severe budgetary constraints and the limitations often imposed by foreign policy. Outside rural areas, these policies had no strong political appeal, and they did not generally find a significant place in economic planning. As governments of different political shades came and went, agricultural policy was accorded a benign neglect.

This period of political atrophy lasted perhaps from the early 1950s to the late 1960s. It was broken by the increase in the rate of inflation in industrial countries which began about 1967. Agricultural matters started to be taken seriously again when the food-price explosion ended, for a time, agriculture's period in the political wilderness.

Economists interested in agricultural policy have in fact attempted to establish the link between this and the objectives of general economic policy. Studies have related the real income cost of market distortions resulting from farm programmes to the general standard of living.[1] The incidence of this cost is sometimes obscure and its measurement is imprecise: and such calculations have had little effect on policy formation. But the results suggest that few farm policy measures would be expected to change national income by any significant extent. Traditional farm policy instruments may look inefficient in relation to their achievements, but are not often important in terms of the absolute magnitude of the burden they place on the non-farm population.[2] Only at a regional level will farm policies tend to have a major impact on employment and income.

There is, however, a potentially important link between agricultural policies and economic growth, in particular through the contribution to growth of the release of farm labour to non-agricultural employment. Such labour mobility is itself largely a function of off-farm employment levels. As the productivity gain of migrants is probably slight in Britain, one would expect the direct influence of agricultural market policies on growth, through the improvement or otherwise of the allocation of labour, to be small. This observation does not negate the possibility of income gains from a removal of excessive protection, but it does suggest that there exists no pool of under-employed or low productivity labour in agriculture in the United Kingdom which can, over time, be released to provide a source of growth in the economy as a whole by manipulating agricultural policy.

Such structural growth occurs in an economy through the aspirations of, and the educational and employment opportunities open to, the individual. Agriculture, as a sector, has shown quite high rates of growth of labour productivity in recent years, even when adjusted for the over-valuation of much of the product. Indeed the actual rise in labour output per hour is probably higher still. But not only is it difficult to tie this down to policy. It is also not clear that this necessarily contributes significantly to the growth in incomes outside the farm sector. The argument occasionally put forward that, because agriculture has a good performance in increasing productivity it is an appropriate industry to subsidise, is rather tenuous; the converse case could also be made.

Stability of real incomes, and the avoidance of major recessions in the level of economic activity, are the province of general demand management policies. At one time it was held that agricultural incomes were causally related to the business cycle – depressions were 'farm-led and farm-fed'. It is doubtful whether under present conditions a recession in British agricultural earnings would have a significant effect on income and employment in general, although the regional effects might be severe. The extension of social security programmes in the United Kingdom to the rural population has itself tended to stabilise spending power. In this regard Britain is significantly ahead of many countries in Western Europe.

The distribution of income and the associated question of the distribution of gains in income from technical change have always been strong arguments in considering agricultural-support measures. As a competitive industry, and in particular one facing a price-inelastic demand for its output, agriculture is in a poor position to retain the income benefits from its own productivity gains.

A well functioning economic system has its own way of distributing productivity gains. The terms of trade would move against agriculture over time if relative demand expansion lagged behind relative productivity increases; and the benefit would be in terms of cheaper agricultural produce and more income to spend on other goods. The parity-price formula used in legislation in the United States was an attempt to arrest the deterioration in the terms of trade and translate agricultural productivity gains into farm income. The cost-recoupment mechanism used in the British annual price reviews made explicit the distribution of such income increases. But the superficial attractiveness of altering the distribution of potential income gains runs foul of the excessive cost of doing so over any prolonged period. Short of making the agricultural industry less competitive, it is not easy to see how consumers can be prevented from benefiting from improvements in farming efficiency.

The other aspect of income distribution that has had prominence has been the implications of different price-support techniques for the incidence of the 'burden' of farm programmes. Clearly families that spend a relatively high proportion of their incomes on food will tend to benefit from the raising of finance to pay for subsidies through the tax system, as against a system which transfers income through higher prices. Such direct payment systems are popular neither with the farm sector nor with finance ministers, and presumably, within the context of the taxation-expenditure system as a whole, the distribution effects can be offset by other measures. A change in system, such as that undertaken in the United Kingdom following the country's accession to the European Community, is bound to lead to opposition and calls for modifications in other items of social expenditure.[3] The whole question of the efficiency of transfers among producer and consumer groups by different mechanisms is basic to the choice of agricultural policy. Although such transfers clearly are a part of the objectives of farm policy, the definition of these objectives is not simple. The problem of defining policy objectives arises in a similar way when considering the efficiency of other programmes such as the policy, adopted by the Wilson Government in 1973, of giving a consumer subsidy on foods in the United Kingdom.

One of the most politically important aspects of farm policy is its effect on food prices and hence on inflation. The emergence of a set of measures to control agricultural exports and to limit domestic price increases was an important new development in agricultural policy. The facility with which governments turned farm price-support policies into instruments to control consumer costs was not only a comment on the flexibility of policy but a challenge to accepted notions about the politics of agricultural support. Despite considerable work on the farm or wholesale price implications of farm policy measures, there is, in general, rather inadequate information on the determination of retail food prices. For instance, retail price behaviour has not been linked with stock positions and with the futures market. It is not clear, in the light of events of the early 1970s, that there is a satisfactory concept of price determination in the world market for agricultural goods.

Turning from the internal to the external value of the currency, the political interest in agriculture as a means of either earning or saving foreign exchange has been periodically investigated. At one level such calculations are mere arithmetic, an extra quantity of output arising from a policy change being evaluated in terms of world prices. These calculations, although defining a change in an item in the balance of trade, do not in themselves give an indication of the impact on the balance of payments. To do this one needs to consider the origin of the balance of payments, the difference between the value of private sector expenditure and earnings, which is then offset by government action in foreign borrowing or lending, or by a change in the level of reserves.

Any change in the pattern of government expenditure – say an additional subsidy to producers of a particular good – will have a series of repercussions on income and on expenditure in the private sector. It is impossible to say *a priori* what will be the net effect, and so a first guess would be to predict a zero impact on the balance of payments no matter what happened to one item of the balance of trade. Those studies that have attempted such a calculation for the United Kingdom have in fact arrived at net figures close to, or a range including, zero. This is not to say that changes in foreign demand or supply of traded goods will not influence the balance of payments, but merely that domestic market intervention in agricultural products is likely to be a very inefficient alternative to conventional macro-adjustment policies.[4]

Few if any countries have a consistent agricultural trade policy in the sense of a set of definable objectives pursued over a period of time. Governments spend considerable diplomatic effort in attempting to modify the policies of other governments in order to complement their own domestic policies: in turn they must take into account the feelings of other countries when formulating their own policies. Through international institutions and negotiations they attempt to regulate condiions on the world market or within regional trading blocks. But the objectives are predominantly domestic – as one would expect. Awareness of this has generated frustration among those advocating a further development of liberal trading practices in agriculture along the lines of GATT principles.

The primacy of domestic motives is responsible, at an analytical level, for the conflict between the view that domestic problems should be dealt with by domestic means, such as producer subsidies, and the desire by many commentators to see the domestic farm-support policies replaced by tariff protection. If one starts from the proposition that tariffs are easier to negotiate away than is the mass of domestic farm legislation then this is a tactical recommendation. But if one allows a legitimate place for domestic agricultural policy objectives, then it is by no means clear that a pure 'GATT approach' is in fact desirable. What may be needed for negotiations is both a quantitative and a qualitative assessment of the externalities inherent in farm-support policies and an evaluation of the beneficial effects of collective action on certain problems of farm trade which are not easily dealt with at the national level.[5]

A further problem has to do with the stability of world markets. An adequate conceptual basis from which to approach this problem is not easy to find. International trade models generally postulate a competitive world market which clears, by adjustments to the quantity demanded or supplied, and settles at an equilibrium price. But until such models incorporate the production lags, the level of stocks, the

policy reactions of governments and the often very imperfect nature
of the market, both with respect to state trading and inter-governmental agreements and with respect to concentration and conflict of
interest among trading companies, they are unlikely to provide a satisfactory basis for analysis. And unless one can then incorporate the
benefits from stability one cannot make policy recommendations on
the degree of market control or freedom which is appropriate in any
situation. Although such work would involve a substantial agenda, it
is necessary if economic analysis is to be of value in resolving international problems of commodity trade.

The interface between domestic agricultural programmes and development policy has been explored mainly in the context of such
measures as 'Food for Peace' in the United States and the European
Community's 'association' agreements. The possible magnitude of the
effect of agricultural protection on developing country incomes is
assessed in an FAO study.[6] The impression given by this and other
studies is that for a limited number of commodities, direct or indirect
impediments to imports, or the indiscriminate subsidisation of exports,
can have damaging effects on the development of agricultural industries in the Third World – even though in the immediate term consumers in these countries may be favoured. As significant as the effect
on the farm sectors of these countries is the impact of high levels of
protection granted to food and other processing activities in developed
countries by hindering the establishment of industries in the developing world which would (i) provide useful employment and profitable
investment, (ii) give a more secure basis for the export trade and (iii)
encourage commerce among these countries themselves.[7] Again the
analysis of the potential benefits of this, and the link between such a
development and traditional trade and domestic policies, is incomplete.

Related to the problems of aid and market stability are those associated with the maintenance of adequate trading reserves. The problems in the grain market following the 1972/73 season, emphasised
that stock accumulation plays a part, not just in the price stabilisation
policies of developed countries and in emergency relief programmes
following natural or man-made disasters, but in the normal commercial trading problems of developing countries which have to ration
foreign exchange availability between imports of foodstuffs and raw
materials and those of capital equipment and investment goods. The
capacity of these countries to withstand commodity price fluctuations
may be limited. To the extent that the domestic price stabilisation and
trading policies of industrial countries can exacerbate the problems of
others, the performance of these policies must be evaluated. Domestic
price stability bought at the price of world instability may be unaccep-
table in an interdependent world.

GENERAL ECONOMIC POLICY AND THE AGRICULTURAL SECTOR

To complete the agenda suggested at the beginning of this chapter it is necessary to consider the effect of general economic policy measures on the farm sector in industrial countries. In one sense this topic raises issues outside the scope of a review of the state of farm policies. The measures to be considered are not decided by the same bureaucracy. Nor are they subject to the same political or commercial influences as those directly operating in agricultural markets. Nevertheless, agricultural policies do operate within a context of general economic policy; sometimes in conflict, and sometimes in cooperation, with these measures. Assessment of the performance of agricultural programmes cannot proceed in ignorance of the interactions among policies. Moreover, non-agricultural policies may, by their nature, be of as great or greater significance to the agricultural sector as more strictly agricultural measures. In this event not only is it important to be able to estimate the impact of other policies so as to be able to evaluate the contribution of farm programmes, but it is also necessary to be able to measure relative performance, in order to be sure that one is not neglecting potentially more efficient instruments for solving a certain problem.

All developed-country governments have accepted responsibility for maintaining a balance, by the use of economic policy, between the availability of resources and their apparent demand; and, in particular, between the demand for and supply of domestic labour and, too, between the aggregate demand for goods and services and the available purchasing power of the population. This twin goal of maintaining full employment and domestic price stability is pursued by a variety of demand management instruments of a short-term nature, by certain structural controls and by a relatively few longer-term policies aimed at (i) stimulating the availability of goods, (ii) improving the quality of labour and (iii) developing the potential of the non-labour resource endowment of the country concerned. As consumers and taxpayers, the farm sector is influenced by these policies much as the rest of the economy; as producers of agricultural goods in a competitive industry dominated by small firms, the effect may be of special interest. From the demand side, changes in money income arising from joint policies may have less impact on agriculture than on producers of goods and services more sensitive to such variations. Although it is usual to conceive of demand reacting to real income fluctuations, there is little doubt that inflation also influences spending patterns and that expansionary, or contradictionary, policy is far from neutral as between goods. Such changes are not likely to be noticeable in staple commodities, but could be of importance in products with high income elasticities.

Of more significance are two effects of macro-economic policy. First, the budgetary constraint associated with a tight fiscal policy may be significant in imposing limits on the spending on farm programmes, at times even leading to a change in farm-support systems. Second, the overall monetary policy of the country could influence farm investment, asset prices, the cost of stockholding, the alternative use of equity capital and the availability of merchants' credit. Despite the work in recent years on agricultural credit, the overall effect of monetary policy is rarely taken into account.

The influence of the rate of inflation itself on agriculture is likely to be complex. Farmers buy goods from the non-farm sector, which is itself going to be affected by inflation and in particular by wage and other industrial costs, so that farmers may have to sell assets in order to maintain consumption standards. Farmers who are net borrowers from outside sources will presumably benefit from the low rates of real interest usually associated with rapid inflation, but farm product prices may tend to lag behind other prices in the economy, except where market imbalances cause temporary shifts in the terms of trade in favour of agriculture. The impact of employment policies is somewhat clearer. High levels of employment are likely to accelerate the exodus of labour from agriculture and, as importantly, moderate the inflow of people into the farm sector in rural areas.[8] The ready availability of off-farm jobs may even lead to an improvement of farm incomes in relation to the earnings of those who work in comparable occupations in the non-farm sector.[9]

A more recent aspect of economic management is the experimentation with price and incomes policies, involving an extension of government involvement with the formation of prices and the determination of wage levels. On the one hand, the common decision of governments has been to avoid where possible the incorporation of agricultural markets within this structure, on the general pretext that farm prices are so strongly influenced by world market conditions that control would be ineffective – a reaction which has had to be modified by the political belief that control of food prices is essential both for the acceptance of other parts of the policy and for their effectiveness. On the other hand, it has been realised that in the existing farm programmes there was already the mechanism of an existing price and incomes policy of the kind adopted for other sectors, and also that within these programmes there was the potential for reducing or holding price levels in spite of world market trends. Hence the rehabilitation of farm policies as measures of general economic regulation in the 1970s.

Of the various structural policies pursued by governments, a few can be singled out as having specific relevance to agriculture. The structure of taxation on income, on property, on capital gains, on intergenerational transfers, on employment, on business profits and on sales, all potentially influence the farming sector.[10] The impact at the farm level of taxation systems has been analysed in some countries, as has the influence of concessionary taxation schemes on land prices. The general impression is of a historical situation of discrimination in favour of agriculture in the taxation structure, offset by discrimination against the rural sector in the provision of personal social security benefits, pensions and general public services, with a trend towards the reversal of both imbalances in the 1970s. But the net effect of the taxation and expenditure structure on the rural sector has rarely been quantified, and hence the place of farm-income programmes in offsetting any imbalance must remain in the realm of opinion.

Other structural policies which affect agriculture are: (i) competition policy, which will regulate the market structure in which agricultural producers buy and sell and, at times, constrain the ability of farmers and farm groups to establish market power for themselves; (ii) regional policy, which may be of particular importance in influencing the pace and pattern of the development of non-farm industries in rural areas; (iii) housing policy, defining in many cases the land use of particular areas and enhancing the capital valuation of farms, both in the affected area and in those areas not designated for property development; and (iv) environmental policy, placing restrictions on farm business and on land use patterns which may or may not be compensated for the individual by the society at large. Conflicts arise in all these areas with agricultural policy, and the outcome often depends on the social priorities of particular governments. These conflicts are the focus of an expanding body of work on rural development, land use and regional problems.[11]

The interaction between foreign economic policy and agriculture is closely related to that mentioned earlier between agricultural policy and foreign policy objectives. As agricultural-support policies influence the diplomatic positions of countries in contact with other nations, so those positions, framed with other objectives in mind, have repercussions for agriculture.[12] And just as agricultural trade can influence a country's foreign balance and exchange rate, so exchange rate policies react on the agricultural sector and may lead to modifications in farm programmes. A country's aid policies will in turn affect domestic farm incomes in the same way that farm policies can conflict with or support overseas aid objectives. There is little evidence that agriculture is at a disadvantage in the conflicts that arise with foreign economic policy. The agricultural sector has, in general, a preference for low industrial tariffs and this position is consistent with the trend of postwar government policy, if not always with the interests of manufacturers themselves, and with organised labour. Regional integration in Western Europe, with an emphasis on enlarging a protected market, is consistent with the interests of agricultural export sectors within the European Community, but not with those excluded; the mechanism for reaching agreement on the pace and method of integration has allowed import-competing interests to withstand the loss of protection that preferential trade implies. But the implications of a common price policy, involving uniform external protection combined with free movement of goods internally, were not acceptable in the European Community when currency changes in the late 1960s forced a return to national prices and an elaborate network of border tax adjustments.[13]

NOTES AND REFERENCES

1. Empirical studies on the costs of various protective measures are numerous. See, for example, P. R. Johnson, 'The Social Cost of the Tobacco Program', *Journal of Farm Economics*, May 1966; and R. Dardis and E. W. Learn, 'Measures of the Degree and Cost of Economic Protection of Agriculture in Selected Countries', ERS Bulletin No. 1384 (Washington: US Department of Agriculture, 1967).

2. At a regional level farm policies can have a major impact on employment and income. But the regionalisation of economic objectives is itself problematic. Governments are not quite at the stage of guaranteeing adequate incomes and employment to people in whatever region of the country they wish to live.

3. This problem has arisen in particular in connection with the adoption by the United Kingdom of the European Community's common agricultural policy. See T. E. Josling and Donna Hamway, 'Distribution of Costs and Benefits of Farm Policy', in Josling *et al.*, *Burdens and Benefits of Farm Support Policies*, Agricultural Trade Paper No. 1 (London: Trade Policy Research Centre, 1972) for an attempt at a quantification of the consequences, briefly reported on in Chapter 6 above.

4. The problems of measurement are discussed in Josling, 'Agriculture and Import Saving: Cautionary Note', in Asher Winegarten and Josling, *Agriculture and Import Saving*, Occasional Paper No. 5 (London: Hill Samuel, 1970). A particularly interesting attempt to extend the analysis to include the foreign 'retaliation' effect of import substitution is given in Truman Phillips and Christopher Ritson, 'Reciprocity in International Trade', *Journal of Agricultural Economics*, Manchester, September 1970.

5. These questions are discussed further in *Agricultural Protection, Domestic Policy and International Trade*, International Agricultural Adjustment, Supporting Study No. 9 (Rome: Food and Agriculture Organization, 1974), and some possible approaches are suggested. The starting point is to express the impact of each policy measure in terms of a 'consumer tax equivalent' and a 'producer subsidy equivalent', which are then related to trade volume and terms of trade effects to arrive at a 'tariff equivalent'. An example of a qualitative externality measure is the ratio of tariff equivalent to producer subsidy – the extent to which the domestic subsidy has a corresponding trade restrictive element. A quantitative measure is, for example,

the absolute size of the reduction in foreign exchange earnings of other countries arising from these domestic policies. Examples for various North American and West European countries show, for instance, that whereas the 'quality' of European policies is more trade-restrictive, in 'quantity' terms American support levels have a more significant impact on trade.

6. The study was done as an adjunct to commodity projections in an attempt to incorporate price movements to reconcile extrapolations of consumption and production. See *A World Price Equilibrium Model*, Agricultural Commodity Projections Working Paper No. 3 (Rome: Food and Agriculture Organization, 1971).

7. For a discussion of the implications of European policy for developing countries, see Marsh, F. Ellis and Ritson, *Farmers and Foreigners* (London: Overseas Development Institute, 1973). American policy in this regard is discussed in D. Gale Johnson, 'Agricultural and Foreign Economic Policy', *Journal of Farm Economics*, December 1964, and Harry G. Johnson, *Economic Policies Toward Less Developed Countries* (Washington: Brookings Institution, 1967).

8. In a British context see K. Cowling and David Metcalf, 'Labour Transfer from Agriculture: a Regional Analysis', *The Manchester School*, Manchester, No. 1, 1968; and for one of a number of American studies, see Dale E. Hathaway and B. B. Perkins, 'Farm Labor Mobility, Migration and Income Distribution', *American Journal of Agricultural Economics*, May 1968.

9. This is documented in an interesting study by Dennis Lucey and D. Kaldor, *Rural Industrialization: the Impact of Industrialization on two Rural Communities in Western Ireland* (London: Chapman, 1969). In Western Ireland it was shown that agricultural output actually increased when farmers took part-time jobs in manufacturing industries. Though the improvement in the balance of a farm implied by the application of more capital and less labour on the same land area may be an important effect of rural non-farm employment programmes, it is not yet clear whether this is a transitional stage in the reduction of the farm population or a stable social system in itself. Do the sons of part-time farmers themselves become part-time farmers?

10. See, for instance, the study on the impact of tax structure on British farming by A. Evans, 'The Impact of Taxation on Agriculture', *Journal of Agricultural Economics*, May 1969.

11. Many of these studies are reported in the survey article by G. Peters, 'Land Use Studies in Britain: a Review', *Journal of Agricultural Economics*, May 1970.

12. Perhaps the clearest example of agricultural programmes following from other commercial and political objectives is the adoption by the United Kingdom of the regulations of the European Community's common agricultural policy. The dual role of the CAP as both an agricultural policy and a European integration device is emphasised in the Wageningen memorandum: Group of European Agricultural Economists, *Reform of the European Community's Common Agricultural Policy*, Wageningen Memorandum (London and Wageningen: Trade Policy Research Centre and the Agricultural University of Wageningen, 1973).

13. The problems of monetary union and its effect on common prices is discussed in Graham Hallet, 'The Problem of Agriculture in a European Economic Union', *Journal of Agricultural Economics*, September 1970; and Josling, 'Exchange Rate Flexibility and the Common Agricultural Policy', *Weltwirtschaftliches Archiv*, Kiel, Vol. 104, No. 1, 1970.

CHAPTER 8

Strategy for the Liberalisation of Agricultural Trade

HUGH CORBET and JANE NIALL

Because farm-support policies have existed for so long, and exert such a major influence in the economies where they operate, as reviewed in the previous chapter, it is difficult if not impossible to isolate their effects on the production of, and trade in, temperate-zone agricultural commodities. To discuss in detail the pattern and volume of production and trade in the absence of farm-support policies would be to enter the realm of speculation. Even so, the position can be discussed in general terms with a fair degree of confidence, complicated as it is from time to time by periods of glut (as in the late 1960s) and shortage (as in the mid-1970s). Any assessment of the impact of farm-support policies depends to some extent, as discussed in Chapter 1, on the view taken of future trends in agricultural supplies and prices, but the situation in the second half of the 1960s might be taken as a frame of reference.

EFFECT OF SUPPORT ON OUTPUT AND TRADE

One approach could be to consider a specific commodity in a specific country and calculate what the effect would be (i) on consumption, (ii) on production and hence (iii) on the balance of trade if the price of that commodity was at a 'world' level rather than at a supported level. The answers for, say, wheat in the European Community during the 1960s, where its price was about twice the world level, would probably have been a substantial increase in consumption and a significant reduction in production with an increase in imports (or a decrease in exports). In the mid-1970s, a similar situation arose in the case of meat, with high prices inside the Community and a glut outside.

Aggregating such analyses across the whole range of commodities to obtain an idea of the effect of farm-support policies leaves a great deal to be desired. Certain realities cannot be ignored. After all, the changes in consumption, production and trade that would result from the elimination, or substantial reduction, of farm-support measures

221

would affect the level of 'world' prices themselves. Second, different commodities are often produced from the same productive resources – root crops and cereals. Third, some commodities are used as inputs in the production of other commodities, such as feed-grains for live-stock. Finally, farm-support measures are sometimes introduced in one country to counteract farm-support measures introduced in another;[1] indeed, such defensive actions have contributed to the escalation of farm-support measures over recent years.

If the commodity-by-commodity approach is subject to serious qualifications, still more so is any attempt to draw general conclusions from the long-run pattern of international trade. Trade in agricultural commodities produced by developed countries has increased more slowly over the longer term than has trade in other goods. But this is not necessarily an accurate indication of the trade effects of agricultural protection.

It can be easily demonstrated that high levels of farm support are maintained in most industrialised countries. In particular, producers of cereals, dairy products, meats and sugar have been heavily protected. Imports of these commodities have consequently become more and more marginal in relation to domestic production and consumption. Before discussing how international trade might be liberalised, which is the purpose of this chapter, an effort should be made to put farm-support policies in some overall perspective.

Measurements of Protection
The problems of measuring levels of protection have been thoroughly explored[2] and several methods have been developed. The choice of method depends on the purpose of the exercise, or whether it is domestic or international comparisons that are required; and the availability of data also affects the choice. Any measurement of the protective effect of a farm-support policy or programme should take into account its efficiency and the distribution of costs. But a quantitative evaluation of success in achieving policy objectives is not often possible, because supply and demand data on the reaction, for example, of producers to increased profitability, or on the effects of a policy-induced change in price on consumption, are not usually available.

For most temperate-zone agricultural products, the main instruments of protection are of a non-tariff character, which means that quoting tariffs alone gives a very false idea of the actual level of protection. Methods have therefore been devised for taking into account non-tariff instruments of protection in order to obtain an 'equivalent nominal tariff'. Adjustment of this rate to allow for changes in input costs attributable to a policy produces a rate described as the 'adjusted nominal tariff'.[3]

The adjusted nominal tariff is perhaps the most useful measure for the agricultural sector, (i) because it is comparatively easy to calculate[4] and (ii) because, not being dependent on structural characteristics, it is appropriate for the purposes of international comparisons. In this last respect, the 'effective tariff' (as opposed to the nominal tariff), measuring the level of protection of value added in a given industry, is not appropriate. Because the measurement of effective protection is dependent on the structural characteristics of the industry in question and, in the case of the farming sector, on the proportion of non-farm inputs in total costs, it is more appropriate for inter-industry comparisons *within* an economy.

Policies act either as a cost or a benefit to producers and either as a subsidy or a tax on consumers. An import duty, for instance, protects domestic producers by raising the domestic price to domestic consumers. On the other hand, a direct subsidy to producers will raise the price they receive for their product, but will not directly affect the price paid by consumers. The effects on producers can be quantified in terms of a 'producer subsidy equivalent' (PSE): the estimated tariff that would be necessary to maintain the revenue received by producers if existing policies were to be replaced by a simple *ad valorem* duty. A similar measure, the 'consumer subsidy equivalent' (CSE), can be calculated to indicate the effects on consumers. In Tables 8.1 and 8.2 the producer subsidy equivalents and consumer subsidy equivalents for six agricultural commodities are shown for six countries. (Notes at the foot of each table briefly explain how the figures are calculated.)

The more governments resort to farm-support measures, the more they deny domestic consumers the benefits of comparative advantage, lower costs, that foreign competitors can provide. The effect is a lowering of real incomes which shows up partly in the use of more resources than necessary to produce a given volume of food and agricultural raw materials. More generally, these costs (lower real incomes) are reflected in higher relative prices or, maybe, in budgetary subventions.

Table 8.3 shows the low level of inputs of fertiliser and machinery, here exemplified by tractors, employed in agricultural production in North America and Australasia. In spite of generally better yields obtained by more intensive farming methods employed in Western Europe and Japan, the high level of inputs combined with the small size of farms accounts, in large part, for the farm income problems which give rise to farm-support measures.

The consumer subsidy equivalents in Table 8.2 indicate the extent to which consumer prices have been affected by policies during the period 1968–74. A negative figure shows that prices were higher than they would have been in the absence of farm-support measures. For

TABLE 8.1
Producer Subsidy Values

	Average annual output 1968–74 (m tonnes)	Producer subsidy ($US per tonne)						
		1968	1969	1970	1971	1972	1973	1974
Wheat								
Australia	9.6	15.23	6.55	6.65	9.43	11.00	8.86	−17.48
Canada	15.0	4.24	5.64	10.44	10.25	8.55	2.41	2.35
European Community (Six)	21.5	32.98	38.76	38.56	41.06	26.85	−55.98	−42.08[a]
Japan	0.5	62.55	67.28	74.64	88.91	110.28	112.92	291.31
United Kingdom	4.5	16.80	16.73	13.54	22.36	15.27	2.35	−23.92
United States	43.0	18.39	27.53	31.83	24.78	35.20	10.66	0.19
Barley								
Australia	1.9	12.60	9.59	7.38	5.79	4.70	−1.38	−11.62
Canada	9.6	3.94	4.16	10.09	7.84	3.89	4.03	4.16
European Community (Six)	16.7	33.13	44.45	28.83	44.34	26.30	−1.57	−16.59
Japan	—	—	—	—	—	—	—	—
United Kingdom	8.6	49.42	18.68	9.44	9.88	8.11	4.22	1.80
United States	8.9	0.34	5.65	5.97	0.81	12.39	8.45	—
Maize								
Australia	—	—	—	—	—	—	—	—
Canada	2.5	3.10	2.93	2.99	3.14	3.19	3.10	2.93
European Community (Six)	13.1	44.44	37.80	28.14	41.70	34.56	6.24	1.01
Japan	—	—	—	—	—	—	—	—
United Kingdom	—	—	—	—	—	—	—	—
United States	125.5	10.96	12.19	12.23	6.42	10.79	6.80	0.65

Sugar

Australia	21.24	25.80	34.16	22.62	14.72	10.58	8.44	3.16
Canada	0.9	6.70	3.25	1.88	0.89	0.71	0.78	0.87
European Community (Six)	53.3[b]	29.11	26.48	25.83	26.33	22.62	22.56	−40.62
Japan	0.6	49.40	45.65	34.67	24.92	47.07	32.12	32.12
United Kingdom	6.5	25.96	53.60	67.68	81.26	143.36	24.27	26.73
United States	46.4	127.81	102.57	100.55	93.00	42.12	19.81	−31.06

Dairy Products[c]

Australia	7.1	29.06	29.06	27.74	33.12	34.79	39.04	44.19
Canada	8.1	79.35	77.75	81.69	85.30	85.90	99.62	99.62[a]
European Community (Six)	74.6	64.5	67.7	58.4	30.7	33.0	47.6	—
Japan	4.7	30.82	35.94	35.77	29.99	31.65	40.29	—
United Kingdom	13.5	44.00	44.41	47.43	42.37	30.52	31.24	29.77
United States	53.4	61.24	72.33	76.73	58.23	37.34	67.92	99.50

Source: *Agricultural Protection and Stabilization Policies: A Framework of Measurement in the Context of Agricultural Adjustment*, C75/LIM/2 (Rome: FAO, 1975) pp. A.10–A.69.

Note: To arrive at each estimate of Producer Subsidy Value –

1. The value of the year's production of the commodity to the producer was calculated, usually by multiplying the volume of production by the producer price. Where the producer price did not include certain direct payments made by the government to producers the total direct payments were added to Producer Value to obtain Total Producer Value.

2. All the policies affecting the producer were listed and the Producer Subsidy Value attributable to each indicated. This figure could be positive or negative depending on whether the policy benefited or imposed a tax on producers.

3. The sum of these amounts was then expressed per tonne produced. For ease of comparison this is expressed in terms of US dollars.

[a] Estimates
[b] Production of sugar beet
[c] Average annual output includes butter, cheese and skimmed milk powder expressed in terms of their milk equivalent.

TABLE 8.2

Consumer Subsidy Values

	Average annual consumption 1968–74 (m tonnes)	Consumer Subsidy ($US per tonne)						
		1968	1969	1970	1971	1972	1973	1974
Wheat								
Australia	2.8	-12.49	-16.80	-11.01	-11.50	-13.70	-9.06	57.59
Canada	4.7	-4.92	-7.37	-5.98	-23.20	-20.87	-7.03	-5.82
European Community (Six)	26.2	-34.01	-41.19	-40.59	-43.18[a]	28.13[a]	55.98	42.08[a]
Japan	5.1	-21.06	-23.07	-22.15	-27.12	-29.57	18.96	94.57
United Kingdom	8.4	—	—	—	-1.11	-5.28	-6.69	-22.86
United States	21.0	-17.89	-21.60	-24.64	-19.11	-30.87	1.91	2.36
Barley								
Australia	1.1	-14.43	-12.75	-12.50	-11.08	-12.17	2.34	17.44
Canada	6.6	-3.17	-3.16	-3.27	-3.37	-3.45	-3.38	-3.45[a]
European Community (Six)	15.6	-33.10	-44.38	-28.80	-44.27	-26.28	1.58	16.60
Japan	—	—	—	—	—	—	—	—
United Kingdom	9.0	—	—	—	—	—	-0.46	-0.89
United States	—	—	—	—	—	—	—	—
Maize								
Australia	—	—	—	—	—	—	—	—
Canada	3.3	-2.95	-2.93	-3.08	-3.20	-3.12	-3.04	-3.16
European Community (Six)	20.4	-44.44	-37.80	-28.14	-41.70	-34.58	-6.24	-1.01
Japan	—	—	—	—	—	—	—	—
United Kingdom	3.0	—	—	—	-2.33	-5.30	-0.47	-0.88
United States	108.7	0.05	0.05	0.12	1.37	0.05	0.04	0.05

Sugar

Australia	0.73	−89.24	−92.13	−64.31	−45.32	−36.02	−19.38	−2.07
Canada	1.08	−4.37	−4.76	−5.00	−4.98	−5.16	−5.28	−5.38
European Community (Six)	6.6	−215.82	−176.63	−173.38	−164.20	−155.77	−159.51	296.40
Japan	3.1	−7.6	—	8.45	12.54	12.12	12.12	
United Kingdom	2.7	−89.46	−75.79	−51.22	−61.92	−5.82	−8.68	26.98
United States	9.6	−132.84	−100.40	−103.64	−95.09	−40.97	−15.40	21.93

Dairy Products

Australia	4.8	−33.23	−34.43	−34.69	−36.10	−38.00	−46.41	−63.30
Canada	8.3	−50.83	−52.04	−56.23	−51.96	−52.16	−49.14	−58.72
European Community (Six)	71.3	−65.4	−67.7	−68.4	−30.7	−28.9	−40.9	−38.2[a]
Japan	4.8	−25.66	−31.22	−30.31	−23.25	−23.81	−29.85	—
United Kingdom	20.7	−19.80	−19.20	−20.41	−21.70	−12.33	−3.07	25.33
United States	53.4	−21.77	−25.13	−26.94	−20.78	−11.91	−26.25	−29.94

Source: *Agricultural Protection and Stabilization Policies: A Framework of Measurement in the Context of Agricultural Adjustment*, C75/LIM/2 (Rome: FAO, November 1975) pp. A.10–A.69.

Note: To obtain estimates of Consumer Subsidy Value –

1. Using the volume of consumption and an appropriate wholesale price for the commodity the consumer value was calculated. Where the wholesale price did not include a particular policy-induced expense to the consumer this was added to arrive at the Total Consumer Value.

2. All policies affecting consumers were listed with the extent to which they acted as subsidies or taxes. These were then added to arrive at the total Consumer Subsidy Equivalent.

3. The total Consumer Subsidy Equivalent was divided by the volume of consumption and the result expressed in terms of US dollars is shown here for ease of comparison.

[a] Estimated

TABLE 8.3

Average Farm Size, Fertiliser and Tractor Use, Milk and Cereal Yields for selected countries

	Average farm size 1970 (ha)	1973 Fertiliser Use		Arable land[h] per tractor 1973[jk] (ha)	Average Yields 1974	
		per 100 ha farm land (tonnes)	per cent nitrogen (%)		Milk per 1000 cows (Kg/year)	Cereal yield (Kg/ha)
European Community						
Belgium	8.4	33.9	31.5	9.0	3669	4608
Denmark	16[b]	25.0	49.6	14.9	4042	4190
France	22.1	16.6[j]	31.5	14.1	2945	4196
West Germany	9[a]	14.9	34.6	5.7	3945	3884
Ireland	na	na	25.9	12.3	2448	3626
Italy	7.0	5.6	47.5	21.5	2688	3208
Luxembourg	17.8	22.2[j]	46.7	8.0[m]	3620	3185
Netherlands	11.8	28.8	64.2	4.9[m]	4500	5041
United Kingdom	55.1	10.3	47.2	15.9	4162	4338
Other Western Europe						
Austria	20[a]	2.0	85.7	5.8[m]	3043	4070
Norway	18[b]	2.4	41.1	7.9[m]	4441	3875
Portugal	6.2[c]	5.0[ij]	57.3	112.5	2423	1130
Sweden	18.7[d]	18.7[n]	46.3	17.9[m]	4105	4223
Switzerland	8.7[e]	11.5	28.4	4.9[m]	3686	4372
North America						
Canada	188[d]	1.7[j]	42.1	71.0	3639	1719
United States	158[e]	4.1[j]	47.3	45.8	4666	2975
Pacific						
Australia	1993	0.3	12.1	144	2749	1339
Japan	1.0	42.7[j]	35.7	18.7	4048	5576
New Zealand	303[c]	3.4[j]	4.9	9.8[m]	2661	3833

Sources: *Production Yearbook 1974* (Rome: FAO, 1975); *New Zealand Official Yearbook 1974* (Wellington: Department of Statistics, 1974).
[a] 1960; [b] 1959; [c] 1968; [d] 1971; [e] 1969; [f] 1972; [g] excluding holdings without land; [h] including land under permanent crops; [i] arable land includes 800,302 ha of temporary crops in association with permanent crops and forests; [j] estimated; [k] wheel tractors developing more than 8 horsepower with 3–4 wheels; [m] includes crawler tractors; [n] arable land.

most of the products considered, the extent to which prices were raised decreased over the period; and in 1974 sugar prices in four of the six countries were actually lower as a result of farm-support policies. Consumers in the European Community were subsidised in respect of wheat during 1972, 1973 and 1974 and in respect of barley during 1974, although when world prices for wheat and barley were low there was a heavy tax on consumers.

Attempts have been made to quantify the overall effects of farm-support policies. One noted authority, D. Gale Johnson, of the University of Chicago, put the world cost of protection at the border plus domestic price supports and subsidies, prior to the dramatic turn-around in world markets of 1972–3, in the region of $40,000m a year.[5] International bodies such as the Food and Agriculture Organisation (FAO), a United Nations agency, have obtained even higher estimates. Although numbers vary, it is clear, after all the necessary qualifications, that the costs of agricultural protection are very high. According to Professor Johnson, and others, the consumer-plus-taxpayer costs of farm-support policies in the late 1960s were around $13,000m a year in the European Community and around $10,000m a year in the United States.[6] Reverting to the earlier calculations of subsidy equivalents, the estimated total producer and consumer subsidy values for wheat, barley, maize, rice, sugar and dairy products in the six countries under consideration are shown in Table 8.4 below. The estimated producer subsidy value in 1968 for this fraction of world production was $20,000m falling to $13,000m in 1974.[7] All these figures are indicative. But they suggest a major impact on production and trade in general and, in particular, on Atlantic trade in agricultural products.

The impact of farm-support measures on the incomes of producers and the impact on consumers of higher food prices can be combined to give an indication of the trade displacement effects. Cost reduction, direct price support and general market protection are included in the calculation of producer subsidy equivalents, while direct consumption measures and general market protection are included in consumer subsidy equivalent. When quantitative restrictions on production and consumption have been taken into account, the modified figures could be used to analyse the implications for trade of different policy measures, providing a basis on which international negotiations could be conducted.

Effects of Trade Liberalisation

Different forms of farm support have different effects on production. In the United States and some other countries, efforts have been made to reduce the effects on production and trade of farm-support policies, using various means – including supply-management measures. American agriculture has been gradually oriented, since the mid-1960s,

TABLE 8.4
Estimated Total Producer and Consumer Subsidy Values, by Countries

	1968	1969	1970	1971	1972	1973	1974
				US $m			
Total producer subsidy values[a]							
Australia	394	391	349	368	386	356	79
Canada	774	809	872	951	865	857	845
European Community (Six)	8,374	8,706	7,355	6,231	5,590	3,193	−559
Japan	4,002	4,278	4,988	4,828	6,316	8,711	6,804
United Kingdom	749	798	798	853	722	530	317
United States	5,969	6,926	7,069	5,702	5,433	5,281	5,155
Total	20,262	21,908	21,431	18,933	19,312	18,928	12,641
Total consumer subsidy values[b]							
Australia	−262	−280	−254	−258	−265	−270	−27
Canada	−462	−490	−513	−579	−574	−500	−570
European Community (Six)	−8,200	−8,582	−7,253	−5,907	−5,127	−2,607	846
Japan	−2,509	−2,775	−3,217	−3,880	−4,672	−5,454	−2,628
United Kingdom	−638	−608	−561	−639	−342	−144	375
United States	−2,770	−2,752	−2,957	−2,340	−1,717	−1,536	−1,325
Total	−14,841	−15,487	−14,754	−13,603	−12,697	−10,511	−3,329

Source: *Agricultural Protection and Stabilization Policies: a Framework of Measurement in the Context of Agricultural Adjustment*, C75/LIM/2 (Rome: FAO, 1975) p. 29.

[a] Total producer subsidy values are the notional instantaneous loss of producer revenue if the policies considered were to be removed.

[b] Total consumer subsidy values as derived in are the notional instantaneous gain to consumers if the policies considered were to be removed.

towards international markets. In the European Community, however, the effects of farm-support measures are continuing and can be expected to increase, particularly on commodities covered by the common agricultural policy. An analysis of the effects of the Community's enlargement on international agricultural trade is shown in the Appendix at the end of this volume. Self-sufficiency ratios increased in the original Six after the adoption of the common agricultural policy and this is likely to happen in the countries which joined in 1973. Some of the impact of the Community's enlargement will be trade-diverting. But much of it will simply restrict trade still more.

International discussion continues, though in less high-pitched tones, on the effects of the European Community's farm-support measures on the exports of the United States, with both sides of the Atlantic having substance in their arguments. Trade has declined substantially in the products covered by the common agricultural policy such as cereals and poultry-meat. But in products not covered by the policy, such as soya beans, trade has continued to expand. There can be little doubt, however, that in the absence of government intervention there would be a significantly higher volume of trade.

In the Flanigan Report, submitted to President Nixon in 1972, there is an estimate of the effects on trade between the United States and the European Community of removing trade-distorting measures. It suggests that American exports of agricultural commodities would increase by 1980 (by some $9000m) to about twice the level that would be achieved without trade liberalisation. American production and exports of grains, soya beans and meat would benefit substantially. Imports from the European Community, particularly of dairy products, would similarly increase although the magnitude of the increase would be considerably less.[8]

Estimates such as these should not be regarded as predictions of what will happen if a particular course of action is taken. They are only meant to indicate the relative effects of alternative courses of action and care has to be taken over the use to which they are put in formulating policy. Three points might be noted: (i) Any such analysis must cope with an extensive range of assumed prices. When one price in a system is changed it usually precipitates a sequence of changes in other prices. These relative price changes are difficult to determine. (ii) The postulated changes in production and trade may be large enough to affect the balance-of-payments position of the countries concerned. As a result, some changes in rates of exchange might occur, thereby limiting the effects of trade liberalisation. (iii) By maintaining excessive resources in agriculture, industrialised countries have reduced their real incomes, but there is a limit to the speed at which adjustments can be made in the agricultural sector. In both the United States and the European Community the labour force on the land dropped by over half between 1950 and 1970. It is not clear by how much the decline could have been accelerated. For the opportunity cost of farm labour tends to be very low.

Nevertheless, it is difficult to deny the basic proposition – supported, as discussed in Chapter 1, by the Haberler Report in 1958, and by later studies under the auspices of the General Agreement on Tariffs and Trade (GATT)[9] – that moderate changes in farm-support levels would substantially increase trade in temperate-zone agricultural commodities. And the benefits would not be limited to agricultural trade. Reciprocal trade – in manufactured goods – could be expected to benefit.

STRATEGY FOR COMMERCIAL NEGOTIATIONS

In spite of the Haberler Report's conclusions, the rising trend of protection continued through the 1960s, culminating in the 'world food crisis' that resulted in the World Food Conference of 1974. In a sense, the climate for negotiations on agricultural trade improved in the early 1970s, since buoyant commodity prices relieved governments of the kinds of pressures normally associated with depressed prices. But the opportunity was allowed to pass. What is all too often overlooked is that the income benefits from buoyant prices tend to be capitalised into high values on farm assets and costs of production tend to rise.

Action on Disruptive Measures

Any strategy for multilateral trade negotiations on farm-support measures must reflect, if it is to be viable, the political realities of independent nation states, each with its own government responsible for pursuing the welfare of its own people. This means, first, that the social objectives of governments with respect to the relationship between farm and non-farm incomes are likely to differ from country to country, which is to say the objectives of governments on the stabilisation of market conditions are bound to differ. Second, in the event of an attempt being made to eliminate international differences in food prices, political realities could well oblige a government to impose trade restrictions, either to protect its domestic price objectives or to prevent a redistribution of income in favour of other countries.

This last point calls attention to the difficulty of making progress with a policy, or negotiating strategy, of deterring governments from achieving 'high price' stabilisation objectives. What would be more viable is a strategy aimed at getting governments to agree to limit the extent to which the burden of domestic adjustment in the agricultural sector is shifted, though trade measures, to producers in other countries. Negotiations should therefore focus on measures which have been most disruptive of international trade.

For a start, governments should have no difficulty in reaching an understanding, especially in a period of tight supplies, on the use of export subsidies. Another objective, at this level, should be the negotiation of codes of behaviour with respect to the various technical measures which – either by design or accident – impede imports of agricultural products, principally the wide range of health standards and regulations relating to food additives and so on.[10]

Just as export subsidies disrupt markets when supplies are plentiful, so also do export controls when supplies are tight.[11] Several countries, not only the United States, have stopped or rationed exports of key commodities once shortages have developed, creating uncertainty in world markets and in policy-making circles everywhere. Reaching an understanding on export controls will be more difficult while shortages exist. With the likelihood of rising inflation, resort to export controls, not only of agricultural products but of minerals and other raw materials, can be expected to increase. Establishing a code of behaviour will be complicated by the variety of purposes to which export controls are put: (i) to underpin a prices and incomes policy; (ii) to protect the establishment of processing industries; (iii) to provide a counter in trade negotiations; (iv) to safeguard exhaustible supplies; or (v) to maintain prices through a cartel arrangement.

Action on International Reserves
Commodity shortages have made importing countries realise that they must be prepared to share the responsibility, and therefore the cost, of stockpiling instead of leaving it all to the exporting countries. Until the early 1970s, the world benefited from the reserves built up by the United States, unintentional as those stockpiles may have been. In retrospect, it is recognised that American stocks helped to maintain a reasonable balance between supply and demand, as well as meet the obvious requirements of famine relief.

With the importing countries interested in security and stability of supplies, governments should be able to reach agreements on the financing and management of reserve stocks of storable commodities, mainly grains. Following the World Food Conference in 1974, negotiations were initiated under the aegis of the International Wheat Council on a system of international grain reserves, the expectation being that the outcome would become part of the overall agreement being sought in the Tokyo Round of the multilateral GATT negotiations. By then there was a substantial degree of consensus among specialists on the objectives and principles that might govern such reserves.[12] They would be aimed at (i) mitigating wide swings over a period of years in the availability of supplies and therefore in prices, (ii) moderating year-to-year fluctuations in the volume and value of international trade in farm commodities and (iii) developing strategic reserves against the threat of famine in poor countries. With the cost of international reserves being shared by both exporting and importing countries, the management of them would have to be by international agreement, involving consultation and negotiation for which it would be necessary to introduce firm procedures.

The issues involved in establishing, and managing, a system of international grain reserves are analysed in Chapter 9. Suffice it here to suggest that there are two basic challenges to be faced. First, what arrangements can be negotiated between exporters and importers of grain on how they will behave during periods of shortage and periods of surplus and, in those arrangements, what is to be the aim of reserve policies? Second, what rules can be devised to take into account the fact that stabilisation objectives differ from country to country and, in particular, how can reserve policies facilitate the development of rules that will ensure that countries seeking a greater degree of stabilisation bear the cost of such greater stability.

Action on Levels of Support

Having established a framework in which some semblance of order might be achieved in agricultural trade, the negotiations should take up, and carry a stage further, the *montant de soutien* proposal of the European Community. Instead of arguing about appropriate and inappropriate *methods* of support, negotiations should concentrate on *levels* of support, leaving governments to decide for themselves – as they will anyway – what is appropriate in their circumstances. What this would involve first of all is agreeing a basis on which to determine the level of support afforded to agricultural producers by the various methods of support – one possible basis being to use producer and consumer subsidy equivalents along the lines discussed earlier in this chapter. Those levels might then be 'bound' and afterwards gradually reduced by negotiation.

At the outset, an implicit objective of the Tokyo Round negotiations was that they should establish a more or less continuous process of consultation and negotiation, mainly on non-tariff interventions in the market. In a sense, therefore, if the negotiations are a success they will never end. As levels of support become the subject of negotiations in the GATT framework, the effectiveness of the policies which underlie them should come, in due course, to be questioned more closely.

To what extent are farm-support policies fulfilling their objectives? Professor Johnson has posed five questions that governments never seem to ask themselves:[13] (i) How much have farm-support policies increased net farm incomes? (ii) What effect have farm-support policies had on farm output and on domestic consumption of farm products? (iii) How much do farm-support policies cost taxpayers and consumers? (iv) How are the economic benefits of farm-support policies distributed between high-income and low-income families in agriculture? (v) What part of the total costs borne by consumers and taxpayers actually accrue to farm people as additional income? These are the questions that need to be answered if ever the fundamental problems of agricultural trade are to be overcome.

NOTES AND REFERENCES

1. Even in New Zealand, the lowest-cost producer of dairy products, it has occasionally been necessary to provide a marketing subsidy to assist farmers.
2. The problems of measuring protection, and of developing a methodological approach for analysing farm-support policies, are presented in *Agricultural Protection: Domestic Policy and International Trade*, International Agricultural Adjustment Study No. 9, Doc. C/73/LIM/9 (Rome: Food and Agriculture Organization, 1973), pp. 23–9. The ideas in this paper are further developed and tested in *Agricultural Protection and Stabilization Policies: a Framework of Measurement in the Context of Agricultural Adjustment*, Doc. C/75/LIM/2 (Rome: Food and Agriculture Organization).

   For a theoretical discussion of protection, see W. M. Corden, *The Theory of Protection* (Oxford: Clarendon Press, 1971).
3. If *TR* is the total value of output under free trade,

   VA is value added and

   TC is the total cost of inputs purchased,

   Let *TR'*, *VA'* and *TC'* be the corresponding values under protection, then $TR = VA + TC$ and $TR' = VA' + TC'$.

   Nominal (or equivalent) tariff $\dfrac{TR' - TR}{TR}$

   Adjusted nominal tariff $\dfrac{VA' - VA}{TR}$

   Effective rate of protection (or effective tariff) $\dfrac{VA' - VA}{VA}$

   For further discussion of this formal presentation, see *Agricultural Protection: Domestic Policy and International Trade, op. cit.*, p. 26.
4. From a computational point of view, the adjusted nominal tariff has the following advantages: (i) it requires less information, as it is not necessary to specify all non-agricultural inputs; (ii) it is more 'stable' in the sense that it is not so sensitive to the size of value added relative to output; (iii) it gives values in the same range as that found in nominal tariffs in non-agricultural markets; (iv) it avoids many of the technical problems of the effective rate such as negative value added at free-trade prices, the classification of inputs into traded and non-traded, the problem of traded inputs with rising supply curves, etc.; (v) it allows the use of conventional supply elasticity estimates in calculating the output effect rather than having to relate protection to the supply of farm resources.
5. D. Gale Johnson, *World Agriculture in Disarray* (London: Macmillan, for the Trade Policy Research Centre, 1973) pp. 45–52.

6. *Ibid.*
7. *Agricultural Protection and Stabilisation Policies, op. cit.*, p. 29.
8. Assistant to the President for International Economic Affairs, *Agricultural Trade and the Proposed Round of Multilateral Negotiations*, Flanigan Report (Washington: US Government Printing Office, for the Committee on Agriculture, Congress of the United States, 1973).
9. For references, see notes 29 and 34 at the end of Chapter 1.
10. See J. S. Hillman, 'Negotiations on Trade-disruptive Measures', in Wilhelm Henrichsmeyer *et al., Trade Negotiations and World Food Problems* (London: Trade Policy Research Centre, 1974).
11. In this connection, see C. Fred Bergsten, *Completing the GATT: Toward New International Rules to Govern Export Controls* (London, Washington and Montreal: British–North American Committee, 1974).
12. See, for instance, Edward F. Fried *et al., Toward the Integration of World Agriculture: a Tripartite Report by Fourteen Experts from North America, the European Community and Japan* (Washington: Brookings Institution, 1973), pp. 20–7.
13. Johnson, *op. cit.*, pp. 257–62

CHAPTER 9

Role of Grain Reserves in an International Food Strategy

T. E. JOSLING

When cereal prices rose with the coincidence of events around 1972/73, as described in Chapter 1, greater attention began to be given to the problems of maintaining grain reserves.[1] At the World Food Conference, held in Rome in November 1974, proposals were advanced for an international system of nationally-held grain reserves.[2] The place of such a system in an international strategy for broaching the 'disarray in world agriculture'[3] has been discussed in Chapter 8. In this chapter the problems posed by a system of reserves will be explored in more detail. In one way the problems are a restatement of the problems of shortages.[4]

If, by luck or good management, there had been a higher level stocks in the world at the time, many of the problems of 1973–74 would have been less acute. The balance-of-payments problems of importing developing countries would have been eased by the greater availability of grain at less onerous prices and the aid authorisations of developed countries would have covered a larger physical quantity of food aid. Inflationary pressures would have been reduced in the world as a whole and concerns about the political power of grain exporters would hardly have arisen.

ROLE OF RESERVES

But all these desirable consequences would have followed equally if 1974 had yielded bumper harvests. A case for reserves has to rest on more than an *ex post* desire for an alternative source of supply when crops have failed. In particular, it must take into account the implication of stocks in years when current production is adequate, and be argued as an alternative to other forms of policy for security of supply and for price stability. The costs must be assessed in relation to the benefits both in total and in their distribution. And the management of such stocks has to be considered as explicitly as the level of reserves. Stocks are not a panacea for the ills of the world's food-

237

situation. But they may have an important part to play in the smooth operation of national and international agricultural markets.

By their nature, stocks are a part of short-term stabilisation policy; they do not correct any long-run imbalance between food needs and available supply. Some level of reserves or stocks is necessary to even out the natural discrepancy between the time path of production and that of consumption. Within a year, normal marketing channels will perform this function; that is, of matching availability to demand. The more refined the distribution system, the less likely there is to be a serious problem of seasonal supply. Access to credit will enable both producers and users to spread the seasonality of the harvest cycle. In developed countries, therefore, stocks should not need to be held by government, or some official authority, to even out seasonal or regional fluctuations in supply. World grain stocks are likely to be a rather blunt instrument with which to tackle problems of market systems which have not allowed the basic functions of place and time distribution to be performed. At this level, there is doubtless a need for further measures, especially in developing countries, to improve the smooth operation of marketing systems.

Of more direct relevance in the present context is the role of carry-over stocks which attempt to smooth the fluctuations in production from year to year. Stocks of this type are likely to be more costly, relative to benefits, no matter how sensible the operation of the stocks themselves. If, at a particular time, current consumption has to come from crops harvested in earlier years, as well as in the preceding harvest, then the maintenance of consumption levels will be more expensive by the extra cost of storage in the interim. A private market system will weigh this extra cost against the consumers' willingness to pay – and an easily storable commodity with price-inelastic demand will tend to be stored quite extensively because the cost can be passed on to the customer.

Price inelasticity, in a commodity market based on cereals, is presumably likely to be found in the very rich countries (for whom the income effect of price changes is negligible) and in the very poor (for whom physical consumption levels are a matter of necessity in the absence of income to buy substitutes). In the latter case, that of poor countries, a humanitarian argument can be made for governmental or inter-governmental action to absorb some of the cost of evening out consumption patterns. Hence a *prima facie* case for government stocks might exist even when market institutions are performing adequately. The corresponding argument in affluent societies would presumably be based on the objective of price stability. Governments might wish to hold themselves, or induce traders to hold, stocks at a level higher than the market would choose in order to support prices when supplies are in excess so that these can be put back on the market in times of shortage.

Not all government buying of foodstuffs comes under this definition of stocks policy. Many countries have accumulated reserves and held them at high cost as a security against the cessation of supplies during periods of embargo or war. If the level of these reserves does not fluctuate with normal changes in the market situation, they can be considered 'dead' stocks, having little if any impact on the market. Occasionally a country's view of its 'security' requirements is influenced by the scarcity or otherwise of those goods, but in general these 'emergency rations' are outside the normal trading system. The 'world food security' undertaking sponsored by the United Nations Food and Agriculture Organization (FAO) has strong overtones of a 'dead stock' approach to reserve policy.[5] The minimum 'safe' level of stocks of basic cereals for the world should be maintained by adoption and adaptation of national stock policies.

But the role of government stocks in bridging the gap between good and bad harvest years needs closer examination. For the world as a whole the concept is impeccable. But for each individual country the logic is less clear. In an open economy, fluctuations in domestic production from year to year, and within a year, can be offset by international trade. Indeed much of agricultural trade is of this nature. The implication of the possibility of such trade is to weaken the national case for holding reserves. Such reserves cannot be justified solely in terms of variability of domestic output in relation to demand. Stock policy becomes a part of trade policy and trade measures can substitute for the holding of stocks.

FUNCTIONS OF AN INTERNATIONAL SYSTEM OF RESERVES

This link between stocks and international trade is at the heart of the current discussion over the need for an international system of grain reserves.[6] So far the analysis has been concerned with government stocks. In focusing the analysis on international reserves it is worth noting the different forms they could take: (i) reserves held by an international authority; (ii) reserves held nationally, but managed by an international body; and (iii) coordination of nationally-held reserves.

To spell out, then, the interrelationship between international reserves and international trade it is useful first to mention first the various functions that have been ascribed to such an international policy. These functions are usually said to include

(a) provision for the relief of emergencies,
(b) availability of basic foodstuffs for developing countries at a time of domestic shortfall in production, and
(c) the stabilisation of price levels.

The first of these functions might be met by a limited, pre-funded and pre-located stock that could be released for humanitarian purposes, perhaps on the authority of an international agency. Indeed, the World Food Programme has, in the past, acted partly in this way. The main advantage of a truly international system of reserves would be in the timeliness and efficiency of the response to an emergency. No one would query the value of such a scheme in principle; in practice, it is difficult to see how one prevents it from becoming open-ended. The definition of an emergency could be made narrow enough to include only natural and not man-made disasters – but that is hardly humanitarian. It could be limited to small or isolated catastrophies, but that is somewhat hard on those affected by a widespread flood or monsoon failure. And in practice the ultimate authority to release stocks of food held in a country is unlikely to repose elsewhere but with the government of that country. This does not destroy the case for such stocks, or deny the need for their careful location and adequate finance, but it does mean that the 'emergency relief' function is hard to distinguish in practice from the second function, that of security of supplies. There seems no intrinsic reason why the operation of emergency stocks should be separate from that of other stockpiles, although in practice there could be some administrative advantages.

The second function of an international reserve, that of underwriting supplies to developing countries in times of need, is somewhat more controversial. Two types of situation can be distinguished.

In the case where food is available in the rest of the world, the main impact of extraordinary food imports for a developing country will be on the balance of payments. A sudden increase in the import bill could have severe repercussions on development plans. But the problem is financial rather than physical; and the solution is more likely to lie in better balance-of-payments aid than in the international accumulation of food. As a reserve asset, grain is inherently expensive to accumulate, both for the world as a whole and for each country in particular. It would seem more sensible to consider, for instance, an extension of the present scheme of the International Monetary Fund (IMF), which operates for primary commodity exporters to allow them to offset excessive variability in export earnings, to include the case of food importers in the developing world.

The other situation is where food itself is scarce in the year when the developing country has high import requirements. In this case, some allocation mechanism may be necessary, in order to ensure that a scarcity problem does not turn into one of widespread deprivation. (There may be a case here for the allocation to take the form of contributions, in the shape of cash and grain, to an international reserve, with disbursements from the reserve being according to need. The pressure for such a reserve is likely to come from those countries who wish to reduce the degree of their dependence on the willingness of particular developed countries to come to their assistance at such times; the resistance would be from nations which prefer bilateral to multilateral channels of aid.

Although a rationale can be stated for such a reserve it is not necessarily the best way of handling the situation. Withdrawals from such a reserve in times of shortage represent a form of food aid. And whereas food aid has previously tended to be linked with concessional sales of food, accumulated under domestic price-support programmes in the developed exporting countries, the placing of such aid on a continuing basis would to a large extent cover the needs of developing countries faced with production shortfalls in times of scarcity. In other words, a medium or long-term food-aid arrangement in a donor country would ensure that *that* country kept the necessary stocks to underwrite those commitments. While there might be some economies to be gained from a global stock to ensure concessional sales to developing countries, the practical politics of food aid are that donors would probably not be willing to support such a measure.

The third suggested function of an international system of reserves is that of stabilising prices by evening out fluctuations in available supplies from year to year. A commonly-held argument runs that since the total fluctuation of world production is bound to be less than the sum of the variability of that of individual nations – on the principle that bad harvests in one country will be offset in part by good crops in another – there are economies to be had in an international stock. Various estimates have appeared on the level of stocks required to counter world uncertainty in output in grains, and these are invariably a fraction of the sum of those necessary to offset such fluctuations in each country individually. But such calculations are largely meaningless. As mentioned above, an important role of trade is to offset national fluctuations. In fact, in a world of smooth trading relationships, the levels of stocks held individually by nations would correspond in total to that which a benevolent world authority would accumulate. Moreover, it would be irrelevant whether the management of such stocks was at a national level or at an international level, and their physical location would be immaterial. It is precisely because the trading system does not work smoothly that (i) some degree of international coordination or management is likely to be beneficial, and (ii) that independently determined national reserve levels will tend to exceed in aggregate those that would be necessary under an international authority. It is in an examination of the problems of the trading system and in the trade policies of various countries that the reasons for an international system of grain reserves emerge.

NATIONAL ALTERNATIVES TO A RESERVES POLICY

For one country, and in particular for a developed country, the distinction between policies for emergencies, for security of supplies and for price stabilisation become essentially meaningless. Whereas for the world as a whole one could argue that certain stock policy objectives had implications for the distribution of the burden of shortages and surpluses among countries, within a country the management of a stock is likely to operate equally on supply availability and on the stability of prices. The individual country can control availability by artificially raising or lowering the price of its imports or exports – a luxury not open to the world as a whole. This gives the country a powerful alternative to stock policies, and one which has been widely used.

But one further distinction must be made in the case of the individual country which is not applicable to the world as a whole: fluctuations in price and availability may emanate either from within the country or from outside. If one country alone suffers a crop failure, it can presumably import its extra needs; to have counselled the holding of stocks in this situation is to have recommended that the country invest in an asset which is costly to hold and store rather than in foreign exchange in one form or another. It is by no means clear that it is in the interest of a country with a reasonable internal marketing system to hold grain against the possibility of its own crop failure.

Equally, though, if it is trying to insure against possible world price rises, a domestic grain stock will also increase in value along with the price of imports. To release that stock at a lower price is to sell at a loss relative to the true price of grain in that year. Moreover, to stabilise domestic prices in the face of world price increases by means of stocks requires a trade impediment if it is to be effective, unless the stock can influence world prices, otherwise the stocks will go abroad. But then the stock policy must be compared with other means of price control, and is likely to be more expensive. Taxes and subsidies on trade, or on domestic production or consumption, will perform the task at less cost. And if the source of instability is domestic then removing trade impediments will again be a preferred policy to the holding of stocks. In an open and free economy, a reserves policy is unlikely to be of itself either effective for price stability, or necessary for security of supplies for each individual country. Hence the danger in recommending such policies as a cure for the problems of food supplies without adequate consideration for the international framework.

Not all economies are open to the influences of world trade and not all marketing systems are adequate to perform arbitrage over time. One function of stocks, then, is to compensate for these imperfections – to be contrasted with 'surpluses' which can be thought of in general as being the result of such imperfections. Stocks and surpluses look alike: the distinction is in terms of motivation and management. Just as removal of these trade barriers reduces the incidence of surpluses so it also reduces the need for stocks. The place of reserves of basic foodstuffs, both national and international, has to be seen not as a straight reflection of variability in production, but as a complex result of a set of institutional and physical restraints on international and national marketing.

This interpretation of the need for governmental reserves as a result of market imperfections suggests that importers and exporters have a somewhat different motivation in this regard.

Motivations of Importers
Taking first the case of the importer, a prime reason for stocks is to reduce vulnerability to overseas *political* action, such as the withholding of supplies for one reason or another. This rationale differs somewhat from the case for reserves against economic events, such as harvest failures, although these might in turn precipitate political developments. In the case of a genuine crop shortfall, the real value of a ton of grain increases and the release of stocks either involves a subsidy, as seen above, together with export controls to prevent leakage, or it has no immediate economic effect in that the opportunity cost of the reserves has risen to that of potential imports. The country holding reserves might make a windfall gain to offset against losses when prices fall, but unless a government has prior knowledge denied to the trade and to other governments it is not easy to see how such a policy can show long-run social returns. But against political actions, the reserve would reduce the scope for such behaviour and act to deter other governments from using this tactic. This might be particularly necessary when the sanctity of forward contracts and inter-governmental agreements is in jeopardy. On the other hand, importer stocks may make it easier for exporter governments to impose trade controls for their own internal reasons; their existence may provide their own rationale, just as the existence of surpluses in exporter countries provided justification for surplus-producing policies in importing countries in the conditions of the 1960s.

Importing countries with state-trading systems also need public stocks to the extent, more or less, that private traders would be willing to hold if they were allowed to operate. Thus centrally planned economies will always appear to be more involved in reserve stock schemes at a national level. But whereas private stocks can usually be reckoned to respond to market situations, those held by public bodies may be effectively insulated from the market. The Soviet Union's purchases in 1972 can be presumed to have increased the size of strategic reserves in that country; the effect on the market was as if total reserves had decreased. Predatory stock accumulation by state traders can be destabilising and increase the demand for countervailing stocks by others. The regularisation of trading patterns and the spread of information on crop prospects may reduce this need for reserves. Until that happens the prospects are that free market economies will need some means of preventing the impact of occasional incursions by state-buying monopolies.

Even leaving aside insurance against political trade controls and predatory purchasing by centrally-planned economies, the grain market may not be willing to hold the optimum level of stocks. Problems might be created by the nature of the markets themselves. Traders need to contract forward for future purchases and sales and governments, too, can anticipate their requirements and availabilities. To set a price on these forward contracts requires that someone bears the risks. Trade in these contracts allows others besides traders to assume this function in the case of many commodities. But these markets are often limited to periods of a few months and rarely extend beyond a year or so. And no such regular market exists for inter-governmental contracts. Under these situations, public reserves might be required as a way of countering the rigidities of the private market – or alternatively of reducing the element of risk and thus the rewards for assuming that risk by 'speculating' in commodity markets. But again the choice remains to improve the market functions rather than hold costly reserves.

Motivations of Exporters

Turning to exporting countries, reserves hold for them special advantages. On a diplomatic level, the existence of reserves may be necessary to convince importers of the reliability of supplies. In other words, the exporter can add a premium for reliable service to the annual cost of the commodities to cover the cost of stocks and the importer may be willing to pay this premium rather than insure in some other form such as domestic protection. But if this overhang persists in times of adequate supplies then the effect might be counter-productive. Commodity reserves can also be seen by the exporter as a preferable domestic alternative to supply control in times of incipient surplus. If productive capacity and storage facilities exist and have few alternative uses then such a policy may be sensible. More important is the fact that agreement among exporters to coordinate stock levels is likely to be much more effective than an equivalent arrangement to cut supplies by such policies as land retirement.

MOVES TOWARDS AN INTERNATIONAL SYSTEM

The important point about these arguments is that the role of international and national reserves is bound up with the way in which the trading system operates. There is a *prima facie* case for the improvement of the operation of the grain market which might have a reserve policy as a key element. In this regard (i) the FAO-sponsored 'undertaking' on food reserves, (ii) the deliberations at the World Food Conference and (iii) the Tokyo Round of multilateral trade negotiations under the General Agreement on Tariffs and Trade (GATT) are a part of that revision.[7]

The essence of the FAO 'undertaking' is that countries should develop and declare national policies on stocks, in particular of grain, together with information on their stock levels. These levels are at the discretion of governments and the operation of the stocks is under national control. If this increases the consciousness of governments to the possible benefits in this area it is useful, if perhaps superfluous, in a climate of uncertainty. But since no rules are imposed on the management of these stocks (besides some less-than-specific guidelines) they cannot truly be regarded as international reserves. And to the extent that the undertaking is obsessed with the concept of a 'minimum' level of stocks, it is unlikely to be an effective policy for improving market stability and ensuring supplies.

The World Food Conference in Rome, convened by the United Nations, presented governments with an opportunity to go further. On the question of aid, it encouraged nations to break into the link between the provision of food aid – unpopular in some importing developed countries, but still of vital significance to many of the world's poor – and the state of the domestic markets in the developed world. Long-term food-aid commitments need either the security of stocks or the flexibility of finance to enable aid supplies to be purchased in times of general shortage – and the former would seem to be preferable.

On the question of price stability, a second line of attack is required. Again the World Food Conference laid the foundations to be built on by others. The Conference made progress along two fronts:

> On one front there was an agreement to develop an improved system of information. This provided for the coordination of information on national stock positions and crop forecasts. This information should form the basis of decisions on reserve behaviour and possibly production policy.

> The other contribution of the deliberations at the World Food Conference was in the more traditional area of trade negotiations. Not that the Conference itself provided a forum for such negotiations. It did, however, highlight the agenda for other discussions to follow under the auspices of the GATT and the United Nations Conference on Trade and Development (UNCTAD).

In spite of everything the Tokyo Round of GATT discussions have proceeded in an atmosphere of mutual suspicion about the motives of both the importers and the exporters of agricultural goods. But the coincidence of interests has never been greater. The main focus of the Tokyo Round talks on agriculture will be the extent to which domestic anti-inflation policies can be made complementary, rather than competitive, with the subsidiary theme of how a potential reversal of the strong terms of trade for agricultural goods can be met without resort to the costly policies of the 1960s and early 1970s. Agreements on stockholding – the rules rather than the levels – could provide the answer to both sets of problems, but with the need for intensive discussions on financial shares and on adequate safeguards.

Whether such discussions on stock policies take place within the multilateral trade negotiations in Geneva or in some parallel session, although not always clear, is hardly likely to affect the outcome. Neither has it been of great importance whether such an outcome is given the title of an International Grains Agreement. Nor has it been particularly relevant whether the arrangements are taken to form part of an 'overall integrated programme for commodities' within the remit of UNCTAD, or of a 'world food security policy' supervised by the FAO.

The impetus comes from (i) the frustration of past conflicts on agricultural trade policy, (ii) the salutory shock of two-digit inflation, (iii) the fear of a return to the old-style farm-support policies and (iv) uncertainties about the direction of price trends. In this climate the institutional focus becomes irrelevant. Agreement on the management of stocks can substitute in large part for the protective levies and quota systems of importers and for their consumer subsidy and forward purchase commitments in times of shortage; exporting countries use coordinated stock management to replace to a significant extent export subsidies, production quotas and, in periods of scarcity, export taxes.

Paradoxically, the strongest case for such an international system of reserves is that it removes to a large degree the reasons why the level of reserves in recent years has seemed inadequate. By obviating the need for trade-disruptive policies, coordination of reserves would bring the level of stocks held by the public and private trading bodies closer to the optimum level required for a smooth functioning of the world agricultural market, without having to know in advance that optimum level, and without having to face the problems of international control of reserves of basic foodstuffs.

NOTES AND REFERENCES

1. For a general discussion of grain reserves, see T. E. Josling, *An International Grain Reserve Policy* (London, Washington and Montreal: British–North American Committee, 1973).

2. The proposals were advanced by the United States, but not all the relevant agencies in the Washington administration appeared to support them.

3. For a major review of the state of world agriculture, see D. Gale Johnson, *World Agriculture in Disarray* (London: Macmillan, for the Trade Policy Research Centre, 1973; and New York: St. Martin's Press, 1973).

4. This chapter is based on a paper first presented in Wilhelm Henrichsmeyer *et al.*, *Trade Negotiations and World Food Problems* (London: Trade Policy Research Centre, 1974).

5. *World Food Security*, Proposal of the Director-General of the FAO (Rome: Food and Agriculture Organization, 1973).

6. In this respect, see Fred Waugh, 'Reserve Stocks of Farm Products', in Presidential Commission on Food and Fiber, *Food and Fiber for the Future*, Technical Papers, Vol. V (Washington: US Government Printing Office, 1967); Edward Fried *et al.*, *Toward the Integration of World Agriculture: a Tripartite Report by Fourteen Experts from North America, the European Community and Japan* (Washington: Brookings Institution, 1973); and J. S. Hillman *et al.*, *The Impact of an International Food Bank*, a Report for the Senate Committee on Agriculture (Washington: United States Congress, 1974).

7. Issues before the Tokyo Round of GATT negotiations are discussed in *European and American Interests in the Multilateral Negotiations on Agricultural Trade*, Staff Paper No. 2 (London: Trade Policy Research Centre, 1973).

CHAPTER 10

Domestic and International Implications for British Agricultural Policy

JOHN ASHTON, T. E. JOSLING and ALISTER McFARQUHAR

In this concluding chapter an attempt is made to present an overall qualitative assessment of the efficacy of British policy. Before beginning to draw overall conclusions, however, it would be useful to consider the conclusions of previous chapters in the light of recent developments in the British economy.

FUTURE ECONOMIC DEVELOPMENTS

Over the past few years, from 1972 to 1976, agriculture in the United Kingdom has experienced more instability than in any period since World War II. At the same time, changes in the general economy have been spectacular. Inflation, as measured by the annual increase in the Retail Price Index, reached a level of almost 25 per cent in 1975: over the years 1972 and 1973 growth in GNP averaged about 5 per cent, but fell in 1974 by 1 per cent; and 1975 GNP recovered slightly, increasing by around 1.0 per cent, although GDP growth in that year was near to zero.

Between 1972 and 1973 food prices rose about 15 per cent, considerably above the rate of increase in the Retail Price Index of 9 per cent, while non-food prices rose by only 6 per cent. In 1974, the rate of increase in food prices remained around 18 per cent, with inflation at 17 per cent and an increase in non-food prices of around 15 per cent. By 1975 the rate of increase in food prices had caught up with the rate of inflation (measured by the increased Retail Price Index) at around 25 per cent. Consequently, over the period 1972 to 1976, while food prices were increasing rapidly the real price of food was falling since 1972 and appeared to have stabilised at around the rate of inflation by 1975. Meanwhile, over this period, the international value of the pound had fallen by about 40 per cent, heralding a further increase in food prices over the remainder of the projection period. (see Table 10.1).

TABLE 10.1

Changes in GNP, Consumer Expenditure and Prices: 1972–75

	1972	1973		1974		1975	
	Actual	*Actual*	*Per cent inc.*	*Actual*	*Per cent inc.*	*Actual*	*Per cent inc.*
GNP	100	106	6	107	0	108[a]	1
Consumer expenditure	100	105	5	103	−1	103	0
Retail price index	100	109	9	127	17	157	24
Food prices index	100	115	15	136	18	171	26
Non-food prices index	100	106	6	122	15	150	23

[a] Estimated on the basis of incomplete year's data.

Over the same period the instability in farming income in the United Kingdom was even greater (see Table 10.2). Between 1972/73 and 1973/74 farming income increased by 40 per cent in money terms; that is, by over one-third in real terms, after allowing for changes in the Retail Price Index – in other words, it was a very good year for farmers. In 1974, however, some of the benefit was clawed back, since money income actually decreased by 1 per cent while prices increased by 17 per cent, giving a fall in real income of 15 per cent. On the forecast figures for 1975/76 there has been a modest increase in money

TABLE 10.2

Changes in British Farm Income: 1972–76 (£m)

	1972/3	1973/4		1974/5		1975/6[b]	
	Actual	*Actual*	*Per cent*[a]	*Actual*	*Per cent*[a]	*Actual*	*Per cent*[a]
Farming net income	£866	£1275	+47	£1263	−1	£1357	+7
Retail price index	100	109	+9	127	+17	157	+24
Real farm income	866	1169	+35	998	−15	863	−14

[a] Per cent of previous 12 months.
[b] Forecast. MAFF

farm income of around 7 per cent, but the effect of inflation has been to reduce real income by 14 per cent (cf. Figure 5.11, p. 149 above).

This is not the kind of environment to demonstrate the art of forecasting or the science of projection. The preliminary estimates carried out for this study covered the period 1973–78, being the six years over which the United Kingdom was to undergo the process of adjustment towards becoming a full member of the European Community, involving the adjustment of agricultural price supports to those operating under the CAP. An attempt was made to update projections to take account of the emerging effect of inflation. Subsequently it was possible to repeat the projections at the end of 1975 to include the actual changes which had taken place between 1972 and 1974. At this time, data on food consumption and production were not available for the 1975 year, so the current projections given in Chapter 3 and Chapter 5 cover the four years 1975 to 1978. Summarised projections relate to the 1978 year and figures for intermediate years are not presented here.

It might be noted, at this point, that where projections appear implausible it is usually because results are expressed on a 1972=100 base. In fact the projections include the effect of actual events up to the end of 1974. Consequently, where a zero growth is assumed this means zero growth in consumer expenditure 1974–78, but includes the effect of actual growth in the years 1972/73/74.

Even at the beginning of 1976 it was an open question as to whether growth in GNP would be positive or negative over the next few years and as to how the economy would adapt to rapid inflation as well as to changes in relative prices. By 1978 it is to be hoped that some kind of stability will have emerged, but the assumptions made about growth in consumer expenditure, which influences the demand for food over the projection period, are on the optimistic side. Nevertheless, some view has to be taken and the figures which form the basis for the projections are given in Table 10.3. It has been assumed that GNP will grow by a total of 6 per cent over the four years 1975 to 1978. Alternative views exist about the rate of recovery in the United Kingdom as far as magnitude is concerned, but the annual figures are not important if the aggregate recovery in GNP by 1978 approaches 6 per cent above the 1975 figure. The most important figure which influences the projections of demand in 1978 is the change in consumer expenditure measured in money terms. Table 10.3 shows that this change is expected to be of the order of 10 per cent over the 1976 to 1978 period, while inflation, measured by the Retail Price Index, is estimated to average around 20 per cent in 1975 falling to 15 per cent in 1976 and moderating to 10 per cent per annum in 1977 and 1978.

Against this background two alternative assumptions have been made about the change in consumers' expenditure between 1975 and 1978. The first assumption is shown in line four of Table 10.3 indicating a fall in consumers' expenditure, measured in real terms, in 1975 and 1976 of 3 and 5 per cent respectively, with a recovery of the same order of magnitude in real terms in the years 1977 and 1978. The overall effect of this is to postulate no change in consumers' expenditure measured in real terms in 1978 compared with 1974. A more pessimistic assumption is that consumer expenditure will have to fall in real terms over these four years by an average of 1.5 per cent per annum composed of a fall in real expenditure in 1976 amounting to 5 per cent, no change in real expenditure in 1977 and a slight increase in expenditure of 1 per cent in 1978.

TABLE 10.3

Assumptions about Economic Trends: 1975–78

	Percentage change over previous year				*Per cent per annum 1975–78 mean*
	1975	*1976*	*1977*	*1978*	
Growth in GNP	0	1	2	3	1.5
Growth in consumers' expenditure	15[a]	10	10	10	
Change in retail price index	20[b]	15	10	10	
Change in consumers' expenditure[c]	−3	−5	+3	+5	Zero
Change in consumers' expenditure[c] in real terms	−2	−5	0	+1	−1.5

[a] Actual figure for first 9 months is 22.2 per cent [in current prices].
[b] Actual figure for first 9 months is 24.3 per cent [in current prices].
[c] Alternative estimates in constant prices.

Apart from these critical parameters of growth, the other vital assumption which affects the projection of demand is the assumption which had to be made about the change of relative food prices by 1978. This estimate of food prices in 1978, originally made in 1972, had to take account of the effect of British adjustment to the European Community and, in particular, to the price-support policy of the CAP, to the effect of rapid inflation, to slow if not negative growth in consumer expenditure, to wide fluctuations in food prices in the United Kingdom and, too, to a period of very rapid change in primary commodity prices in the world as a whole. Accordingly, it seems wise to check how far the estimates of real prices in Chapter 3 and Chapter 5, after adjusting for inflation in 1978, are in line with the most recent information (at the time of writing) on food prices for 1975. This comparison is made in Table 10.4, which measures the percentage change in real prices since 1972 for the two years 1975 and 1978.

Encouragingly, there seems to be no evidence that the relative prices which were forecast for 1978 need to be changed, even if re-estimated

TABLE 10.4

1978 Food Prices compared with 1975 Prices (1972 = 100)

	Index of 1978 deflated retail prices	Index of 1975 deflated retail prices		Index of 1978 deflated retail prices	Index of 1975 deflated retail prices
Fresh milk	85	78	Butter	134	70
Milk products	96	108	Margarine	105	111
Cream	105	90	Other fats	115	125
Cheese	104	86	Sugar	143	178
Beef/veal	115	93	Sugar preserves	115	123
Mutton/lamb	116	101	Potatoes	115	160
Pork	102	106	Fresh vegetables	95	104
Bacon/ham	105	116	Vegetable products	91	107
Poultry	118	111	Fresh fruit	89	97
Other meat			Fruit products	98	107
products	106	102	Bread and flour	99	99
Fish	111	106	Other cereal		
Eggs	106	112	products	97	107
			Beverages	98	86

at the beginning of 1976. The following commodities are expected to increase slightly their relative price between 1975 and 1978, namely fresh milk, cream, cheese, beef, mutton, poultry and fish and, perhaps most of all, butter. The following commodities are expected to follow a downward adjustment in relative real price compared with their present level, namely condensed milk, bacon and ham, other fats, sugar, sugar preserves and potatoes, which is very much what would be expected in the light of the record high prices experienced for some of these commodities, in 1975. For the remainder of the commodities, real price assumptions for 1978 are very close to the 1975 level; that is to say, they involve changes each way of not more than around 5 per cent. Consequently, even if account is taken of changes that have taken place between 1972 and 1975 there is not yet any evidence that would necessitate a change in the assumption about food prices in 1978. The estimates of demand for foods, based on these assumptions about prices and growth in consumer expenditure, are set out in Chapter 3 for 1978.

In Chapter 5 trends in supply of home-produced food in the United Kingdom are discussed in detail and many alternative estimates of projected output in 1978 and 1980 compared. As in the case of food consumption and prices, wide fluctuations in prices have occurred in supply of agricultural products, partly due to weather conditions and partly due to instability in farm product prices and costs. Additional information is now available regarding possible agricultural output in 1978 from the estimates given in the British Government's White Paper, *Food from Our Own Resources*.[1] These estimates are provided by MAFF for the year 1980 and seem to take the form of target figures rather than forecasts or projections. Further, it is presumed that the figure given by MAFF in 1980 constitutes a trend estimate of production, rather than an estimate of production taking into account expected weather conditions in that year. Taking the MAFF target figures for 1980, an intermediate figure in 1978 has been inferred by measuring the trend value for 1978 which relates the 1980 target to production in 1973 to 1976. In the case of individual products, the MAFF figures do not state whether the 1980 target figure will be achieved by linear expansion or by an accelerating or decelerating rate of growth. Whatever the case, the 1978 MAFF figure provides a useful comparison with the forecasts for production for 1978 which are presented in Chapter 5. It is encouraging to note that in no case does the equivalent MAFF output for 1978 differ from the Chapter 5 forecasts of output in 1978 by over about 10 per cent (see Table 10.5). In the case

TABLE 10.5

British Food Supply in 1978: Comparison of Estimates in Chapter 5 with those from the 1975 White Paper
('000 tons unless otherwise stated)

	TPRC 1978	MAFF 1978[a]	Difference
Total cereals	16,500	16,644	+0.9
Raw sugar	1,065	942	−11.5
Milk (output for human consumption)			
mn gals[b]	3,100	3,340	+7.7
Beef	1,150	1,143	−0.6
Pigmeat	1,071	999	−6.7
Mutton/lamb	250	276	+10.0
Poultry	700	685	−2.1

[a] Data in *Food from Our Own Resources*, Cmnd 6020 (London: HMSO, 1975) are for 1980. The figures above are interpolated between the 1980 input figures and the mean yields for the three-year period 1973–74 to 1975–76.
[b] Excludes milk retained on farms for stock-feeding.

of total cereals, milk and mutton and lamb, the MAFF estimates are very slightly higher than those in Chapter 5, while in the case of raw sugar, beef and pigmeat and poultry they are slightly lower. This is interesting because the White Paper was taken in some quarters to

imply a significant change in the direction of British agricultural production: in reality, however, it was estimated in 1972 that this level of
production was likely to emerge on the basis of trends in technology,
costs and prices current at that time.

Consequently, in terms of total output, agricultural production may
in the early 1970s have been appropriate to the 'world level' of primary commodity prices. It is difficult to conclude that future expansion
of the British agricultural production, over and above what is expected
up to 1978 (Table 5.4, p. 165), will reflect better resource allocation in
the late 1970s, except in so far as benefits can be derived in the short
run from the support policies of the CAP.

Considering individual commodities, major 'exports' in 1978 will be
soft wheat,[2] at over 1m tons, and barley at nearly 3m tons. There is no
obvious market for these surpluses except the European Community's
intervention pools. Britain will benefit to the extent that her share of
surplus support is less than her earnings from foreign exchange from
exported cereals.

INTERNATIONAL VALUES

The wealth and material well-being of any modern open economy can
only be enumerated at international values. This applies to agriculture
as much as to any other sector. The crucial problem facing the British
Government revolves around the fact that international values are
themselves ambiguous. This ambiguity arises from two causes. First,
the implication of adopting the European Community's common
agricultural policy, as distinct from participating in its common agricultural market, is that 'international' values are themselves administered as an act of policy and, secondly, that the price of sterling –
which provides the link between national values and domestic prices
and profits – is itself erratic, although not necessarily unrealistic.

The implication of using international values to monitor and evaluate domestic trends is that national policy should be directed to making
sure that resources are employed in a way which appears most profitable at international prices. A corollary of this is that any direct
government attempt to use the economy to achieve other (quite legitimate) objectives – such as redistribution of income, security of supplies
and regional balance – will in general have a cost in terms of national
wealth. Agricultural policies are replete with programmes to achieve
social objectives through the manipulation of the economic system. In
the remaining sections of this chapter we discuss policies at British and
European Community level in terms of the problems associated with
returning to a sound basis for British agriculture.

It is easier to recognise a good policy than to describe it. A sound
agriculture in the European Community would be one that produced

those commodities – mainly raw materials to the food sector – which found a market in competition with other sources of supply. This is the only basis which is likely to be satisfactory, in the longer run, to those who invest their capital and their skills in farming. Uncertainty is in many cases the result of attempts by governments to hide the inevitable. The position in the dairy sector illustrates the extent to which delays in providing producers with realistic expectations as to their future markets can build up problems which then, in turn, act as justifications for the continuation of the policies themselves.

To expect that a reasonable agricultural policy would also be simple is to deny the complexity of modern government. At a time when all sectors of the economy have come to look to government to guarantee incomes and jobs, to underwrite investment and to protect the size of the markets,[3] one cannot expect the farming industry to welcome a policy which allows international values alone to determine its standard of living. But the converse is also true. To expect the government to determine incomes in isolation from the international valuation of output is to ask a sacrifice from other parts of the economy and a degree of government involvement which is politically unstable. This applies, *par excellence*, to the policy of the European Community, but it also holds for the United Kingdom.

CURRENT POLICY CONCERNS

The complexities of farm policy in the European Community are familiar. At the political level, the Community itself survives on a precarious balance between advance (based on cooperation and integration) and disintegration (threatened by the predatory nature of national self-interest). Thus British policy hovers between a feeling that there should be some benefit in organising agriculture on a Community basis, and a view that the political capital that might be expended in promoting such changes would detract from Britain's ability to pursue other national interests. And the fact that the budgetary 'cost' of the CAP has been hidden by a set of *ad hoc* monetary arrangements (to delay the effects of the weakness of sterling) which has led to a tendency to postpone serious consideration of the more important question relating to the direction of the policy as a whole.

The pressures on the CAP have been discussed briefly in Chapter 2. We have tried to approach questions of agricultural policy from a longer perspective. But policy in the long run is only the reflection of a succession of short-run decisions, taken often with little foresight as to their cumulative implications.

The concerns of the moment relate to such things as the control of consumer price rises, the modification of the regulations surrounding the European Community's common agricultural policy, the stability of production in the livestock sector, the effect of taxation on land ownership, and the availability of reliable supplies from abroad. The introduction, in Britain, of consumer food subsidies in 1974 represents an example of a policy fashioned for an occasion – a sudden rise in food prices and a need to get political support for other aspects of government policy. Within a year, the expenditure on such subsidies exceeded by far the level of payments to agriculture under previous British farm-support policies. Will these measures become a permanent feature of food prices? It is too early to tell, but the history of farm-support policies would suggest that the removal of government programmes is not a simple matter. Should such policies be adopted on a European scale? There would be advantages to an importing nation such as the United Kingdom, but the financial problems may prove to be too great.

At European Community level, a number of related issues arise. How effective are existing institutions at formulating an approach to the development of agricultural strategy? Are decisions on price levels taken on the basis of adequate information and in the interests of all the parties concerned? Perhaps more conscious decisions need to be taken on the location of production within the Community in order to avoid, or at least make explicit, the potential conflicts of interest among farmers in the Community. Is livestock production to develop further on the basis of purchased feedingstuffs or on a fuller use of indigenous pasture? To what extent should the development of non-agricultural animal feeds be encouraged? How should the Community develop policies to deal with income disparities in various regions? Should exchange rate changes be allowed to impinge directly on the agricultural and food sectors? Can the European Community's policies adjust to a period of oversupply in agricultural markets such as might follow a series of good harvests and an exaggerated response by producers to recent levels of prices? These and many other questions remain to be answered in terms of Community policy, but many of them would also have to be faced by a British government formulating policy outside the Community.

It is in the current concern with the supply price of agricultural goods from overseas that more fundamental issues arise. At the root of the problem is the ease with which the world is likely to be able over the next decade to feed its growing population. The FAO's assessment of the food situation was optimistic in this regard: per capita consumption could be maintained by a rate of expansion of agricultural capacity similar to that achieved in the early 1970s. But the cost of such expansion could well lead to price levels higher, relative to those of manufactures, than we have been used to in the past. And such projections do not allow for the fact that current consumption levels themselves are barely adequate for large numbers of people. Moreover, attention is beginning to focus on rural poverty, and its causes, in developing countries where there is a consequent lack of effective demand for food. Measures directly related to alleviating this poverty, and improving incomes, will lead to increases in effective demand for food which, in turn, will lead to higher food prices, thereby stimulating food production, especially in developing countries.

Add to these facets the vulnerability of supply to natural and other disasters and the prospect is not so secure. There is a need for a fundamental review of the workings of international markets in agricultural goods to ensure that countries have available to them output from farms outside their own borders. In addition, more satisfactory allocation procedures need to be fashioned to ensure that the burden of shortages fall on those who can afford to modify consumption patterns. Farm policies have a new-found importance, and the response of policy makers to the challenge will be closely watched.

FARM INCOME QUESTION

Historically, a major concern of agricultural policy, in the industrialised countries, has been the influence of market-intervention measures on the average level of agricultural incomes. The effect of price-support measures on agricultural incomes can be approximately represented by the increase in money received by the farm sector at constant levels of production – the 'effective protection' afforded by the price supports. This measure gives a useful guide both to relative resource use within an economy and to the direct income-support effect of policies within agriculture. The measure will tend to underestimate the full impact of protection in that output response will increase profit (or reduce loss) relative to the 'fixed output' calculation.

For individual sectors, the figures given in Table 6.12 (p. 198), can also be interpreted as rough measures for effective protection in the United Kingdom. In international studies, effective rates of protection for agricultural sectors have been shown to be high, relative to other sectors of the economy. This suggests that resources in industrial countries are often encouraged into agriculture even though they would tend to have a higher earning-power in other employment (see Table 10.6).

Not all the benefit, though, from effective protection can be said to increase income to farmers. Much of the benefit will be reaped by those who supply the capital equipment to the farm sector and, in particular, by those who own the land on which the agricultural industry is based. In many cases, the landowner will also be the farmer; and he may be indifferent as to whether his income is explicit, through farming profits, or implicit in the returns to capital on land. Tenant farmers may find that much of the benefit that they expect to receive from price-support measures are dissipated by higher rents. This in turn leads to a desire to take the level of rents into account as a 'cost' of production in formulating government price levels.

TABLE 10.6

Levels of Effective Protection for Several Agricultural Products
(percentage)

	Wheat	Barley	Maize	Sugar	Milk and products
Canada	17.2	23.7	12.9	55.6	169.9
United States	83.9	17.2	43.0	182.8	139.8
United Kingdom	56.8	61.7	—	133.3	128.4
West Germany	87.5	94.1	61.3	111.6	129.1
France	40.0	45.0	40.0	76.7	121.7

Source: *Agricultural Protection: Domestic Policy and International Trade*, International Agricultural Adjustment: Supporting Study No. 9 (Rome: Food and Agriculture Organisation, 1973).

Agricultural policies have a marked effect on the stability of income levels in the farm sector; indeed, stability of farm incomes has been an important motive for much of the intervention in agricultural markets since the 1930s. The success of income-stabilisation policies depends to a certain extent on the cause of instability.

Fluctuations in levels of domestic output under conditions of inelastic demand will lead to demand for support in periods of high levels of production. The response of governments is often to remove goods from the market, thus increasing the effective demand facing producers, thereby generating 'surpluses' which then have to be disposed of or stored.

But fluctuations in domestic output may also be a function of the lack of knowledge of future prices and the consequent over-reaction to prices ruling at the time of the production decision. The analysis of such cycles has so far produced little in the form of policies to improve price expectations. To some extent production cycles will be damped by government market intervention. This puts a considerable burden, however, on the information available to the intervention authorities and can lead to expensive programmes.

A large part of British agricultural policy, and of policy in the European Community, is defensive in nature. Incomes and livelihoods are protected against sudden change, either from domestic disturbance (usually in the form of variability in weather patterns, incidence of disease or changes in the rate of inflation) or from foreign events (ranging from crop failures to aggressive marketing policies by other countries). For the major products in advanced industrial countries, the 'demand' facing domestic producers – the schedule that determines at which price their output will sell – is likely to be quite price-elastic. Government action usually has the effect of increasing the price elasticity still further and, in the extreme, guarantees a price at which all of the commodity can be sold.

Under these conditions the impact of fluctuations in supply and consumption are absorbed in the volume of trade, often with undesirable implications for foreign policy and for the stability of the world market. The advantages, though, in terms of a stable environment for investment in the agricultural sector, could be considerable even if the incentive for improvements in marketing may be reduced. Stabilisation of this type is an important motivation for farm policy; the potential benefits of the reduction of risk on profitable investment decisions can be considerable. It is no part of the normative theory of the workings of markets that short-term disturbances should be allowed to interfere with production planning. On the other hand, an efficient capital market, supplemented by such devices as crop insurance programmes, may reduce the importance of business risk as effectively as market intervention and price-guarantee schemes run by governments.

The impact of farm-support policies on income distribution within the agricultural sector has come to be of some political importance in most countries. At a conceptual level the point has now been established that a price-support scheme which benefits farmers according to the volume of their output is likely to favour those who least need income support. If one extended the analysis to include the asset appreciation accepted as a consequence of price-support policies, the distribution of these capital gains would probably be even more skewed. But the interpretation of this evidence is not so clear cut. Whereas from an equity point of view, at any particular time, it may appear to be desirable to bias payments towards those farmers with inadequate incomes, a system of support which discouraged efficiency and investment could itself either generate or perpetuate an undesirable farm structure. This leads to the conclusion that price policy in itself is unlikely to deal effectively with the problem of absolute poverty in the rural sector; and that this role should be left to instruments more sensitive to income needs, and less related to output decisions.

Another aspect of inter-farm income distribution is the recurrent conflict of interest between producers and users of animal feed – in particular cereals, but increasingly oilseeds and other feedstuffs. One aspect of farm-support policies common to many industrial countries is the imbalance between the extensive support given to cereals and other arable crops, relative to the often meagre protection afforded the grain-based livestock industry, in spite of the growing importance of the latter in affluent diets. Protection of the value-added in the production of poultry and eggs, of pigs and, to a lesser extent, of beef and milk has in general been more modest than a simple price comparison would indicate. This 'arable bias' has exacerbated the general tendency of farm-support policies to enhance land values rather than to encourage the return to farm-family labour. It remains to be seen whether the period of high cereal prices will serve to reduce this aspect of support policies or to reinforce them on the basis that shortages of cereals should be avoided in the future at almost any cost.

STABLE SUPPLY OBJECTIVES

Whereas in the past it has been usual to discuss agricultural policy in the light of its impact on farm income, one major implication of the upheaval of world commodity markets in the mid-1970s has been a revival of interest in the role of such measures in giving a degree of security of supply. Supply security itself is hardly an objective concept and hence the impact on security of a set of policies is not easy to gauge. But one can detect trends which enhance or diminish security. It is generally true that an increased level of domestic self-sufficiency (as measured by the ratio of domestic production to domestic consumption) will enhance security. But this statement must be modified in a number of ways:

(*a*) If increased domestic production of a product renders the level of output less certain (such as by risking disease in cereals by more intensive rotations, or by growing sugarbeet on less suitable land), then supply security may not be advanced.

(*b*) If extra domestic output relies heavily on imported inputs (such as cereal or protein feeds for livestock, fertiliser for arable crops, or heating oil for horticulture), then the vulnerability of the enterprise to changes in availability of these inputs may be such that the degree of security is impaired.

(*c*) If expanded output itself reduces international trade to the status of 'occasional' residual source of supply, the variability in such supply may be exacerbated and the increased degree of security from the higher self-sufficiency may be offset by shortages in the world market.

For these reasons, supply security must be seen as a function of both domestic production levels in relation to demand requirements, and also to the performance and reliability of the international market. The record of industrial countries in preserving this balance is mixed. Western Europe as a whole, and Britain in particular, has enjoyed rising levels of self-sufficiency in agricultural products of temperate-zone origin. But this security has been to a large extent offset by the growing dependence on imported high-protein animal feeds and on oil-intensive inputs. Equally important, the residual nature of many of the international agricultural markets has itself been a reflection of the internal price-support policies in Western Europe and elsewhere. Insufficient attention has been given to the way in which trade can perform the function of securing supplies of agricultural products if the market is allowed to operate smoothly.

RESPONSIBILITY IN POLICIES

The inherent weaknesses in the common agricultural policy which threaten to undermine its continuation are well known.[4] It is costly to taxpayers and consumers. It is, as yet, open-ended as far as the commitment to farmers is concerned. It generates supplies in many products for which markets are difficult to find – in fact, for some, such as dried skimmed milk, they do not even exist.

At the same time, general economic pressures will, to an increasing degree, constrain agricultural policymakers. Hence there is a growing awareness and hostility among consumers about the monetary cost of agricultural support measures. Trade union interest and antipathy is becoming more evident. Moreover, the uneven incidence of the cost and benefits of the common agricultural policy among the nine member countries of the European Community shows no sign of being corrected, thus weakening the political stability of the Community.

Against this background, it is likely that measures will be required, to an increasing extent, to separate those aspects of the CAP which are directed towards primarily social ends from those which are related to the promotion of an efficient European agriculture. In short, major changes are required within the CAP to bring it more into line with international economic conditions and obligations.

It is unlikely that a rich, industrial group of nations such as the European Community can continue to pursue an agricultural policy that is totally isolated from general world conditions, while benefiting from a relatively open system for the rest of its economic activity. The contribution of European agriculture to the world economy will only become clear when investment and resource employment decisions are based not on artificial national or Community prices, but on the international value of the output which is produced. The mechanics of policy, the instruments of price support and the method of financing them are all of importance. But until a realistic price level is reached, no amount of ingenuity in devising policies[5] will solve the problem – and if the price levels are appropriate, the choice between farm policy instruments becomes a technical matter related to the situation in each commodity market.

NOTES AND REFERENCES

1. *Food from Our Own Resources*, Cmnd. 6020 (London: HM Stationery Office, 1975).
2. 'Exports' may of course be reduced by legislation in the European Community, requiring the substitution of wheat for imported maize in feedstuffs.
3. See pp. 21–23 above.
4. The weaknesses are briefly stated on pp. 26 and 27 above, quoting *Reform of the European Community's Common Agricultural Policy*, Wageningen Memorandum (London and Wageningen: Trade Policy Research Centre and the Agricultural University of Wageningen, 1973).
5. Various proposals have been made for reforming the CAP. Three possibilities were advanced in the Wageningen Memorandum, *op. cit.*, which reflected the general views of twenty-two agricultural economists from the nine member countries of the European Community.

APPENDIX

International Effects of the European Community's Enlargement

T. E. JOSLING

The accession of the United Kingdom, Ireland and Denmark to the European Community will have not only significant effects on the markets for agricultural goods within Europe, but also implications for external trade. The extent to which the enlarged European Community might disrupt the market for temperate zone products is discussed in this section. But first it is necessary to examine the prospects for world trade in agricultural commodities.

A study prepared by the Food and Agriculture Organisation (FAO) provides a general outlook for agriculture to 1980.[1] This study projects, for most countries of the world, levels of production and consumption assuming the continuation of present national policies and of recent trends. Price effects are ignored by assuming that prices would be constant throughout the projection period.

Because the results arrived at using this approach were not altogether meaningful, an attempt was made to provide a more realistic set of estimates. A research working paper was prepared which describes and quantifies the implications of including price effects on the commodity projections.[2] The results of this working paper, together with the original production and consumption estimates, provide a satisfactory picture of the prospects for agriculture over the next decade.

For our purposes, the major findings of the FAO study lie in the trade indications for those commodities covered under the CAP. The results suggest that a number of commodities could face severe surplus problem on world markets. The largest surpluses are projected for wheat and coarse grains despite the operation of production controls and other disincentives. This is caused by higher yields in grain production and by a continued emphasis on national self-sufficiency. The implication of this surplus for trade in grains is a downward pressure on world prices.

At the same time, surpluses are not projected for all commodities. Beef and veal, pigmeat, and mutton and lamb are expected to be in

263

short supply. This implies a likely rise in the prices of these commodities relative to other agricultural products. Prices of milk products are expected to remain reasonably firm.

One thing which might affect world price levels is a change in the size of the European market. In order to assess the effect of the enlargement of the Common Market on world prices, it is necessary to examine the impact of enlargement on Community trade. The possible magnitude of trade changes for the community of nine over the decade to 1980 are shown in Table A.1. Along with the calculations are given estimates of changes in trade terms which indicate the potential pressure on world prices caused by enlargement. The first column of the table indicates the world market shrinkage over the decade due to changes in the nine country area. A positive figure implies either an increase in (net) exports or a decrease in (net) imports for the enlarged Community. The amount of this market contraction which is attributable to enlargement is shown in the second column. A third column indicates the comparison between the trading position of the enlarged Community in 1980 with the six (1968). A positive figure here indicates a further contraction in the Community market.[3]

TABLE A.1

Impact of Community Enlargement on Internal Trade in Agricultural Goods and on World Price Levels ('000 metric tons)

	Change in total trade 1968–80[a]	Change due to enlargement[b]	Change in Community trade, 1968–80[c]	Effect on world prices (%)
Coarse grains	2076	459	−1091	−0.48
Wheat	7910	312	2819	−1.30
Beef and veal	64	296	280	−6.20
Mutton and lamb	−190	−65	−507	9.50
Pigmeat	407	163	639	−0.74
Milk (in b.f. equivalent)	258	278	−104	−13.60[d]

[a] Net exports of nine-country group in 1980 minus net exports of nine countries in 1968. Positive figures show increase in net European exports (or decrease in net imports) over decade.

[b] Net exports of nine country group in 1980 minus net exports of nine-country group if the Community is not enlarged in 1980. Positive figures show increased net exports due to enlargement.

[c] Net exports of nine-country group in 1980 minus exports of Community of six in 1968. Positive figures show increased net exports from the Common Market due to enlargement over the decade.

[d] Effect of Community enlargement on world price, calculated by applying volume changes in the second column to world market elasticities implicit in in the FAO study.

Suppliers will find a smaller European market for their grain exports. The displacement of ten million tons of grain imports will exert a downward pressure on world prices. The enlargement of the Community accounts for 8 per cent of this market shrinkage in grains and this indicates a further depression of world market prices. Traditional overseas grain exporters will suffer a considerable loss in potential income as they are displaced from the European market. A further loss of income can be expected due to unfavourable changes in the trading terms for grains.

The market for beef contracts marginally over the decade for the nine-country area. Again, the enlargement implies a larger market contraction, indicating that the European market would have expanded by 230,000 tons if it had not been for the adoption of the CAP by the new members. This contraction of the European market is largely due to the fall in consumption in the United Kingdom. Traditional beef exporters will suffer a further potential loss of income, since the decrease in import demand for beef due to enlargement results in a 6 per cent drop in the price of beef and veal sold on the world market.

The situation in the market for mutton and lamb is somewhat different. Protection to sheep farms increases less than that to competing enterprises, and supply is not so greatly stimulated. The market for European imports is expected to increase over the decade as demand remains firm. The calculations suggest that the Community will become a significant importer of mutton and lamb. About one-third of the expansion is due directly to enlargement. The effect of this increase in import requirements is a 9.5 per cent rise in the world price level.

The interpretation of the table is somewhat different for pigmeat. No internal price level is maintained for this commodity under present CAP arrangements. In the case of pigmeat there is an intervention system which operates spasmodically. Without an export subsidy scheme, however, intervention buying can only even out market fluctuations in price. An increased surplus of 407,000 tons would therefore indicate a downward pressure on prices. Less than half this pressure on prices comes directly from Community enlargement; an expansion in European pigmeat production is projected even without the effect of CAP on the new members. Hence the pressure on pigmeat prices from enlargement of the Common Market should be fairly small.

The world market for milk products is expected to contract as European production exceeds consumption. The whole of this contraction can be explained by the enlargement of the Community. In particular the market shrinkage is explained by the fall in the British demand for butter. It is interesing to note that the 'enlargement effect' is larger than the total market contraction, indicating that the European market would have expanded for third countries over the period if enlargement did not take place.

Of the industrial countries, those which appear on balance to gain from the enlargement of the European Community are countries which are either major importers or are primarily exporters but are fortunate enough to have the loss of producer income more than offset by the consumer gains. Countries which appear to benefit are Western Europe and Japan which are major importers and New Zealand which gains through improved world prices for mutton and lamb. The United States gains, on balance, through her pattern of trade. Australia, as a major exporter, and Canada both stand to lose from enlargement of the European Community.

TABLE A.2

Impact through Terms of Trade of Community Enlargement on Developed Countries: 1980[a] (£m)

	Real income change[c]			Balance of trade[d]
	Consumer gain	Producer loss	Net	
Australia	15.4	29.8	−14.4	−29.1
Canada	41.7	44.5	−2.8	−30.8
Japan	15.3	10.3	5.0	−3.6
New Zealand	5.8	2.8	3.0	0.10
Western Europe[b]	63.9	55.0	8.9	−29.2
United States	393.0	384.8	8.2	−232.6

[a] Excludes cheese
[b] Excludes Community members
[c] Change in consumer and producer surplus
[d] Increase in export earnings or decrease in import costs shown as positive figures

This calculation is presented in Tables A.2 to A.4. Producer real incomes in Australia are seen to decline; this will particularly involve producers of beef and veal and butter, but grain producers would also suffer from the depression of world grain prices. Firming of world prices for mutton and lamb, however, provide some benefit for sheep producers. Australian consumers are also affected. Here again the price effects on beef and veal and mutton and lamb are important. The effect of enlargement on Australian export earnings is significant. Total earnings would appear to be less by £29m in 1980, owing to the enlargement of the Community.

The effect on Canadian incomes is again dominated by terms of trade change in the beef and veal sector. There is a potential loss in export earnings of nearly £31m. More than half this loss is due to increased import costs.

TABLE A.3

Impact through Terms of Trade of Community Enlargement on Developing Countries: 1980[a] (£m)

	Real income change			Balance of trade
	Consumer gain	Producer loss	Net	
Argentina	50.1	84.1	−34.0	−77.4
Latin America[b]	149.6	157.7	−8.1	−105.5
Africa	58.9	56.6	2.3	−33.1
Near East	41.1	24.8	16.3	1.9
Asia and Far East	130.7	110.3	20.4	−78.4

[a] Excludes cheese
[b] Excludes Argentina
[c] Change in producer and consumer surplus
[d] Increase in export earnings or decrease in import costs shown as positive figure

TABLE A.4

Impact through Terms of Trade of Community Enlargement on Centrally Planned Economies: 1980[a] (£m)

	Real income change			Balance of trade
	Consumer gain	Producer loss	Net	
Soviet Union	238.98	213.03	25.95	−131.77
Eastern Europe	96.02	94.61	1.41	−67.99
Asian CPE	122.14	109.51	12.63	−53.72

Japan is a less important market, particularly in per capita terms. As an importer of most commodities, Japan's import bill increases implying a foreign exchange cost of over £3 million. This increased import bill is due to additional expenditure on beef, mutton and butter imports. The cost is somewhat alleviated by decreased value of grain imports.

New Zealand is the only country whose export earnings increase due to enlargement. This is a result of more favourable world prices for mutton and lamb, due largely to the diversion of British demand away from beef and veal to mutton. At the same time New Zealand loses on terms of trade changes for beef and veal, butter and pigmeat.

The United States, as a major producing and consuming country, stands to gain potentially from enlargement. This somewhat un-expected finding is a result largely of the effect of depressed prices in the beef and veal sector. Although producers of beef and veal suffer a decline in income of £288m, this loss is more than offset by a con-sumer gains equalling £310m. The United States grain sector loses £67m while users of wheat and coarse grains benefit by £54m. Export earnings from the grain sector decrease by £40m. In addition to this imports of beef and veal cost an extra £165m. The United States stands to lose, in total, £233m on balance of payments.

Of the developing countries, those regions which are major pro-ducers of beef and veal and grains, clearly stand to lose. This is illus-trated in Table A.3. Looking at the case of Argentina, which suffers a net loss of £34m, the £50m gain to consumers in terms of lower prices is more than offset by a loss of producer income equal to £84m. Argen-tinian producers of beef and veal, in particular, stand to lose. This effect is larger than the total real income loss incurred by United States grain producers. The change in balance of payments due to Community enlargement is larger for Argentina than the combined effect on Canada, Australia, New Zealand and Japan. This provides some indication as to the pressures which are likely to prevail for nego-tiating a continuing trade arrangement between the European Com-munity and Argentina.

The effects of enlargement on the rest of Latin America are roughly similar to Argentina. On balance this group loses £8m. Again this is largely due to a loss of producer income from the beef and veal enter-prise. A decrease in export earnings from beef and, to a lesser extent, from wheat is responsible for an unfavourable change in trade balances totalling £105m.

Of the lesser developed regions, there is a slight net advantage to Africa. Gains to consumers of £59m outweigh the loss to producers. However, the effect on Africa's balance of payments through decreased export earning and increased import costs is a loss of £33m.

The Near East as a significant importer of beef and grains stands to gain £16.3m. The effect of enlargement of the Community on the balance of payments of this area is a decrease in import costs. Simi-larly, Asia and the Far East gain, on balance, £20m. However, the import bill for this region increases by a substantial £78m.

The impact of enlargement of the Community on the major centrally planned economies is presented in Table A.4. All three regions of this group are seen to benefit as consumer gains outweigh producer losses. The Soviet Union, as an importer of beef, food-grains and butter, stands to gain £26m. After the United States, the Soviet Union suffers the second largest loss on balance of payments. Eastern Europe and centrally planned economies in Asia also face increased import bills.

NOTES AND REFERENCES

1. *Agricultural Commodity Projections 1970–80* (Rome: Food and Agriculture Organisation, 1970).
2. *A World Price Equilibrium Model*, Agricultural Commodity Projections Working Paper No. 3 (Rome: Food and Agriculture Organisation, 1971).
3. The author is indebted to Donna Hamway for assistance in the calculations presented in this Appendix.

Selected Bibliography

Set out below is a selected bibliography relating to agricultural policy and international trade. All the entries are monographs or volumes. Journal articles have not been included, but are cited in the notes and references at the end of each chapter, as and when relevant.

Thus the bibliography has been designed for both general and specialist readers. In no sense is it meant to be comprehensive. Included in the bibliography are a number of publications of the Trade Policy Research Centre, which has taken a special interest in agricultural trade problems. The bibliography begins with a background section. This is followed by one on the European Community and a final section listing specialist studies on other parts of the world and on international trade problems.

BACKGROUND

Agricultural Protection, Domestic Policy and International Trade, International Agricultural Adjustment Supporting Study No. 9 (Rome: FAO, 1974).

AMERICAN ECONOMICS ASSOCIATION, *Readings in the Economics of Agriculture* (London: Allen & Unwin, 1970).

LESTER BROWN, *Seeds of Change: the Green Revolution and Development in the 1970s* (New York: Praeger, for the Overseas Development Council, 1970).

EDWARD F. FRIED *et al.*, *Toward the Integration of World Agriculture*, a Tripartite Report by Fourteen Experts from North America, the European Community and Japan (Washington: Brookings Institution, 1973).

J. GEORGE HARRAR, *The Green Revolution in Perspective* (New York: Rockefeller Foundation, 1970).

HIGH-LEVEL GROUP ON TRADE AND RELATED MATTERS, *Policy Perspectives on International Trade and Economic Relations*, Rey Report (Paris: OECD Secretariat, 1972).

D. GALE JOHNSON, *World Agriculture in Disarray* (London: Macmillan, for the Trade Policy Research Centre, 1973).

T. E. JOSLING, *An International Grain Reserve Policy* (London, Washington and Montreal: British-North American Committee, 1973).

T. E. JOSLING, BRIAN DAVEY, ALISTER MCFARQUHAR, A. C. HANNAH and DONNA HAMWAY, *Burdens and Benefits of Farm-support Policies*, Agricultural Trade Paper No. 1 (London: Trade Policy Research Centre, 1972).

PANEL OF EXPERTS, *Trends in International Trade*, Haberler Report (Geneva: GATT Secretariat, 1958).

UGO PAPI and CHARLES NUNN (eds), *Economic Problems of Agriculture in Industrial Societies* (London: Macmillan, for the International Economic Association, 1969).

ERNEST H. PREEG, *Traders and Diplomats* (Washington: Brookings Institution, 1971).

PRESIDENTIAL COMMISSION ON INTERNATIONAL TRADE AND INVESTMENT POLICY, *United States International Economic Policy in an Interdependent World*, Williams Report (Washington: US Government Printing Office, 1971).

PRESIDENTIAL COMMISSION ON RURAL POVERTY, *Rural Poverty in the United States* (Washington: US Government Printing Office, 1968).

PRESIDENTIAL COMMISSION ON FOOD AND FIBER, *Food and Fiber for the Future*, Berg Report (Washington: US Government Printing Office, 1967).

VERNON RUTTAN, A. D. WALDO and J. P. HOUCK (eds), *Agricultural Policy in an Affluent Society* (New York: Norton, 1969).

THEODORE W. SCHULTZ, *Transforming Traditional Agriculture* (New Haven: Yale University Press, 1964).

PETER J. O. SELF and HERBERT J. STORING, *The State and the Farmer*, revised edition (London: Allen & Unwin, 1971).

THE EUROPEAN COMMUNITY

DENIS BERGMANN *et al.*, *A Future for European Agriculture*, Atlantic Paper No. 4 (Paris: Institut Atlantique des Affaires Internationales, 1970).

MICHAEL BUTTERWICK and EDMUND NEVILLE ROLFE, *Agricultural Marketing and the EEC* (London: Hutchinson, for the Home-Grown Cereals Authority and the Meat & Livestock Commission, 1971).

SIR ALEC CAIRNCROSS, HERBERT GIERSCH, ALEXANDRE LAMFALUSSY,

272 *Agriculture and the State*

GIUSEPPE PETRILLI and PIERRE URI, *Economic Policy for the European Community: the Way Forward* (London: Macmillan, for the Institut für Weltwirtschaft an der Universität, Kiel, 1974).

JOHN FERRIS *et al.*, *The Impact on US Agricultural Trade of the Accession of the United Kingdom, Ireland, Denmark and Norway to the European Community*, Research Report No. 11 (East Lansing: Institute of International Agriculture, Michigan State University, 1971).

T. E. JOSLING, *Agriculture and Britain's Trade Policy Dilemma*, Thames Essay No. 2 (London: Trade Policy Research Centre, 1970).

GAVIN MCCRONE and E. A. ATTWOOD (eds), *Agricultural Policy in Britain* (Aberystwyth: University of Wales Press, 1965).

ALISTER MCFARQUHAR (ed.), *Europe's Future Food and Agriculture* (Amsterdam: North-Holland, for the Association Scientifique Européene pour la Prévision Economique à Moyen et à Longe Terme, 1971).

JOHN MARSH and CHRISTOPHER RITSON, *Agricultural Policy and the Common Market* (London: Royal Institute of International Affairs, 1971).

HERMANN PRIEBE, *Landwirtschaft in der Welt von morgen* (Düsseldorf: Econ Verlag, 1970).

HERMANN PRIEBE, DENIS BERGMANN and JAN HORRING, *Fields of Conflict in European Farm Policy*, Agricultural Trade Paper No. 3 (London: Trade Policy Research Centre, 1972).

MICHAEL TRACY, *Agriculture in Western Europe: Crisis and Adjustment Since 1880* (London: Jonathan Cape, 1964).

ADRIEN ZILLER, *L'imbroglio agricole du Marché commun* (Paris: Calmann-Levy, 1970).

OTHER COUNTRIES

BRIAN FERNON, *Issues in World Farm Trade: Chaos or Cooperation?* (London: Trade Policy Research Centre, 1970).

F. O. GROGAN (ed.), *International Trade in Temperate Zone Products* (Edinburgh: Oliver & Boyd, for the Agricultural Adjustment Unit, University of Newcastle upon Tyne, 1972).

YURIJO HAYAMI and VERNON W. RUTTAN, *Resources, Technology and Agricultural Development: an International Perspective* (Baltimore: Johns Hopkins Press, 1971).

D. GALE JOHNSON and JOHN A. SCHNITTKER (eds), *U.S. Agriculture in a World Context: Policies and Approaches for the Next Decade* (New York: Praeger, for the Atlantic Council of the United States, 1974).

KAZUSHI OHKAWA, B. F. JOHNSON and HIROMITSU KANEDA (eds), *Agriculture and Economic Growth: Japan's Experience* (Tokyo: University of Tokyo Press, 1969).

ANTHONY S. ROJKO and ARTHUR B. MACKIE, *World Demand Prospects for Agricultural Exports of Less Developed Countries* (Washington: United States Department of Agriculture, 1970).

MICHAEL TRACY, *Japanese Agriculture at the Crossroads*, Agricultural Trade Paper No. 2 (London: Trade Policy Research Centre, 1972).

GERALD I. TRANT, DAVID L. MACFARLANE and LEWIS FISCHER, *Trade Liberalisation and Canadian Agriculture* (Toronto: University of Toronto Press, for the Private Planning Association of Canada, 1968).

Index

Page numbers with the following letters added refer to:
   n – note
   t – table
   fig – figure.